Theory of Media Literacy

Theory of Media Literacy

A Cognitive Approach

W. James Potter

University of California at Santa Barbara

SAGE Publications
International Educational and Professional Publisher
Thousand Oaks ▪ London ▪ New Delhi

For information:

Sage Publications, Inc.
2455 Teller Road
Thousand Oaks, California 91320
E-mail: order@sagepub.com

Sage Publications Ltd.
1 Oliver's Yard
55 City Road
London EC1Y 1SP
United Kingdom

Sage Publications India Pvt. Ltd.
B-42, Panchsheel Enclave
Post Box 4109
New Delhi 110 017 India

Printed in the United States of America on acid-free paper.

Library of Congress Cataloging-in-Publication Data

Potter, W. James.
Theory of media literacy: a cognitive approach / W. James Potter.
    p. cm.
Includes bibliographical references and index.
ISBN 0-7619-2951-7 (cloth)—ISBN 0-7619-2952-5 (pbk.)
    1. Media literacy. I. Title.
P96.M4P685 2004
302.23—dc22   2003026516

04   05   06   07   08   09   10   9   8   7   6   5   4   3   2   1

Acquiring Editor:	Margaret H. Seawell
Editorial Assistant:	Jill Meyers
Typesetter:	C&M Digitals (P) Ltd.
Indexer:	Molly Hall
Cover Designer:	Janet Foulger

Contents

Preface

As I began working on the third edition of *Media Literacy*, it became apparent that my plan for revision was too ambitious for one book. Besides updating the facts and figures, I wanted to strengthen two features of the book, but the two features were at cross-purposes with each other.

One of those features was the self-help nature of the book, which made it appealing to undergraduates. To increase this appeal, I would need to add more anecdotes and examples to make the ideas more concrete. I would need to add more detail about the media industries, audiences, and content. I would need to make the tone more personal as I talked directly to readers and encouraged them to incorporate the information into their own knowledge structures. As a textbook, it needed to be written for consumers of information; it needed to put forward the knowledge structures that people require to be media literate; and it needed more exercises to help readers acquire and use the information.

The other feature of the book I wanted to strengthen was its theoretical vision, which made it more appealing to researchers and graduate students. To increase this appeal, I would need to add more critical analyses of the media literacy literature and to synthesize more theoretical propositions to make the ideas more abstract. I would need to focus *less* on detail about the particulars of media industries, audiences, and their content and instead focus *more* on general patterns. I would need to make the tone more scholarly as a way of appealing to the imagination of researchers and stimulating them to test the ideas I synthesized from the literature. As a theory book, it needed to put forward a systematic explanation about what media literacy is and how it works; it needed to be written for researchers who would be interested in testing those claims and thereby generating more information.

The balance between these two features in the first and second editions of *Media Literacy* could no longer be maintained if I were to attempt a significant revision to increase the book's appeal to two different audiences at the same time. I had to make a choice about whether *Media Literacy* should remain primarily a textbook written for undergraduate students or whether it should be a theory book written primarily for researchers and graduate students.

The obvious solution to this dilemma was to revise *Media Literacy* as a textbook for undergraduates and to write a second book that would have a different purpose and different primary audience. This is that second book, *Theory of Media Literacy: A Cognitive Approach*. This solution had worked well for me before on the topic of media violence. Primarily for researchers, I wrote *On Media Violence*, wherein I critically analyzed the social science literature and synthesized a broad explanation I called *lineation theory*. My purpose was to provide a systematic vision of the phenomenon that researchers could test. Then, I took a different approach in *The 11 Myths of Media Violence*, which was written for undergraduates as well as a general trade audience. In this second book, I organized the information around major controversies so that readers could consume the information in a way that would lead to a more informed debate about media violence.

In this book, *Theory of Media Literacy*, I offer a general theory of media literacy. In developing this theory, I drew heavily (but not exclusively) from the social science literature, particularly psychology. But this theory does not look like typical psychological theories, which focus on one or two hypothetical constructs, then link these constructs with other constructs, demographics, or situational variables in a small set of propositions that are essentially predictive. Those are narrow range theories that offer precision and depth of explanation as their greatest assets.

In *Theory of Media Literacy*, the theory is much broader than any single psychological theory because my goal was to provide a map of the relatively large, complex phenomenon of media literacy. This phenomenon has more facets than could be explained in a small set of predictive propositions. Also, so much has been written about media literacy by scholars from different paradigms and with different purposes that I needed to draw together many literatures. Thus, this book was *not* written because there is a void of thinking about media literacy. Instead, this book was written to build on many of the existing ideas and try to move past some of the constraints in the individual writings to present a big picture about what media literacy can be.

This theory is offered to several audiences: new scholars interested in media literacy, empirical researchers, and practitioners. For new scholars, this book can provide an introduction to much of the research dealing directly with media literacy as well as contiguous research literatures that provide an infrastructure to media literacy. The major components of concern within the broad construct of media literacy are presented and linked together in a model that incorporates both scientific propositions and normative suggestions for techniques of achieving higher levels of media literacy. The scholarly citations will tell readers where to go to find more in-depth treatments of each topic.

For empirical researchers, I offer the theory as a kind of table of contents of what needs to be examined. Many of the chapters include a list of propositions that need further testing as well as research questions that need answering.

Practitioners are those educators and social activists who are dedicated to improving the level of media literacy in individuals as well as society. This book includes a review of techniques that have been found successful in achieving various goals of media literacy.

Organization of Book

This book presents 12 chapters that are organized into four sections. The first section lays the foundation for a theory of media literacy and is composed of two chapters. In the first chapter, I make a case that the study of media literacy is essential by analyzing both the cultural and the scholarly contexts. Our culture is saturated with information, and this makes considerable demands on individuals to deal with it all. Among scholars, there has been considerable activity in trying to delineate what media literacy is. In Chapter 2, I analyze a good deal of the scholarly thinking and writing about media literacy. As you will see, there are many different definitions incorporating numerous interesting elements.

The second section introduces the theory. Chapter 3 provides definitions of the key terms in the theory, then uses these terms to build a synthesized definition of media literacy. Chapter 4 presents a model that displays the major components of the theory and illuminates its structure. It also presents the major assumptions on which the theory is based. Each of the next three chapters explicates a major component of the media literacy model and provides a rationale for the importance of that component in the overall flow of thinking. Chapter 5 lays out the foundational knowledge structures. Chapter 6 illuminates the locus, which is the hypothetical construct that governs a person's media literacy. Chapter 7 deals with competencies and skills, which are the tools that people use to work with information.

The third section presents the component tasks of information processing. Chapter 8 examines the task of information filtering. Why do people pay attention to certain media messages and not others? Chapter 9 focuses on the mental processes involved in meaning matching. How do people recognize symbols and patterns in messages, then associate meaning with them? Chapter 10 examines the cognitive processes that people use to construct their own meaning of media messages. This section concludes with Chapter 11, where I illuminate many of the traps in meaning construction.

The fourth and final section of the book presents a brief overview of what practitioners do to help others increase their media literacy. Chapter 12 examines practitioners in interpersonal and institutional settings. Interpersonal settings are primarily parents working with their children. The institutional setting raises issues of teaching media literacy as part of an educational curriculum.

In summary, this theory attempts to explain how the human mind works when dealing with the flow of media messages in our information-saturated culture. It addresses how people make decisions about the thousands of media messages they are exposed to every day; how people make sense of the enormous variety of stimuli across those messages in many different channels; and how people construct their own meanings for those messages. Most important, it shows how these things can be done better in a more media-literate manner.

Acknowledgments

There are many people I need to thank for helping me with this book. First, I am indebted to the students in the media literacy courses I have taught over the last decade at UC Santa Barbara (UCSB), Florida State, UCLA, and Stanford. These hundreds of students have patiently listened to my ideas in class, then let me know what did and did not make sense to them. While that feedback was often humbling, it never failed to teach me a great deal. Paramount among all those students is Sahara Byrne, a graduate student here at UCSB who carefully read not one but two full drafts—line by line—of this manuscript and gave me incredibly detailed and useful feedback.

Also, I thank all the creative scholars who have dedicated a good portion of their professional careers to thinking and writing about this important topic. These people are too numerous to mention, but I must name the few who stimulated my thinking the most: Jim Anderson, Erica Austin, Jim Brown, David Buckingham, Bill Christ, Renee Hobbs, Sut Jhally, Bob Kubey, Paul Messaris, Josh Myrowitz, and Amy Nathanson. There are many others who have also stimulated my thinking about media literacy and help me formulate my own perspective. These people include social science theoreticians, especially those in the cognitive and social psychological arenas; empirical researchers who have examined how people attend to the media and how exposure affects individuals and institutions; social and media critics; consumer activists concerned with the power of the media; and educators who have developed and tested practical techniques to help people understand media influence and teach people how to be better consumers of the media. Thanks also to the reviewers who helped me clarify and extend my arguments: Deborah Dunn, Stuart Fischoff, Timothy P. Meyer, and Timothy J. Moreland. Thank you all!

Last but certainly not least, I thank the people at Sage Publications: Margaret Seawell, the greatest of all acquisition editors, and her many serial assistants. Also I extend a sincere thank you to Claudia Hoffman for managing the production process with grace and effectiveness.

PART I

Background

CHAPTER 1

Why Do We Need a Theory of Media Literacy

1

Why Do We Need a Theory of Media Literacy

This introductory chapter presents an argument for why media literacy is so important. The beginning point for this line of argument is that the media provide so much information that we cannot physically avoid it, so we psychologically protect ourselves by processing it automatically. While this automatic processing does shield us from having to deal consciously with a large majority of those messages, it comes with some high costs. We risk avoiding too many messages, which would narrow our experience. Also, we risk turning too much control over to the automatic processes, which are themselves substantially conditioned by the media. Because the media have a very different motive for presenting their messages than we have for receiving them, we end up satisfying the media's goals at the expense of our own. Thus, we risk misperceiving the real world and misunderstanding its true nature. Also, as we become comfortable employing automatic processing with its focus on efficiency, we let our skills of meaning construction atrophy. With weaker skills, we come to depend more and more on the media to tell us what is important and who we should be.

I. Problem of Access to Information

For centuries, getting access to information was a major problem for virtually all humans. The elites who had the education and the wealth could get the information they needed to make them knowledgeable and powerful. The others—and that included almost all people—could not get access to learned scholars, could not buy or borrow books, and were not able to read. Without access to information, most people were prevented from becoming knowledgeable.

A. Culture Flooded With Media Messages

With the rise of the mass media throughout the 20th century, the barriers to access were substantially reduced, especially with the spread of radio, then television, and then the computer. By the late 20th century, access to existing information ceased to be a major problem (see Table 1.1). For example, this year in the United States alone, about 65,000 books will be published, and each of these is available in public libraries or through online bookstores for a relatively modest price. Furthermore, books are only one channel of information. Throughout the world, radio stations send out 65.5 million hours of original programming each year, and television adds another 48 million hours. In this country alone, the seven major film studios have an additional 169,500 television programs in their archives.

Table 1.1   Information Vehicles

Medium	United States	World
Books (titles per year)	64,711	968,735
Radio stations	12,600	43,973
TV broadcast stations	1,884	33,071
Newspapers	2,386	2,386
Mass market periodicals	20,000	80,000
Scholarly journals	10,500	40,000
Newsletters	10,000	40,000
Archived Web pages	3×10^9	7.5×10^9

SOURCE: Information is from Lyman & Varian, 2001.

With personal computers connected to the Internet, people have access to more information than ever before. In the early 1980s, fewer than 5% of all American households had a computer; within 20 years, that number had climbed to almost two thirds of households (Statistical Abstract, 2002). The Internet gives people access to about 3,000 newspapers (Kawamoto, 2003). Also, the World Wide Web offers access to about 2.5 billion documents. These are the publicly available pages, referred to as the surface Web. There is also what is called the deep Web, which consists of pages that require memberships and fees or are otherwise private. This deep Web has been estimated to be 400 to 550 times the size of the surface Web (Lyman & Varian, 2001).

B. Information Production Accelerates

Not only is information easily available to almost anyone today, information keeps getting produced at an ever increasing rate. In 1984, Peter Large computed that more information had been produced in the 30-year period after 1954 than in the 5,000 years before that date. Writing in *Megatrends*, John Naisbitt (1984) estimated that in the early 1980s, scientific and technical information was doubling every 5.5 years; he expected this rate to accelerate to a doubling of information every 20 months by the 1990s. As startling as these figures are, they are likely to be hopelessly outdated as estimates of the speed of information generation in 2004, because half of all the scientists who have ever lived on Earth are alive today and producing information.

C. Keeping Up

The information problem is no longer about how to get access. The much more pressing problem is how to keep up with all the information. For example, if you were to try to read only the new books published in the United States this year, you would have to read a book every 8 minutes for 24 hours each day with no breaks over the entire year. All that effort would be needed just to keep up with the new titles in only one country. You would have no time left to read any of the other 66 million book titles in existence worldwide (Lyman & Varian, 2001). Also, if you wanted to watch all the television programming broadcast in this year alone, it would take you about 550 centuries—if you took no breaks.

We have long since reached a saturation point; there is no hope of keeping up with information. As a result, the problem of gaining access to information has quickly shifted to trying to keep up, and then finding a way to avoid information. Information providers are now aggressively competing for our limited attention. This can be seen with advertising messages, which rapidly accelerate in terms of number, venues, and aggressive nature (see Table 1.2). The average person is now exposed to more than 300 ads on any given day, almost all of which were not sought out by the person exposed. If you asked people at the end of a typical day how many ads they remember being exposed to, most people could not recall more than a handful. This amounts to an unconscious exposure to more than 110,000 messages per year, or about 2 million by the time a person graduates from high school. That is a very large number of unplanned and unconscious exposures.

Table 1.2   Submersion in Ads

- From 1967 to 1982, the number of print and broadcast ads doubled. Since 1982, the number has quadrupled. In 1971, the average American was targeted with at least 560 ad messages per day; in 20 years, that had climbed to 3,000 per day. Third class mail (junk mail) in the 1980s grew 13 times faster than the population.

- Television: The average American household has the TV on more than 47 hours per week. Out of this time, about 12 hours are ads. From 1965 to 1995, ads on network TV got shorter and more frequent—the average length shrank from 53.1 seconds to 25.4 seconds, and the number of ads per minute increased from 1.1 to 2.4. In 2002, commercial clutter had climbed to 20:57 per hour in daytime television and 16:08 per hour in primetime (*MediaWeek*, February 18, 2002). Children's TV programs contain a high proportion of ads. Cable networks had the least amount (10:38 per hour on average) compared to broadcast networks (12:09) and independent stations (13:29) (Kunkel & Gantz, 1992)

- In America, radio programming can consist of 40 minutes of ads per hour.

- Newspapers are primarily ads now. The average newspaper is now more than 60% advertising; some are more. For example, the *New York Times* Sunday edition contains 350 pages of ads, which is well over 60%. Newspapers have given about the same amount of space to news content since 1910, however, because the overall size of newspapers doubled during that time, the percentage of the newspaper that contains news has shrunk by half.

- Sporting events and stadiums are themselves vehicles for ads.

- There are companies that sell ads in bathrooms. Stall-Boards places about 350 ads in public bathrooms in Southern California and has revenues of about $1 million.

- Pepsi-Cola produced a TV commercial in space by filming Russian cosmonauts launching an oversized Pepsi can from their space station Mir.

- Even the Pope has been commercialized. The Vatican acknowledges that the Pope's visits are costly, so they have agreed to sponsorship. The Pope's 4-day visit to Mexico in the winter of 1999 was sponsored by Frito-Lay and PepsiCo.

- In Sweden, they have tried interrupting personal phone calls with ads.

- Half of all the money spent on advertising in the world is spent in the United States.

Marketers rely on quantity of exposures, not quality. As a result of this clutter, advertisers operate on a principle that each member of their target audience must be exposed to an ad a minimum of three times in order for it to make any kind of an impression. But such an operating principle itself causes the clutter to expand greatly each year.

We live in an environment that is far different than any environment humans have ever experienced, and the environment changes at an ever increasing pace. This is due to the accelerating generation of information, the sharing of that information through an increasing number of media channels, and the heavy traffic of media vehicles traversing those channels. Messages are being delivered to everyone, everywhere, constantly. We are all saturated with information.

II. Information Fatigue

The information explosion has changed the way we deal with messages from the media. Along with the quantity of information, the qualitative nature of information has changed. These effects are profound. However, they have happened so gradually over generations that they are not noticeable on a day–to-day basis.

A. Devaluing Messages

No single piece of information has any special significance to us any longer because so many pieces are coming at us all the time. If a person owns a single book, he or she will likely treasure it. But the owner of a library of 6,000 books is not likely to have a special attachment to many of them. And if instead, a person knows that she or he has access to the words in more than 60 million books through the Internet, that person is even less likely to think that any one of those books is indispensable or even much better than the rest in value. Also, if a person has to work hard to find a fact, he or she will likely feel it has great worth. But people who have to fight off an onslaught of facts every day are likely to develop an avoidant or even adversarial stance to information.

With so many facts and opinions circulating, it is difficult to decide consciously which to regard as the most valid or important. Because it is so difficult to know which are more valid, there is a temptation to avoid a careful assessment of the validity of each fact and instead to be satisfied to regard the validity of all facts as the same, even when they contradict one another. Over time, we come to believe that all facts have only ephemeral validity at best; if we regard a fact as correct, that characteristic is not especially compelling because the fact is likely to lose its validity quickly as the world changes. Also, because the information comes at us so fast, there is no sense of loss if we miss a message. Instead, we feel secure that in a few minutes the same message or an even better one will come along.

Thus, when all these low value messages rain down on us, we do not feel blessed; instead we feel defensive. How can we deal with it all? We know we cannot, so we have to ignore the flood without thinking about it. If we think about all the messages we are ignoring, there is a tendency to begin hating the pressure from the relentless flow.

B. Nature of Information Has Changed

The sheer amount of information has also affected the quality—or character—of that information. Over the course of the last century or so, the nature of information has changed. Messages have become shorter. When messages become shorter, they lose the detail that can provide people with a context for interpreting those messages.

Almost all media messages are fleeting, quick, and superficial. The length of messages is kept short to minimize the demands on us and thus to increase the chance that we will attend to the message. But the shortness of messages forces them to be superficial. Ideas presented in a 15-second advertisement cannot be developed in any depth. Nor can the ideas in a 60-second news story.

When messages become shorter, the context we ourselves bring to the understanding of those messages becomes more important. However, the superficiality of the messages makes it harder for us to construct a good context. For example, it used to be easy to categorize messages as being either information, entertainment, or ads. But now, news shows are using the entertainment formula, so they provide less information and more entertainment. Ads are becoming more like information and entertainment to mask their purpose. For example, info-mercials on television look like information shows but are really half-hour paid ads. Entertainment vehicles, such as Hollywood films and TV shows, are becoming advertising vehicles as ads are embedded in them. There are 30 companies operating in Hollywood to place products within movies and TV shows. For example in *Santa Claus—The Movie,* McDonald's paid $1 million to the filmmakers to have a scene set in a specially constructed McDonald's restaurant; McDonald's also spent $18 million on promotion and network advertising related to the film. CBS-TV's *The Price is Right* gets $1 million in payments from product producers each year, in addition to the prizes the manufacturers give away on the show. What we commonly think of as purely entertainment messages are becoming hybrids where the senders of those messages have a different intention than the one we perceive.

Another factor that makes it difficult to construct context is the decoupling of messages from their senders. It is difficult—sometimes impossible—to tell who the sender is and, therefore, what the sender's intentions are.

With television, most people now have no idea what a broadcast station is and how it is different from a cable network. They do not understand that the two are very different entities with different regulatory constraints, means to access audiences, audience configurations, programming philosophies, and criteria for success (Walker & Ferguson, 1998). With Internet providers, it is difficult to tell who the sender really is and what the sender's intentions are.

Even when a television channel, radio station, or a magazine is named as a source, it is not always clear who controls it and who is making the decisions about the content. With the concentration of ownership in the media industries, very different messages may be controlled by the same people. Bagdikian (1992) conducted an analysis of media ownership patterns in 1983 and found that the control of the media was essentially in the hands of 50 people: These were the CEOs of the largest media companies, which in combination controlled more than half of the revenues and audiences in their media markets. Less than a decade later, Bagdikian found that the number had shrunk to 23 CEOs of corporations that control most of the country's 25,000 media businesses. The less we know about the media industries and their messages, the greater is our risk for being powerless to use those messages to fulfill our own needs for information and entertainment.

III. Automatic Processing

A. Response to the Information Flood

In a society characterized by aggressive media, we can try to avoid exposure. We can stop buying and reading books. We can cut back on our subscriptions to magazines and stop newspaper delivery. We can reduce our time searching for particular messages in radio, television, and the Internet. Exposures will still occur, however. We cannot avoid all media messages unless we expend a great deal of energy in avoidance, which then defeats the purpose of reducing our effort in dealing with all the messages.

When the goal is to reduce our effort, the strategy is to cut back on exposures that require effort and to tolerate exposures that would require effort to avoid. This tolerated exposure is done in an unconscious manner; that is, people try to expend as little mental energy as possible and default to automatic processing. This means they mindlessly follow habits of avoiding messages in the environment by not attending to them until something in the message triggers their attention.

We realize that it is hopeless to keep up with the information. The only sane response seems to be to protect ourselves. This means we must screen out almost all the information. However, we still need to pay attention to some information; we cannot simply screen it all out and hope to survive in our information society. The challenge, then, becomes one of being able to pay attention to those info-bits we need while screening out all the rest of the flood of information. The way we meet this challenge is to rely on automatic processing of information: Our minds stay on automatic pilot, screening out all information until something of value to us triggers our attention.

The obvious advantage of automatic processing of information is that it provides us with an efficient means to avoid all the messages we do not need while giving us a means to filter in the few messages we want. However, there are negative consequences associated with this automatic processing. One of these consequences is that the automatic processing does not eliminate physical exposure. It only reduces attention, which is conscious exposure; there are still unconscious exposures. The information that gets into our minds unconsciously through automatic processing is more likely to lead to faulty interpretations than information that is consciously processed. Unconscious exposure is still exposure. When people are in a message-saturated environment, they are still being bombarded by information; even though they are not paying attention. Messages still get into people's minds, if only subconsciously. For example, we might have the radio on in the car as we concentrate on driving, and when ads come on, we do not pay much attention. Then, later, we find ourselves humming a jingle; or a word phrase occurs to us; or we pass by a store and "remember" that there is a sale going on there. These flashes of sounds, words, and ideas emerge from our sub-conscious where they had been put by ads to which we did not pay atten-tion. Over time, all those images, sounds, and ideas build up patterns in our subconscious and profoundly shape the way we think about health, body image, success, relationships, time, and happiness.

Almost all exposure to advertising is unconscious, yet it still works. Advertising works because it gets into the audience's unconscious without the audience attending to those messages and analyzing them. A very sophis-ticated marketing research industry spends more than $7 billion each year to find out how to shape people's needs and behaviors; this is more money that the federal government spends each year on all of education.

B. The Default Model of Information Processing

The default model describes what happens when people have little aware-ness of media effects, the process of influence, and their own selves (see Figure 1.1). With default processing, the media are in control. The designers and programmers of media messages exert a strong influence over exposure

Figure 1.1   The Default Model

decisions by conditioning people to accept habitual patterns of exposure. As a result, most exposure is automatic with little mindfulness or planning. Meaning matching is done automatically. With little mental effort or awareness invested in processing the flow of messages, people are left to accept the obvious surface meaning of messages rather than constructing meaning for themselves.

When processing information from the media, people most often use a default process. The advantage of using this process is that it requires the least mental effort. The media set and shape expectations, which are rarely not met. So people have a relatively pleasant experience with the media. With their expectations unchallenged, people then continue to let the media set those expectations and shape their behavior. People stay in the automatic mode, which is the default.

The problem with following the default model is that people maximize the media's control. On a superficial level, this may not appear to be a problem; that is, many times, people do not have strong conscious preferences for media exposure so they fall into a habit. They just want to relax, and it does not matter what they watch, especially because they are really not paying that much attention to the actual content. When following this habit, people do not think much about possible negative consequences, such as wasting a few hours watching television. If negative consequences do occur to them, those consequences are regarded as trivial.

What people miss in this superficial reasoning is the bigger picture. Their exposure is not an isolated event with no consequences; instead, it is part of a pattern that has many serious consequences. As people spend more time in habitual, mindless activity, the media are conditioning them by defining what news is, what entertainment is, and how to solve problems with advertised products. These associations are shown with attractive images and pleasant emotions. Also, these associations are repeated endlessly. When people then ignore the challenges of meaning construction and instead default to only matching meaning, people are left with only media conditioned associations.

With the default model, the media largely determine the exposure. This means that either people have not made a decision to expose themselves at all to the media (thus messages inject themselves into their environment without their seeking them out) or people have sought out a kind of exposure, which has opened the door for many other messages and other exposures have attached themselves to that selection. For example, a person decides to watch a particular TV show but is also exposed to ads, promotions for other shows, etc. The exposure is automatic, that is, the person continues in the exposure environment without actively processing any or much of the messages. Meaning matching happens automatically, and the person does not challenge any of the meanings presented.

The media are conditioning us to accept their control. This can be seen in the way the newer media deliver their messages compared with the way the older media deliver messages. With print, which is the oldest of the mass media, consumers have had almost total control over exposures. Books cannot expose themselves to consumers; people have to take the initiative to go out to a store or a library. Magazines and newspapers are a bit more intrusive because they are delivered to our doors, but we need to subscribe for this to happen. Also, with all forms of print, we control the exposure sequencing and pace. We can begin reading a magazine with any story, read the stories in any order, and read the stories as fast or as slow as we want. Thus, with the print media, we exert a relatively high degree of control over all the important exposure decisions: whether to be exposed or not, which stories to read and in which order, the timing of the exposure, and the pace of the exposure.

With the arrival of electronic media, new forms of control were established that contrasted with print media. In the 1920s, radio was introduced and people began to lose some of their control over the media exposure. Of course, radio requires that someone turn on a radio receiver in order for information to flow, but once the audio is in the environment, everyone is exposed. In this way, radio is more intrusive than print. Also, radio controls the timing, sequence, and pacing of the messages. If you want to listen to a particular show, you have to tune in when the program is broadcast. You have to listen to the messages in the order they are broadcasted. Radio producers control the interruptions (for ads) and can suspend the story (as in serialized stories). Of course, some magazines present serialized stories, but an audience member can wait for all issues to be published, then read them all at once; this is not possible with serialized radio dramas. Radio and then television trained us to structure our lives around certain times when their shows were broadcast; they trained us to tolerate interruptions for commercial messages; and they trained us to develop weekly habits of exposure.

Over time, some technological innovations have been made available that potentially give people more control over media exposures. For example, tape recorders, then MP3 players, enable people to rearrange audio messages through editing; also, people can control the playback time. VCRs do the same for video. Computer software seems to give people more control over searching for information (Web browsers and search engines). However, to use these technologies, we have to expend more effort. We have to scan more messages to make our decisions about what to record or use, and this serves to increase our exposures. Therefore, most people stay with their media-shaped habits of exposure most of the time. Also, these technologies have hidden features that serve to reduce our control while making it appear that they are increasing our control. For example, Internet Service Providers (ISPs) and search engines make people feel that they are in control of their Internet searches, but these devices constrain people's access. ISPs have links to favored Web sites while excluding others. Search engines cannot possibly access more than a small percentage of Web pages, so the decisions concerning which pages to access lies at least as much with the search engine company as with the user.

Today, the number of messages bombarding us is at an all time high, and it continues to grow. The providers of those messages are at a high point in being able to control our knowledge, our attitudes, and our behaviors. However, at the same time, we have more potential now than ever before to control our own exposures and their effects on us, but sadly, few people recognize this potential. Most people are either too fatigued by the onslaught of messages to confront the situation consciously, or if they want to confront the problem and gain control for themselves, they are not sure about what to do.

This constraining of choices would be less dangerous if there was a balance of choices across the potential range of audience interests. However, media businesses construct the constraints to achieve their own economic objectives; that is, they provide only those services that they feel will generate the greatest revenues while keeping their expenses as low as possible. Of course, revenue is associated with audience size, so people do have an influence on what messages get offered. However, it is not as simple as saying that the largest audiences will command the messages. This is because audiences are not the only source of revenue for the media; with some media, the message providers are also a source of revenue. For example, cable television companies charge cable networks to carry their signals, and they charge subscribers to access these signals. There are two sources of revenue. Let's say a cable company finds it has an open slot on its channel menu and is considering whether to schedule Service X or Service Y. The cable company knows that demand for Cable Channel X among its subscribers is very high but that the provider of Cable Channel X is not willing to pay to get on the cable company's menu. Let's say that demand for Cable Channel Y among subscribers is low but that the provider of Cable Channel Y is willing to pay a good deal of money to get on the cable company's menu. In this case, it is likely that the cable company will fill the open slot with Service Y to make more money, even though the demand is much higher among subscribers for the other service.

C. Faulty Meaning Construction

The information-saturated environment and our response to it leave us vulnerable to faulty beliefs. Either we accept the beliefs presented to us in the media, or we construct our own beliefs, which tend to be faulty if we rely on the superficial and spotty information we absorb during automatic exposures.

Three factors converge to maximize the conditions that would lead us to accept faulty beliefs about the world. One of these factors is the superficial nature of most information presented in the endless stream of short snippets. Second, the media businesses do not want our attention as much as they want our exposure. Entertainment providers do not want critical awareness that might lead to objections about content; they want simple, habitual exposure that they can count on week to week. News providers do not care if audiences engage the issues as much as if they maintain their habits of buying the newspaper and watching the evening news each day. Advertisers do not want attention that would lead to a critical analysis of their claims; instead, they want unfettered access to people's unconscious where they can plant images, jingles, and logos. The media have conditioned us to become comfortable with a lack of context for the information they provide. Without context, we cannot construct our own meaning for the messages; instead, we must accept the superficial meaning provided by the short messages. Over time, we either get used to liking messages with no context (superficial entertainment) and unattributed news accounts or accept the media constructors' context. Thus, we are being trained to tune down our powers of concentration. Over time, we lose the ability to look for a sustainable argument supported with reasonable evidence.

The third factor is that we encounter almost all of these messages in a state of automaticity, that is, mindless acceptance, where we are not interested in investing the effort for conscious attention, much less the effort to analyze and evaluate the messages and to find more information to construct more accurate interpretations. This combination of factors leads us to accept many beliefs that are faulty.

1. *Faulty beliefs.* A fruitful place to observe faulty beliefs in the general population is to examine the results of public opinion polls. Often, these polls ask people about issues that would seem to be very important. However, when we look at the patterns of public beliefs, we can see that many people are not really well versed about these seemingly important issues. We can see that these beliefs are clearly faulty either because they are not accurate reflections of reality or because they are not logically consistent.

In public opinion polls about crime, for example, only 17% of people think crime is a big problem in their own community, whereas 83% of Americans think crime is a big problem in society (Whitman, 1996). Most people do not experience crime in their own lives and therefore do not think it is a big problem where they live. However, they are convinced it is a big problem in society. Where could the public get such an idea? From the media's fixation on deviance in the news. Also, the news media prefer to present sensationalized events rather than typical events. When a crime is reported, it is usually a violent crime, following the news ethic of "if it bleeds, it leads." Watching evening newscasts with their highlighting of crime and violence leads us to infer that there must be a high rate of crime and that most crime involves violent assaults. In reality, less than 20% of all crime is violent. More than 80% of all crime is property crime committed when the victim is not present (U.S. Department of Justice, 1999). Furthermore, the rate of violent crime has been declining in this country for the past decade, in terms of both crimes reported to the police and actual victimization rates. Yet, in a recent poll, only 7% of Americans believed that violent crime had declined in the past 5 years (Whitman & Loftus, 1996). People have remembered a few crime stories and gory images, but they have not taken an active role in finding out what the true crime rates are. They have fashioned their opinions based on sensationalized events, and this type of information provides no useful basis to infer an accurate picture about crime.

In a wide range of public opinion polls, we find that people not only exaggerate problems with crime but also overestimate problems with health care, education, religion, and family, believing that they are all serious, growing problems. For example, with health care, 90% of adults think that the health care system is in crisis, but at the same time, almost 90% feel that their health care is of good quality. About 63% of people think other people's doctors are too interested in making money, but only 20% think their own doctor is too interested in making money. As for education, 64% give the nation's school's a grade of C or D, but at the same time, 66% give their public school a grade of A or B. As for religion, 65% say that religion is losing its influence on American life, whereas 62% say religion is becoming a stronger influence in their own lives. As for responsibility, almost 90% believe that a major problem with society is that people don't live up to their commitments, but more than 75% say they meet their own commitments to families, kids, and employers. Nearly half of the population believes it is impossible for most families to achieve the American dream, whereas 63% believe they have achieved or are close to the American dream. From 40% to 50% think the nation is currently moving in the wrong direction whereas 88% of Americans think their own lives and families are moving in the right direction (Whitman, 1996).

Most people think that the media, especially television, have either a very strong effect on other people or no effect at all. They have an unrealistic opinion that the media cause other people to behave violently. Some people believe that if you allow public service announcements (PSAs) on TV about using condoms, children will learn that it is permissible and even a good thing to have sex. This is clearly an overestimation. At the same time, people *under*estimate the influence the media have on them. When they are asked if they think the media have any effect on them personally, 88% say no. These people argue that the media are primarily channels of entertainment and diversion so they have no negative effect on them. The people who believe this say that they have watched thousands of hours of crime shows and have never shot anyone or robbed a bank. While this may be true, this argument does not fully support the claim that the media have no effect on them; this argument is based on the false premise that the media only trigger high-profile, negative behavioral effects that are easy to recognize. However, there are many more types of effects, such as giving people the false impression that crime is a more serious problem than it really is or that most crime is violent.

There is a faulty belief in this country that television is to blame for the educational system not being very good. The media often present reports about how poorly this nation's youth do on learning compared to youths in other countries. The 1998 National Assessment of Educational Progress (NAEP), administered nationally by a group established by Congress, reported that one third of high school seniors lack even a basic understanding of how the American government is run, and only 26% of seniors were considered well versed enough in civics to make reasonable, well-informed choices during elections (McQueen, 1999). The NAEP reports that only about one quarter of American school children have achieved the proficiency standard in writing (Wildavsky, 1999). Reports like this lead critics to complain that children in this country watch too much television. However, the same report says that students in Japan rank third on both tests, although they watch as much television as American kids do, but this bit of information is rarely reported.

Many conscientious parents have accepted the belief that it is bad for their young children to watch television. They believe that TV somehow will make their children's minds lazy, reduce their creativity, and turn them into lethargic entertainment junkies. If this happens, children will not value achievement and will not do well in school. This belief is faulty because it blames the media, not the child or the parent, for poor academic performance. It also focuses only on the negative effect and gives the media no credit for potentially positive effects.

This is an important issue, but again, it is not a simple one. When we look carefully at the research evidence, we can see that the typically reported finding is wrong and that when we look more carefully, there are several effects happening simultaneously (see Potter, 1987). For example, the typically reported finding is that television viewing is negatively related to academic achievement, a fair amount of research supports this conclusion. What makes this faulty is that this relationship is explained better by something else: IQ. School achievement is overwhelmingly related to IQ. Also, children with lower IQs watch more television, so it is IQ that accounts for both lower achievement and higher television viewing. Research analyses that take a child's IQ into account find that there is no overall negative relationship; instead, there is a much more interesting pattern. The negative relationship does not show up until the child's viewing has passed the threshold of 30 hours per week. Beyond that 30-hour point, the more television children watch, the lower their academic achievement, and that effect gets stronger with the more hours they watch beyond that threshold. This means that academic achievement goes down only after television viewing starts to cut into study time and sleep. Children who view less than 30 hours of viewing per week experience no negative effect. In fact, at the lowest levels of television viewing, there is actually a positive effect, that is, a child who watches none or only a few hours a week is likely to do less well academically than a child who watches a moderate amount (12 to 15 hours per week). Thus, the pattern is as follows: Children who are deprived of the source of information that television provides do less well in school than children who watch a moderate amount of television; however, when a child gets to the point where the amount of television viewing cuts into needed study time, academic performance goes down.

What effect does viewing television have on a child's academic performance? We could give the simple, popular answer: There is a negative effect. However, now you can see that this answer is too simple. It is simple-minded and also misleading because it reinforces the limited belief that media effects are negative and polarized and that the media are to blame. The reality is not so simple and does not lend itself easily to a short sound bite or flashy image, so it is not likely to be presented in the mass media.

2. *Misguided criticism*. Public opinion polls consistently reveal that people think there is too much violence in the media (see Potter, 1999). When we examine what bothers the public the most about the violence they see, it is graphicness. Violence that is portrayed as gory with lots of blood and harm to the victims is what offends audiences and stimulates their criticism. Programmers are aware of this criticism, and they respond to it by changing the way violence is presented. Instead of reducing the amount of violence, they sanitize it so that little harm to the victims is usually shown. Thus, the graphicness is reduced and public criticism along with it.

The public criticism and the industry's response display a sad irony. The kind of violence that upsets people the most is precisely the type of violence that they need to be exposed to more. In contrast, the violence that most people do not complain about—or even perceive—is doing them the most harm. If a show presents a highly graphic act of violence, people will complain, but this is a good thing. It shows that people are sensitive and that these portrayals can outrage them. When these portrayals fail to outrage them, this is clear evidence that they have succumbed to the negative effect of desensitization. The fact that people do not complain about the moderate- or low-level graphic acts is an indication that they have become desensitized to much of the violence (see Potter, 2003).

Desensitization is only one of many possible negative effects. Let's examine another negative effect, loss of inhibition. We have natural inhibitions toward being physically aggressive to the point of harming others. When we are exposed to a portrayal of a relatively minor physical act of aggression in which the characters are attractive, justified in their actions, and get away with the action without punishment, our inhibitions erode a bit. When we are exposed to a half dozen of these portrayals every hour for years, our inhibitions substantially erode. If we are totally unaware that this is happening, we cannot stop or control its effect on us.

Also, the public is sensitive to the fear that people may imitate the violence they see in the media, and this stimulates criticism. However, the one form of violence, verbal violence, that viewers are must likely to imitate is the target of almost no criticism. People complain most about highly graphic acts of physical violence, but these depictions are not likely to lead to much imitation. Much more easy to imitate are the relatively minor forms of physical violence and especially verbal violence. We are much more likely to imitate a character who delivers a wicked tongue lashing that humiliates another character than we are to imitate a character who stabs another character to death. The public does not regard verbal aggression as violence. Yet, insults and harsh criticism can cause more harm to a person than cuts and bruises. The emotional and psychological damage can last a lifetime. Yet, verbal aggression comes to us "flying under our radar;" that is, we do not notice it. The television networks, which are continually being criticized for the amount of physical violence, have not increased those rates over the past 30 years. However, the number of acts of verbal violence has increased dramatically since the 1970s (Potter & Vaughan, 1997). Seldom does the public complain about verbal violence because we do not notice it, or if we do, we are not bothered by it.

3. *Why the faulty meaning construction?* We create most of our opinions using very little information and information that gives us only a superficial understanding of issues. It does not have to be this way, because so much information is available to everyone all the time. Why, then do we still use so little information as a basis for our opinions? The answer is that we have information fatigue. Information fatigue leads us to automaticity, where our minds do not control either our exposures or the way that messages get into our minds. This unconscious exposure increases the probability that the information we receive is inaccurate. By *inaccurate*, I do not mean that the media are presenting biased or nonfactual information to us, although there is some of this. The condition of inaccurate information is traceable much more to the fact that our information base is filled with partial under-standings, facts without context, facts that are out of date, and unsorted impressions where conflicting information resides unresolved in our mem-ories. With this type of information as our base, it is no wonder that many of our beliefs are faulty. As long as we continue with unconscious exposure, our absorption of more information will not translate into better knowl-edge; instead, more information will only increase our stockpile of faulty beliefs. Habitual passive exposure to this constant flow can serve to reduce our literacy if we merely float along in the stream of messages. If we accept unquestioningly the images in these messages, we can end up with faulty beliefs about the world and ourselves.

Our opinions can get started in all sorts of strange ways, and often, they are not based on sound reasoning or in-depth knowledge of a topic. Opinions can spontaneously spring forth in surveys or conversations, without much thought or foundation. When it comes to the media, we often create opinions based on intuition or on partial, anecdotal information. We often look for high-profile anecdotes in the media and in our real lives.

IV. Conclusion

We cannot physically avoid the glut of information that aggressively seeks our attention in our culture. Instead, we protect ourselves by psychologically avoiding almost all of the messages in the flood of information. We do this by following the default model of information processing where our minds are on automatic pilot. This automaticity allows us to avoid almost all messages and to do so efficiently. However, automaticity comes with a price. We allow the media to condition us while we are in this automatic state. The media condition us to habitual exposure patterns to the messages they want to present. This increases the risk that we will miss many of the messages that might have value for us. The media also condition us to accept unchallenged the meaning they present in their messages. This increases the risk we will accept faulty meaning.

Without a good understanding of the media, their messages, and the effects, people can develop misunderstandings and misperceptions about their world. Those who fail to develop their media literacy will get swept along in a tide of messages. Knowing a lot about current events presented by news organizations does not necessarily mean we know what the problems in the world are—or how to deal with them. The media can give us a false sense that we are knowledgeable.

CHAPTER 2

Explicating the Construct of Media Literacy

2

Explicating the Construct of Media Literacy

A wide range of people have been writing on the topic of media literacy for some time now, and it is easy to access all kinds of information on the topic. For example, a search for media literacy on Google results in more than 87,000 hits. Although this is a very large number, it is merely the tip of the iceberg, because Google reported only those writings that use the term *media literacy*. Writings that use other terms in place of media literacy, terms such as *media education, critical thinking,* and *information processing,* were not included, and neither was information not on the Internet.

The availability of so much information on this topic is a very positive characteristic because it indicates that the topic is important to many people. There is a lot of vitality, which produces many ideas. Among scholars, media literacy is really the convergence of three huge bodies of knowledge: media studies (the industries, content, and effects), human thinking (how people attend to messages and construct meaning), and pedagogy (how to help people access information, develop skills, and become educated). Media literacy is not just the overlapping intersection of these three; instead, it is the entire realm covered by all three.

The downside of having access to such a wealth of ideas on the topic is that it creates a big challenge to organize it. For example, to get an idea about the variety of ways people on the Internet define media literacy, see Table 2.1 for definitions from citizen action groups and Table 2.2 for definitions from scholars. Several years ago, Bill Christ and I tried to provide some organization about this complex phenomenon of media literacy in a

Table 2.1   Definitions of Media Literacy: Citizen Action Groups

Group and Source	Definition
Action Coalition for Media Education (http://www.acmecoalition.org/about.html)	Encourage critical thinking and free expression, examine the corporate media system, and inspire active participation in society
Alliance for a Media Literate America (http://www.amlainfo.org/)	Critical inquiry, learning, and skill building rather than on media bashing and blame
American Psychiatric Association (http://www.psych.org/public_info/media_violence.cfm)	Media literacy skills are vital; rather than allow the media to promote unchallenged the quick fix of violent solutions, conflict resolution skills involving patience and negotiation should be taught
Center for Media Literacy (http://www.medialit.org/pd_services.html#crash_course)	"A framework for accessing, analyzing, evaluating and creating media. The development of critical thinking and production skills needed to live fully in the 21st-century media culture." Also defined as a "new vision of literacy for the 21st century: the ability to communicate competently in all media forms, print and electronic, as well as to access, understand, and analyze and evaluate the powerful images, words and sounds that make up our contemporary mass media culture." Also, "through a four-step inquiry process of awareness . . . Analysis . . . Reflection . . . Action, media literacy helps young people acquire an empowering set of navigational skills," which include the ability to access, analyze, evaluate, and create media
Children Now (http://www.childrennow.org/television/tv%2Das%2Da%2Dtool.htm)	Media literacy is a way to foster critical-viewing skills in young viewers
Citizens for Media Literacy (http://www.main.nc.us/cml/)	How to think critically about TV and advertising; special emphasis is placed on the benefits of telling one's own stories rather than being preoccupied with manufactured stories designed to promote the purchase of products

Group and Source	Definition
Coalition for Quality Children's Media (KIDS FIRST!) (*http://www.kidsfirst.org/ kidsfirst/html/whatcq.htm*)	Teaching kids to become more critical media users and to reduce the impact of and exposure to violent and biased media; The coalition teaches them to recognize programs that are intellectually and creatively stimulating; that break down racial, gender, handicapped and cultural boundaries; and that are produced with high technical and artistic standards
Media Awareness Network (*http://www.media-awareness. ca/eng*)	To be functionally literate in the world today, young people need critical thinking skills to "read" all the messages that are informing, entertaining, and selling to them every day
Media Education Foundation (*http://www.mediaed.org/index_ html*)	The tools and vocabulary needed to reexamine media images and their influence on how we think about our personal, political, economic, and cultural worlds
Media Watch (*http://www.mediawatch.com/*)	Challenge abusive stereotypes and other biased images commonly found in the media
National Communication Association (*www.natcom.org/instruction/ k-12/ standards.pdf*)	A media literate person understands how words, images, and sounds influence the way meanings are created and shared in contemporary society in ways that are both subtle and profound; a media literate person is equipped to assign value, worth, and meaning to media use and media messages
National Leadership Conference on Media (Aufderheide, 1993)	The ability to access, analyze, evaluate, and communicate messages in a wide variety of forms of literacy
National Telemedia Council (Considine, 1995, p. 1) (*http://danenet.wicip.org/ntc/ NTC.HTM*)	The ability to choose, to understand—within the context of content, form/style, impact, industry and production—to question, to evaluate, to create and/or produce and to respond thoughtfully to the media we consume; It is mindful viewing, reflective judgment; also, the ability to access, analyze, evaluate, and create information in a variety of print and nonprint media formats

(Continued)

Table 2.1 (Continued)

Group and Source	Definition
New Mexico Media Literacy Project *(http://www.nmmlp.org/nmmlp. htm)* (Moody, 1996, p. 113).	The ability to critically consume and create media. Media literate individuals are better able to decipher the complex messages they receive from television, radio, newspapers, magazines, books, billboards and signs, packaging and marketing materials, video games, and the Internet. Media literacy skills can help one understand not only the surface content of media messages but the deeper and often more important meaning beneath the surface. Media literacy education seeks to give media consumers greater freedom by teaching them to analyze, access, evaluate, and produce media. The New Mexico project "defines media literacy as the ability to access, analyze, evaluate, and create messages in various media" (from Moody)
Northwest Media Literacy Project *(http://www.mediathink.org/ aboutML.htm)*	The ability to critically assess media messages in order to understand their impact on us, our communities, our society, and our planet; it is also a movement to raise awareness of media and their influence
Office of National Drug Control Policy *(http://www.nytimes.com/ learning/teachers/NIE/ medialiteracy/intro.pdf)*	"To (a) recognize how media messages influence us (e.g., develop a vocabulary to recognize manipulative techniques, develop skills to protect oneself against messages about drugs or negative lifestyle choices that are embedded in the media), to (b) develop critical thinking (e.g., know that messages are constructed by people with points of view and commercial interests, uncover value messages inherent in media, evaluate information for accuracy and reliability), to foster self-esteem (e.g., creatively produce satisfying and constructive messages)"

Source: Compiled by Sahara Byrne.

symposium for the *Journal of Communication* (Christ & Potter, 1998). We asked eight media literacy scholars to address the question, What is my conceptualization of media literacy? The authors produced eight great essays, but the strength of the writing was in illuminating a wide range of issues, debates, and concepts more than in suggesting a convergence of meaning.

Table 2.2   Definitions of Media Literacy: Media Scholars

Author/Date	Definition
Adams and Hamm (2001)	"Media literacy may be thought of as the ability to create personal meaning from the visual and verbal symbols we take in every day from television, advertising, film, and digital media. It is more than inviting students to simply decode information. They must be critical thinkers who can understand and produce in the media culture swirling around them." (p. 33)
Anderson (1981)	"[The] skillful collection, interpretation, testing, and application of information regardless of medium or presentation for some purposeful action." (p. 22)
Barton and Hamilton (1998; as cited in Margaret Mackey, 2002, p. 5–6)	"[Literacy is] primarily something people do; it is an activity, located in the space between thought and text. Literacy does not just reside in people's heads as a set of skills to be learned, and it does not just reside on paper, captured as texts to be analysed. Like all human activity, literacy is essentially social, and it is located in the interaction between people." (p. 3)
Hobbs (1997a)	"Literacy is the ability to access, analyze, evaluate, and communicate messages in a variety of forms" (p. 7). She says this definition suggests the following characteristics: inquiry-based education, student-centered learning, problem solving in cooperative teams, alternatives to standardized testing, and integrated curriculum.
Sholle and Denski (1995)	Media literacy should be conceptualized within a critical pedagogy, and thus "it must be conceived as a political, social, and cultural practice." (p. 17).
Silverblatt and Eliceiri (1997)	"[Media literacy is] a critical-thinking skill that enables audiences to decipher the information that they receive through the channels of mass communications and empowers them to develop independent judgments about media content." (p. 48)

The diversity in the *Journal of Communication* symposium as well as the diversity across the broader range of writing about media literacy indicates that the topic has attracted an eclectic range of scholars and concerned citizens. In this chapter, I will illuminate the nature of the definitions proposed for media literacy and analyze that definitional work. I will then make a case for the importance of a synthesized definition. Then, working in a larger frame, I will make a case for why it is important to develop a theory for media literacy.

I. Analyzing Definitions

There are two obvious dimensions for analyzing the definitions of media literacy. One of these dimensions is how scholars conceptualize literacy. The second is the media to which they link the literacy.

A. Literacy

Conceptualizing what is meant by literacy is perhaps the most popular form of definitional work. Some of these definitions focus primarily on skills, others focus primarily on knowledge, and some focus on a combination of skills and knowledge (for a summary, see Appendix A).

Several scholars have noted that a range of perspectives are expressed on the idea of literacy (Hobbs, 1997a, 1997b; Kuhlthau, 1997; McClure, 1997; Meyrowitz, 1998; Zettl, 1998). There has always been and still is a debate about what literacy is, even when the debate is constrained to the ability to read the written word (Tyner, 1998). The debate concerns what literacy is and how it contributes to the good of individuals and society at large. Tyner (1998) also observes,

> Operative definitions for the broad term *literacy* have become so mired in cultural politics and theoretical hairsplitting that a constellation of multiple kinds of literacy has emerged to represent addenda to literacy, or aspects of literacy that are felt to be missing in its common usage. (p. 63)

Also, Kellner (1995) argues,

> The Frankfurt School, for instance, developed a powerful critique of the cultural industries and the ways that they manipulate individuals into conforming to the beliefs, values, and practices of the existing society, but the critical theorists lack

theories of how one can resist media manipulation, how one can come to see through its ruses and seductions, how one can read against the grain to derive critical insights into self and society through the media, and how one can produce alternative forms of media and culture. (p. xiv)

How broadly should literacy be conceptualized? Should it be regarded primarily as a skill (Aufderheide, 1997; Kulleseid & Strickland, 1989; Neuman, 1991), as an accumulation of knowledge (Bianculli, 1992), or as a perspective on the world (Potter, 2001)? In the symposium, we said, "even with the re-emergence of media literacy as a key area of interest, the construct itself remains a complex and dynamic phenomenon" (Christ & Potter, 1998, p. 5).

Using a component type of definition sometimes gives the appearance to the casual reader that the author is restricting the view on media literacy. For example, Messaris (1998) argues that "a central component of media literacy should be an understanding of the representational conventions through which the users of media create and share meanings" (p. 70), especially visual representations. This seems to limit media literacy to a focus on one type of convention. But then later, Messaris says,

Ideally, this knowledge should encompass all aspects of the workings of the media: their economic foundations, organizational structures, psychological effects, social consequences, and, above all, their "language," that is, the representational conventions and rhetorical strategies of ads, TV programs, movies, and other forms of mass media content. (p. 70)

So component definitions can also serve to expand a reader's perspective on the concept by adding new components.

One trend in defining media literacy is to argue that there are multiple literacies, and this serves to use components to expand the idea of media literacy beyond the ability to recognize printed symbols, that is, to read a printed language. For example, Meyrowitz (1998) argues that media literacy is a complex construct and needs to be conceptualized as a number of literacies and that students need to be able to perform a range of analyses to be considered literate. Also, Adams and Hamm (2001) argue for multiple literacies:

At one time literacy was squeezed into an established framework of reading and writing. The meaning has changed as new circumstances and new approaches to teaching have opened up a much wider range of possibilities. The word "literacy" has become almost synonymous with the word "competence." (p. v)

"Being literate now implies having the ability to decode information from all types of media," Adams and Hamm continue, and by media, they include "technological literacy, visual literacy, information literacy, networking literacy, and more" (p. 3). Adams and Hamm (2001) take a broad approach to defining media literacy, calling it "the ability to read, write, speak, listen, think, and view" (p. vii). They say that viewing is especially important and that viewing includes looking critically at visual information in a television production, a movie, a video game, an Internet Web site, or a computer simulation. They also include "media analysis, multimedia production, collaborative inquiry, networking technologies, and more. We view media as a junction point between disciplines that can serve as a vehicle for pulling fragmented elements of the curriculum together" (p. vii). They also say that "literacy now requires an understanding of information and communication technology. It also requires manipulating the processes used to create messages in the modern world" (p. 1). Hobbs (1998) believes the connection between media literacy and production skills is important. She says that media access, analysis, and production skills are all linked.

Some scholars have used the term *critical media literacy* to emphasize the skill of evaluating messages. For example, Alvermann, Moon, and Hagood (1999) say that critical media literacy is "providing individuals access to understanding how the print and non-print texts that are part of everyday life help to construct their knowledge of the world and the various social, economic, and political position they occupy within it" (pp. 1–2). Media literacy is also concerned with creating communities of people who interact in complex social and cultural contexts and use this awareness to decide what textual positions to accept (Buckingham, 1998a, 1998b; Hilton, 1996; Luke, 1998).

Tyner (1998) says there are the multiple literacies of computer literacy, electronic literacy, information literacy, technology literacy, visual literacy, and media literacy. As for media literacy, Tyner says it

attempts to consolidate strands from the communication multi-literacies that correspond with the convergence of text, sound and image, including the moving image. . . Its all encompassing nature is both a strength and a weakness that is reflected in attempts at consensus about its definitions and purposes. (p. 113)

Others have also taken a broader view for literacy. Johnson (2001) says,

The definition of literacy has recently been expanded to include the ideas of communication, functioning in society, and dealing with all forms of information in a technological age. Whereas the former definition of literacy regarded the print media as its focus, a discourse using an expanded view of literacy must include other forms of media. (p. 1)

But this definition is not limited to the media; it also includes interpersonal communication of all forms. When a definition covers everything, it explains nothing. In my theory, I draw the line between mediated and non-mediated communication. The reason this line is important is because the character of mediated communication is different in its sheer magnitude and aggressiveness. It forces us into a state of automaticity so that we can ignore almost all of it, and this is a huge difference. Granted we slip into states of automaticity with interpersonal interactions, but these are usually downstream. For example, when a significant other drags out the same tired argument for the hundredth time or when a college professor is giving the fifth example of a too obvious point, we slip into automaticity. But our normal approach to interpersonal communication is conscious processing; not so with the media.

B. Media

Some writers have emphasized certain media over others. For example, some writers focus their attention on the ability to use oral and written language (Maddison, 1971; Scribner & Cole, 1981; Sinatra, 1986), still and moving images (Messaris, 1994; Metallinos, 1999), television (Goodwin & Whannel, 1990; Zettl, 1998), computers (Adams & Hamm, 1989; Gardiner, 1997), or multimedia (Buckingham, 1993a; Buckingham & Sefton-Green, 1997; Christ, 1998), whereas others span many different kinds of media (Adams & Hamm, 2001; Hobbs, 1997a; Potter, 2001; Silverblatt, 1995). For example, Adams and Hamm (2001) argue that people should understand all technologies that deliver information.

II. Identifying Key Elements Across Definitions

As can be seen in the above analysis of definitional work on media literacy, there are many different types of definitions and many, many elements. The good thing about this condition is that it shows there is a great deal of interest in the topic from many different people.

Another pattern is that the different definitions are more complementary than they are competitive. That is to say, there is little evidence that one group of scholars is rallying around a definition that other scholars reject.

Instead, the differences in definitions seem to involve how much to include in the definitions and what to regard as most important. Thus, it appears that different writers are emphasizing different parts of the complex pheno- menon. The ideas of the many writers substantially overlap, but each writer presents something unique to extend beyond the commonality. It is not as if some writers are saying a thing is green while others say it is red. Instead, it is more like all writers agree that there are patches of green and patches of red. The disagreement surfaces over whether green or red should be empha- sized more. Or more typically, some writers simply choose to write about the green, and others prefer to write about the red. For example, some scholars argue that media literacy should be treated primarily as a public policy issue (Aufderheide, 1993), a critical cultural issue (Alvarado & Boyd-Barrett, 1992), a set of pedagogical tools for elementary school teachers (Houk & Bogart, 1974), suggestions for parents (DeGaetano & Bander, 1996; Kelly, 1983), McLuhanesque speculation (Gordon, 1971), or a topic of scholarly inquiry from a physiological (Messaris, 1994), cogni- tive (Sinatra, 1986), or anthropological (Scribner & Cole, 1981) tradition. Some writers focus primarily on one culture, such as American culture (Manley-Casimer & Luke, 1987; Ploghoft & Anderson, 1981), British culture (Buckingham, 1990; Masterman, 1985), or Chilean culture (Freire, 1985), while others refer to several countries and/or cultures (Brown, 1991; Maddison, 1971; Scheunemann, 1996). Media literacy is a term applied to the study of textual interpretation (Buckingham, 1998a, 1998b; Meyrowitz, 1998; Zettl, 1998), context and ideology (Lewis & Jhally, 1998), and audi- ence (Buckingham, 1998a, 1998b). The term is also used as a synonym for or component of media education (Sholle & Denski, 1995).

All this activity is a positive sign that media literacy is an important con- cern to many sincere, concerned people. However, how can we make sense of all this thought and activity to a broader audience that is also becoming concerned about media literacy? There appear to be five recurring ideas across most of these definitions. Each of these is illuminated below.

A. Media Literacy Is Not Limited to One Medium

The key idea here is that the old idea of literacy was limited to reading and further limited to recognizing symbols. This still seems to be the foun- dation for all print literacy. However, media literacy is something much broader, that is, constructing meaning from experiences and contexts (eco- nomic, political, cultural, etc.). The media differ in terms of the symbols they use, their attitude toward audiences, their motives for doing business, and their aesthetics. The more people know about these differences across media, the more they can appreciate commonalities and the more they can understand how messages are sensitive to the medium in which they are delivered.

In the minds of many people, the term *literacy* is most associated with the print media, so it means the ability to read (Scribner & Cole, 1981; Sinatra, 1986). Some people expand the term to *visual literacy* as they think about other media such as film and television (Goodwin & Whannel, 1990; Messaris, 1994). Other writers have used the term *computer literacy* (Adams & Hamm, 1989). Reading literacy, visual literacy, and computer literacy are not synonyms for media literacy; instead, they are merely components. *Media* literacy includes all these specialized abilities as well as something more. If we don't know how to read, we cannot get much out of the print media. If we have trouble understanding visual and narrative conventions, we cannot get much out of television or film. If we cannot use a computer, we are cut off from what is growing into the most important medium.

B. Media Literacy Requires Skills

On the surface, there is a debate over which skills are required, but this may be a matter of naming or a matter of writers trying to be suggestive of competencies rather than trying to be complete.

Media education is organized around key concepts, which are analytical tools rather than an alternative content. They do not seek to replace "bad" content with "better" content. Media education aims to foster not simply critical understanding but critical autonomy. Masterman (1997) argues that "media education is primarily investigative" (p. 41).

C. Media Literacy Requires Certain Types of Knowledge

Most people agree that in order for people to be media literate, they need good information in at least three areas: content, industries, and effects. With content, people need to understand that media messages are constructions that follow certain conventions and that the conventions distort reality rather than represent it. As for the industries, people need to understand that the media are businesses with particular motivations. For effects, people need to understand that they have the ability to negotiate meaning for themselves.

D. Media Literacy Must Deal With Values

Masterman (1997) argues that media education "does not seek to impose specific cultural values." He continues, "It does not seek to impose ideas on what constitutes 'good' or 'bad' television, newspapers, or films" (p. 41). Of course, that position in itself is value laden. While media educators may not be defining bad and good messages, they are implying that mindless exposure to messages is bad and that interpreting the messages actively is good. The issue is not whether this enterprise of media literacy is value laden or not. Instead, the issue is where are the values and what are they.

III. Need for a Synthesized Definition

The writing about media literacy is like a large complex patchwork of ideas. Many of these ideas are truly inspired, but it is difficult to make sense of it all. Thus, there are people like Herb Zettl (1998), who complained,

> The plethora of available articles, books, classroom materials, and information on the internet dealing with media literacy does not seem to help very much in answering the question, "What is media literacy?" Much of the material consists of recipes for how to prevent children from watching too much or unsuitable television programs. (p. 81)

Now 6 years later, the same observation can be made. There is considerable evidence that the construct is still in flux.

Many scholars have had the same feelings Zettl expressed about the mass of ideas concerning media literacy, and periodically, groups of these people have joined efforts to struggle with crafting a definition they can all accept. For example in 1992, U.S. scholars interested in media literacy convened the National Leadership Conference on Media Literacy and after several days of discussion agreed that literacy "is the ability to access, analyze, evaluate, and communicate messages in a variety of forms" (Aufderheide, 1997, p. 79). Furthermore, the scholars agreed that most conceptualizations include the following elements: Media are constructed and construct reality; media have commercial implications; media have ideological and political implications; form and content are related in each medium, each of which has a unique aesthetic, codes, and conventions; and receivers negotiate meaning in media (Aufderheide, 1997, p. 80).

Such a definition is valuable because it provides a rallying point for lots of different types of scholars and educators. This gives the group identity, and if the definition is general, it appeals to a wide variety of thinkers. The problem is that when committees build definitions, some members insist that their definitional element be included and this detail tends to narrow definitions rather than keeping it general. In the National Leadership Conference definition on media literacy above, some elements are very general, such as not specifying a particular type of message or form of message. But when the definition specifies particular skills—to access, analyze, and evaluate—it begs the question about whether other skills are purposely being rejected, skills such as recognizing patterns, inducing conclusions, synthesizing solutions to problems, constructing messages, and so on.

General definitions have great value as umbrellas; that is, they can provide a sense of the perimeters of concern by showing what ideas are included under a term. But general definitions lack specificity; that is, they cannot provide much detail, especially to people who want to use the definition to design an educational curriculum or even to create some strategies for themselves.

Clearly, a general "big picture" definition is needed to orient readers to the map of media literacy thinking. Then, the details are also needed to show how ideas have developed in each of the components of that definition. In short, conceptualizing media literacy requires a hermeneutic process of learning the context and using that context as orientation to learning the specifics. Furthermore, the more one learns the specifics, the better one understands the context. The process is a spiral where understanding the specifics gives you a better understanding of the context (big picture), which leads to a greater appreciation of any one specific.

Both types of work are necessary if we take a hermeneutic approach. As useful as these definitions are in giving readers an orientation to the big picture, their general nature limits the amount of detail and texture that can be provided. The specifics are important, especially to people interested in doing something with the idea of media literacy. For example, some people want to use the concept to develop a course or a curriculum, others want to develop materials, and others want to show readers how to empower themselves to be media literate. General definitions do not help much in guiding people with these kinds of goals.

How can both the general and the specific be achieved? The answer is to synthesize a definition that has all of the following three features. First, an umbrella definition, which is short and general, is needed in order to provide an overview of media literacy. Second, because media literacy is a process, a definition needs to articulate the steps or components in that process. Third, a purpose definition is needed to illuminate what media literacy can deliver.

IV. Need for a Cognitive Theory of Media Literacy

In addition to a need for a synthesized definition of media literacy, we also need a theory of media literacy. Such a theory needs to illuminate the particulars about why being media literate is good; that is, it needs to elaborate on the purpose definition. This is needed to provide a foundation for articulating processes and techniques. Without such a foundation, there is no rationale for researchers who want to design treatments or educators who need to design teaching modules. Also, because the effort required for people to develop greater media literacy is likely to be substantial, we need to be clear that the payoffs warrant the costs.

A. Why Be Media Literate?

The advantages of being media literate are not addressed in many writings. Rather, it is assumed that readers will accept that being media literate is a good thing, much as it is often assumed that everyone believes it is better to be rich than poor, better to be smart than stupid, and better to be attractive than ugly. I, of course, do not disagree that being media literate is better than not, but I think we need to address the costs that present considerable barriers preventing people from being more media literate. Before we can expect people to expend the considerable effort to develop skills, to build elaborate knowledge structures, and to pay attention during media exposures, we must demonstrate that the rewards for such effort are worth it.

There are reasons to be media literate as well as reasons not to be media illiterate. However, people rarely talk about the positives. While the wide-ranging body of writing about media literacy includes many valuable insights and suggestions, several things are missing that could be helpful. One is a cataloging of the range of negative effects. When reading an essay that convinces us about the danger of one or several negative effects, it is tempting to think: What else? Are there other negative effects? If there are, might some of these other negative effects be more serious? Furthermore, are all the possible effects *negative*? Are there no positive effects? A systematic overview of the variety of potential effects from the media is needed to provide a good context for understanding criticism about particular effects.

Some writers have provided a general purpose definition that illuminates what they think a media literate individual should think and do (for a summary, see Appendix B). Some focus more on what the purpose of educational experiences should be to help people, especially children, become more media literate. Some definitions focus more on personal activism. There is even a definition that illuminates the product of illiteracy. Some of these definitions emphasize what a person should do to become more media literate or to help others become more media literate. Other process definitions illuminate how thinking about media literacy has changed over time or how it ought to change.

The one thing these definitions all seem to have in common is that the purpose of media literacy is focused on improving individuals in some way. The underlying assumption appears to be that if enough individuals experience an amelioration, then society at large will experience benefits. Another common element is that businesses providing messages will need to undergo some changes, changes that are not necessarily harmful to them. That is, the market for certain products may dwindle, but the assumption is that other markets will open up. Thus, the purpose is not to put the message providers out of business, only to shift resources.

What do scholars mean when they refer to improving individuals? This could mean many things. Usually, the goal is expressed in the abstract, such as getting people to understand messages better (Masterman, 1985) or helping people think for themselves (Aufderheide, 1997) and make better choices (Desmond, 1997b). For example, Masterman (1997) argues that the objective of media literacy is

> [to] produce well-informed citizens who can make their own judgements on the basis of the available evidence. In so far as media education deals with value judgements, it does so in the ways which encourage students to explore the range of value judgements made about a given media text and to examine the sources of such judgements (including their own) and their effects. It does not seek to impose ideas on what constitutes "good" or "bad" television, newspapers, or films. (p. 41)

In a general sense, improving individuals means to enable them to make better constructions of meaning from media messages. The assumption is that people are more likely to know what is good for them as individuals than do the media, which are primarily interested in their own marketing agendas and view their audiences as aggregates of people with something in common that defines their niche.

Some media literacy scholars have alluded to problems that can occur and suggest that these problems could be fixed if people were more media literate. But these problems are either presented in an ambiguous way (if you don't understand the media, you will develop false beliefs) or in a limited set of negative effects (typically limited to children being scared by certain portrayals and led to behave badly by other portrayals).

B. Rationale for Techniques

Another reason that a theory of media literacy is needed is to provide a strong rationale for the testing of particular techniques. We desperately need research to provide findings about how people can improve their filtering of messages from the media as well as improve their experiences with the information they encounter. The need for this type of information is high, but the resources available to generate these insights are modest. Therefore, we need to be efficient in addressing the most pressing concerns and designing research that will result in findings that can have the greatest impact on helping people understand how they process information.

One of the current strengths of the writings on media literacy is a wide range of suggestions for exercises people should do to develop competencies and understandings about various aspects of the media. While these suggestions have a great deal of appeal on the surface, they need to be accompanied with a rationale to show how the techniques should be applied and for which type of people. Without such an accompanying rationale, many techniques that look good on the surface may actually cause more harm than good when applied. For example, it is assumed that it is a good thing for parents to watch television or movies with their children. This assumption has obvious validity—on the surface. But let's think this through a bit. What if the parents are not much more knowledgeable than their children? There is evidence that only a small minority of parents are aware of the meanings of the labels on the V-chip (Kaiser Family Foundation, 1999; Schmitt, 2000). Furthermore, even parents who do understand the ratings will frequently find them misapplied or even missing from shows (Kunkel et al., 2002). Parents, of course, have more experience with the media and with life than do their children. But does this experience automatically translate into knowledge about how to help their children reduce their risks of negative effects? It is not clear that it does. In fact, some of those negative effects take years to show up, so it is likely that parents are experiencing some negative effects—such as desensitization and false beliefs about the real world—that their children are not experiencing. It is likely that most parents do not understand the extent to which they have been desensitized to certain portrayals and do not understand which of their beliefs are false and have been conditioned by the media without their permission or awareness. When these parents try to guide their children to be like them, negative effects can get amplified.

On top of all this, children may have some competencies and skills in a far more developed form than their parents, such as programming the VCR or computer, parallel processing of information, and so on. Given all the arguments above, it is risky to conclude that children will benefit from the guidance their parents can provide. In many joint viewing situations, the children may have better skills than their parents and more experience with a genre or a particular show, and they may exhibit fewer negative long-term effects of media exposure than do parents.

Most media literacy scholars focus on helping children. While it is always admirable to help children, people need to ask themselves about their own levels of literacy. Simply being past childhood does not qualify a person to know how to increase a child's media literacy.

My point here is that media literacy is not a simple concept deriving from a singular skill that builds uniformly with age and experience. Instead, media literacy should be conceptualized as a complex of skills and knowledge that vary widely across people, even at a given age. Media literacy is a concern that demands we do something. However, doing something before we are clear about what we need to do is not likely to decrease the risks of harmful effects, and it may end up making the situation worse. This is why we need a set of principles to explain the media potentials (for good as well as for harm), the process of how those potentials grow into actualities, and how people can control that process for themselves. We need a theory of media literacy that can address these fundamental concerns in detail and provide an integrated system of explanation about what the dangers as well as opportunities are from exposures to media messages, how those messages exert an influence on us, and how we can gain more control over that process of influence so we can direct it to our own goals and thus reduce our programming by the media.

V. Conclusion

There has been a great deal of dynamic scholarly activity on media literacy. That activity has many of the characteristics of brainstorming. There is great vitality in the production of ideas about what media literacy should be, its purposes, and the techniques that can be used to achieve it. However, there is little structure to the topic as a whole. I argue that it would be useful to have a unified perspective that would draw from the range of ideas and synthesize a set of operating principles. That is the goal of *Theory of Media Literacy*. In the next chapter, this information will be used to synthesize a definition of media literacy.

PART II

Introducing the Theory

CHAPTER 3

Definitions and Distinctions

3

Definitions
and Distinctions

This chapter introduces the key terms and definitions used in this cognitive theory of media literacy. First, some terms foundational to the theory are defined. Then, seven pairs of constructs are defined through contrasts. Finally, the main construct of media literacy is defined through a synthesis of elements identified in the previous chapter.

I. Definitions of Primary Terms

This theory of media literacy requires an acceptance of definitions for many fundamental terms. In everyday language, these terms are treated as primitive concepts, because people assume there is a shared meaning for them. However, in this theory, I do not treat these terms as primitive and prefer to offer particular definitions that may be different than the meaning held for them by some readers. A few of these terms are briefly defined in this section; then, those definitions are further elaborated in the next section dealing with key distinctions.

A. The Media

The media are the technological means of disseminating messages. They are usually categorized as being print (newspapers, books, magazines) or electronic (radio, CDs, film, television, computer). The media create vehicles as the means of delivering messages. For example, newspaper is a medium; *The New York Times* and the *Wall Street Journal* are vehicles. Television is a medium; *Friends*, *The Evening News*, and *The Sopranos* are vehicles.

There are two kinds of media: Mass and nonmass. This distinction has very little to do with the size of the audience, although that is how most people approach defining *mass*. Nor does it have much to do with the experience the audience has when receiving the messages, although this was the main criterion for defining a mass audience for a long time (for more detail on this, see Potter 2001, Chapter 12). Instead, *mass* has to do with the motives of the sender. In a mass medium, the sender's main intention is to condition audiences into a ritualistic mode of exposure; that is, senders are much less interested in coaxing people into one exposure than they are in trying to get people into a position where they will regularly be exposed to their messages. Senders attempt this conditioning by making the exposures efficient to the audience. Efficiency is achieved when the messages require as little cost to the audience as possible while delivering maximum payoffs. The greater the message efficiency, the greater the audience size. As the mass media increase the size of their audience, their revenues also grow.

B. Information

The key component terms of information are *message, factual information,* and *social information*. Messages are those instruments that deliver information to us. Information is the content of those messages. Messages can be delivered in many different media: television, radio, CDs, video games, books, newspapers, magazines, Web sites, conversations, lectures, concerts, signs along the streets, labels on the products we buy, and so on. They can be large (an entire Hollywood movie) or small (one utterance by one character in a movie).

Messages are composed of two kinds of information: factual and social. A fact is something raw, unprocessed, and context-free. For example, when you watch the news and hear messages about terrorism, those messages are composed of facts, such as the World Trade Center in New York City was destroyed on September 11, 2001. On that day, the United States declared war on terrorism. The person suspected of planning the attack on the World Trade Center was Osama bin Laden. These statements are facts. Facts are discrete bits of information, such as names (of people, places, characters, etc.), definitions of terms, formula, lists, and the like.

Social information is composed of accepted beliefs that cannot be verified by authorities in the same way factual information can be. This is not to say that social information is less valuable or less real to people. Social information is composed of techniques that people learn from observing social interactions. Examples of social information are rules about how to dress, talk, and act to be considered attractive, smart, athletic, hip, and so on.

The media present three general types of messages: news, entertainment, and ads. At base, the media's primary purpose for producing and distributing all messages is to construct audiences to generate revenue. The three types of messages differ in their secondary purposes to the media. With news messages, the intention of the media is to evoke in audience members a sense that they are being informed. With entertainment messages, the intention of the media is to evoke in audience members a sense that they are having pleasant emotional experiences, particularly of laughter, character attraction, or vicarious fear. With advertising messages, the intention of the media is to stimulate in companies paying for the advertising a sense that those ad messages are changing target audiences in terms of their cognitions, attitudes, or behaviors.

Over time, the media have blended two or more of their secondary intentions to achieve their primary purpose more effectively. This has had the result of making it more difficult for audience members to understand the nature of messages. For example, there are messages referred to as docudramas, which are based on actual happenings in real life (from the news) but which have been fictionalized to increase their entertainment value. Thus, audiences are given a sense that they are accruing more value from a single message, that is, receiving information about the real world plus being entertained. Also, there are messages referred to as info-mercials, which use a news show or informational talk show-type format but are paid advertising messages. Thus, audiences are given the sense that they are accruing valuable, objective information on a problem, which they are given an easy and compelling means to solve.

There are also genres of messages. For example, within the set of television entertainment messages there are comedies, dramas, sports, news/information, cartoons, music, and so on. Each has its subgenres. For example, within dramas, there are crime dramas, action/adventure, family drama, continuing drama, and so on.

II. Key Distinctions

Seven distinctions are important to understanding this theory. First, there is a difference between partially specified and fully specified problems. Second, there is a difference between meaning matching and meaning construction. Third, exposure is different than attention. Fourth, there is the difference between automaticity and mindfulness. Fifth, there is the difference between information and knowledge. Sixth, there is a difference between schemas and knowledge structures. Seventh, there is the difference between competencies and skills.

A. Fully Specified and Partially Specified Problems

When we interact with media messages, we are confronted with fully specified as well as partially specified problems. It is important that we know which is which so that we can properly select the best approach to solve the type of problem that confronts us.

A fully specified problem is one where all the information that is needed to solve the problem is available to the person, either in the problem itself or in the person's existing schema on the topic. When people use this full set of information, they can all arrive at the same answer, confident that they have solved the problem in the one correct way. For example, consider the following problem:

$$6 + 18 = \underline{\hspace{1.5cm}}$$

People who understand that 6 and 18 represent numbers with particular values and that the symbol + means addition can arrive at a solution of 24 with ease and have confidence that their solution is the correct one. This is what is called a fully specified problem, because the person has enough information to solve the problem.

Not all problems are fully specified. Some are partially specified. For example, consider this problem:

$$Y + Z = 24$$

This problem has two unknowns—Y and Z—so there is not enough information to arrive at one solution with confidence. You could answer 6 and 18, while I might answer 10 and 14, and we would both be right. There are also many other correct answers to this problem, because it was only partially specified. To most of us, each of these answers intuitively seems faulty. Because many answers are possible, can any one of them be regarded as "the solution?" We prefer a more fully specified problem, such as $5 + Z = 24$; with this problem, we have enough information to know that Z is 19: There is one and only one correct answer.

We can solve fully specified problems with relative ease because we have memorized all the links we need, and the process of making sense is automatic. For example, learning to read in the first grade means learning to recognize symbols for letters, words, and sentences. The better we learn these symbols, the more automatically we can recognize and make sense of them. Learning to read in the elementary school years is largely a task of learning to recognize more and more of these symbols and associating them with their authority-determined definitions. When we see the sentence, "Jane throws the ball to Dick," we need to recognize that *Jane* is a word that is a symbol for a particular girl in the story and that the other words are symbols for particular ideas. We also need to recognize that the sentence is constructed in a way that Jane is the subject who is doing something (throwing a ball) and that Dick is receiving the action. When we are in the first grade, it is a struggle to learn how to do all this, but once we do, we can do it again and again, each time with less effort. Also, everyone learns the same symbols and definitions. This is a convergent task, where all of us must learn the same rules for recognizing symbols and their definitions.

The task of meaning construction is more difficult than the task of meaning matching. The primary reason for this difference is that the task of meaning construction is always a partially specified problem; that is, the challenge always includes one or more of the following characteristics. First, we are not sure what the meaning should be. Second, the beginning point is unclear. Third, there is an incomplete process that links a clear beginning point with a clear goal as a solution to the problem; that is, steps are missing that we need to arrive at one solution.

Now let's bring this idea of fully and partially specified problems into the realm of media literacy. Reading a page in a book is a combination of both fully specified and partially specified problems. The fully specified problems are where to start reading (upper left corner), how to scan eyes (left to right across each successive line in turn), and what to look for (black lines are letters arranged in groups or words that are separated by spaces; words are arranged in sentences, sentences in paragraphs). We need to be able to recognize a word and match its meaning to the definition for the word. These are all meaning-matching tasks. By the time we complete elementary school, these tasks can be performed with relative ease. But this is not all there is to reading. We might be able to make sense of each word and even each sentence but not get much meaning from the effort of reading. To construct meaning beyond the individual words, we need to move beyond competencies and use skills. Skills help us construct our meaning about the theme of the story, how morally the characters behave, how aesthetically pleasing the story is, and how the characters' actions resonate with our own experiences.

B. Meaning Matching and Meaning Construction

This distinction between meaning matching and meaning construction is a major one for this theory. With meaning matching, meaning is assumed to reside outside the person in an authority, such as a teacher, an expert, a dictionary, a textbook, or the like. The task for the person is to find those meanings and memorize them. Thus, parents and the educational institution are primarily responsible for housing the authoritative information and sharing it with the next generation. The media are also a major source of information, and for many people, the media have attained the status of an authoritative source, so people accept the meanings presented there.

While meaning matching is essentially a task composed of fully specified problems, meaning construction, in contrast, is composed of partially speci-fied problems, and this makes it a much more challenging task. Meaning construction is a process wherein people transform messages they take in and create meaning for themselves. Many meanings can be constructed from any media message, and furthermore, there are many ways to go about con-structing that meaning. Thus, people cannot learn a complete set of rules to accomplish this; instead, they need to be guided by their own information goals and use well-developed skills to creatively construct a path to reach their goals.

The two processes are not discrete; they are intertwined. To construct meaning, a person has to first recognize symbols and understand the sense in which they are being used in the message. Thus, the meaning-matching process is more fundamental, because the product of the meaning-matching process then is imported into the meaning-construction process.

To understand how this distinction is important for media literacy, we must focus on how people regard a task of information processing. Figure 3.1 shows that both meaning matching and meaning construction are continua, and they each can be plotted on a larger continuum of how people regard the task. On the left side are tasks that are fairly routine; that is, they are familiar and can be performed with high accuracy and little effort. An example would be reading simple sentences and being able to recognize words and their designated meaning. On the right extreme are tasks that are idiosyncratic; that is, they have never been encountered before and are unusual; there are no algorithms that can be learned to solve these problems. They must be solved in a creative manner.

Notice that the meaning-matching task is not a point on the routine-idiosyncratic continuum; meaning matching is a continuum of challenges. While some of the challenges can be met in a relatively automatic manner, others require more effort. These more challenging meaning-matching tasks

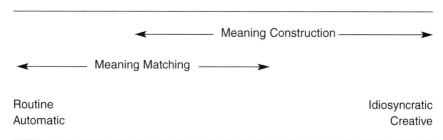

Figure 3.1   Meaning Matching and Meaning Construction

occur when symbol recognition is not yet learned well or when a symbol is ambiguous. Also, a symbol may have more than one meaning so a person has the additional task—beyond recognizing a symbol and associating its definition—of selecting among the definitions to choose the one most appropriate, given the context. Notice, too, that the meaning-construction task occupies a range on the routine-idiosyncratic continuum. Some meaning constructions require more effort and creativity than others.

Finally, notice that there is an overlap between the two processes In many tasks of information processing, people regard the task as one of meaning matching and try to find an automatic association of a message with a definition, when they would be better off making the effort to treat the task as one of meaning construction. The challenge to be more media literate rests in this mid-continuum area. The constant flow of media messages motivates people to be more efficient than accurate and hence to look for automatic ways of processing idiosyncratic messages. Thus, they use shortcuts to do this, and these shortcuts allow them to achieve higher efficiency. But the danger is that people frequently then construct faulty meaning. To avoid this danger, they need to expend the effort to treat these tasks as meaning construction and avoid shortcuts.

The most fundamental of all barriers that hinder people from becoming more media literate is treating meaning-construction problems as if they were simple meaning-matching problems. When this happens, people think that there are correct convergent meanings that they need to learn. Because they have not learned them, they go to the media to find them. They look for news and accept the constructions offered by "experts" as the one and only meaning. They look for political pundits and accept those positions as facts. They look at how characters in fictional stories live their lives and memorize that social information so they can use it, without adaptation, in living their own lives. After years of schooling, people have learned well how to go to sources outside themselves for information and acquire that information as solutions to what they see as fully specified problems. People are less comfortable in regarding these as partially specified problems, which would require them to search out a range of information, carefully analyze it for usefulness, evaluate the various claims, then synthesize their own opinions or conclusions. It is much easier to accept the opinions and conclusions of others.

C. Exposure and Attention

In everyday language, *exposure* is a term that is often used synonymously with the term *attention,* but in this theory, I draw an important distinction between the two terms. Exposure refers to being in physical proximity to a media message such that a person is in contact with that message. Attention is a conscious awareness of the message. Thus, attention is encompassed within the idea of exposure, that is, a person cannot attend to a message without being exposed to it. However, exposure is broader than attention because people could be exposed to messages without attending to them.

Exposure is not a unitary construct. In this theory, there are three modes of exposure: active searching, scanning, and screening. They differ in motive and amount of attention. Active searching is driven by a conscious desire for a particular message; attention is high as people develop their searching strategy, monitor its success, and continually make adaptations to achieve the goal. Scanning, like searching, begins with an awareness of a goal. Unlike searching, however, scanning does not require a particular question to motivate it. Instead, scanning is motivated by a general need, such as a need for entertainment or for information.

Screening is a message-monitoring state that requires the least amount of effort, hence attention. It begins with the default of automatically ignoring messages, that is, screening them out. There is no conscious goal or strategy. The screening out continues automatically with no effort until some element in a message breaks through people's default screen and captures their attention. The switch into the attention mode is usually automatic; that is, something in the message triggered the attention. Thus, message designers are in control of the screening process, because they can condition triggers into the minds of audience members then place certain elements in messages to set off the triggers.

D. Automaticity and Mindfulness

This distinction refers to the degree of awareness in the processing of information. Automaticity refers to cognitive activity that occurs outside of consciousness; that is, it is mindlessness (Fiske & Taylor, 1991, p. 283).

Mindlessness is a state where a person is not especially alert, thoughtful, or creative. Although the person is awake (not unconscious as if asleep or in a coma), the person is not actively thinking through decisions; instead, the person's mind is on automatic pilot where it executes habitual routines with very little mental effort. Automatic processing, according to Posner and Snyder (1975), must meet three criteria: (a) it must occur without intention, (b) it must occur without involving conscious awareness, and (c) it must not interfere with other mental activity.

For most people, driving a car is an automatic task. However, when we first learn to drive, it can be an overwhelming cognitive experience. With practice over time, however, we do not think about all the hand motions we make when we get in the car, turn it on, and get it moving. We do not think about all the visual information we process that guides us to drive safely and arrive at our destination accurately. People who drive to work each day rarely remember any of the details or hundreds of decisions they made on a particular commute. When we know a routine well, we no longer pay attention to individual components of the routine; we accomplish a wide variety of encoding tasks without much bothering our intentional, voluntary, effortful, conscious selves.

When we are in a state of automaticity, we can perform tasks with little effort or attention. Rogers, Rousseau, and Fisk (1999) explain:

> After extensive and consistent practice, some task components may become automatized. As a result, because they no longer require step-by-step application, they are performed faster, are more efficient, and are generally more accurate. Automatized task components generally do not require devotion of attentional resources and, hence, may be performed in parallel with other tasks. Another characteristic of automatic processes is that, once initiated they tend to run to completion unless a conscious effort is made to inhibit them. (p. 39)

The state of automaticity is the opposite of the state of mindfulness; in the automatic state, we are operating on automatic pilot and are unaware of the details of what we are doing. This, however, does not mean that when we are in the automatic state, we have no control over the process and are instead controlled by the media; this might be the case, but it need not be. The key to control lies in how we develop our automatic routines. If we learn the routines through a conscious process (such as driving a car), then we are still in control because we are simply following our own constructed routines. However, if the routines have been built up over years of media conditioning and thereby were formulated when we were in mindless states, then we are controlled by the media routines. It is important to remember that when people are in an automatic state, this is not always indicative of a low level of media literacy. We need to examine the routines that guide the automaticity and analyze whether they were constructed by the individual or conditioned by the media.

E. Information and Knowledge

In everyday language, the terms *information* and *knowledge* are used as synonyms, but in this theory, they have meanings very different from one another. Information is piecemeal and transitory, whereas knowledge is structured, organized, and of more enduring significance. Information resides in the messages, whereas knowledge resides in a person's mind. Information gives something to the person to interpret, whereas knowledge reflects that which has already been interpreted by the person.

Information is composed of facts. Facts by themselves are not knowledge, any more than a pile of bricks is a house. Knowledge requires structure to provide context and thereby exhibit meaning. Think of messages as the raw materials and skills as the tools you use to do something with the raw materials. That "something" is pulling the information out of the messages and turning that information into knowledge, that is, to reconstruct the information so that it will contribute to our knowledge structures. A characteristic of higher media literacy is the ability and habit of transforming information into knowledge structures.

F. Schemas and Knowledge Structures

Schema is a term that has been important in cognitive psychology for a long time. Bartlett (1932) introduced the idea of schema in his book *Remembering*. He defined schema as an "active organization of past reactions, or of past experiences, which must always be supposed to be operating in any well-adapted organic response" (p. 201). Since that time, the term *schema* has been used by many scholars. For example, Rumelhart and Norman (1988) conceptualize a schema as a large unit of organized information used for representing concepts, situation, events, and actions in memory. The purpose of schema is to help with information encoding, retrieval from memory, inference, and evaluation (Fiske & Taylor, 1991).

There has been a wide range of usage of the term *schema*, as well as terms that are synonyms. These alternative terms include *prototypes* (Cantor & Mischel, 1977, 1979), *frames* (Minsky, 1975), *stereotypes* (Lippmann, 1922), *social scripts* (Schank & Abelson, 1977), and *cognitive maps* (Rosch, 1978). A series of schemas are thought to be somewhat like scripts. *Script* has also been defined as a schema for routine events, such as going out to dinner (Schank & Abelson, 1977). If you ask people what they do when they go to a restaurant, most people say the same things in the same order; thus, they share scripts. For example, a script is a "structure that describes an appropriate sequence of events in a particular context" or "a predetermined stereotyped sequence of actions that defines a well-known situation" (Schank 1982, p. 170).

Schemas are networks or grouping concepts (Graesser, Millis, & Long, 1986). How are schemas organized? Typically, they use a series of nodes and links. "The result of the construction process is considered to be an associative structure formed by connecting nodes representing individual objects or concepts with links" (Smith, 1999, p. 252).

Schemas are constructed by remembering simple associations. In their everyday lives, people make informal associations, such as between a name and a face when they meet someone. If they remember the ideas, these are stored in memory as nodes, and if they remember that the two ideas are associated, the two nodes are linked together, such that thinking about one of the nodes brings to mind the other. This is a schema. Schemas are ideas linked together in associative networks. For example, a person sees a word on a page, asks someone what the word means, and remembers the word and the definition. Thus, there are two nodes in memory, one for the visual image of the word (or the sound of the word) and the other for the denoted meaning. The two nodes are linked together. The more a person accesses this association, the stronger the link becomes. Eventually, other related words may become linked to this association; if this happens, the links and nodes grow organically, linkage by linkage.

Schema are composed of memories of sound, smell, touch, taste, and how things feel. They also contain memories of emotions. All of these elements are linked together in networks of associations. Some of those links between elements are strong, and others are much weaker. For example, when some people think of dog, their first reaction might be one of fear as they recall being bit by a dog when they were very young. The next thing they might remember is a visual image of a dog with bared teeth because that has the strongest link from the fear. Then, there might be a link to the sound of the dog barking and the person crying. As we use a schema, we begin with the element that is most salient and work our way to other elements by following the links throughout the network.

Schemas and knowledge structures share some commonalities. Both are constructions by individuals; people are not born with these but must build them as they experience life. Both are composed of information of a cognitive, emotional, aesthetic, and moral nature. Both are used by people to make sense of their world, and both are organic; that is, they are continually in a state of change as people acquire new experiences.

The differences between the two are in how people construct them and how the information is organized in them. Schemas are constructed quickly and efficiently by linking a pair of elements, such as a symbol and a definition or a face and a name. In contrast, knowledge structures are carefully constructed in a conscious and systematic manner. Their goals are accuracy and utility rather than efficiency. People spend more time tracking down useful information, not simply waiting for it to come to them in serendipitous exposures. Also, people check and cross-check the accuracy of the information. Thus, schema are composed of elements that are informally grouped together, usually by expediency. In contrast, knowledge structures are consciously built and maintained with the use of higher level skills.

We can construct a knowledge structure beginning with a schema if we thoroughly examine our schema and clear out all the inaccurate and irrelevant information, then put in the effort to search out new information to fill in the logical gaps. Schema are simple guides, whereas knowledge structures are authoritative maps that provide strong context for helping us work toward the most useful determination of meaning in an accurate manner.

Another important difference is that knowledge structures are formal mapping devices with analytical depth, whereas schema are loose amalgamations of elements that are connected by simple associations. Schemas can be regarded as two dimensional, with the elements lying on the surface. Knowledge structures are more like outlines where concepts are nested within other concepts. Location of a concept matters a great deal to knowledge structures. This is why a knowledge structure is a better mapping tool and why it is better for helping people understand context.

Knowledge structures require some thought to construct and maintain, but they offer great power in long-term efficiency. Thus, I use the term *knowledge structures* to focus attention on knowledge rather than information and also to focus attention on structure instead of organization.

G. Competencies and Skills

There is an important distinction between competencies and skills. Competencies are the abilities people have acquired to help them interact with the media and to access information in the messages. Competencies are learned early in life, then applied automatically. Competencies are relatively dichotomous; that is, either people are able to do something, or they are not able. For example, people either know how to recognize a word and match its meaning to a memorized denoted meaning, or they do not.

Skills, in contrast, are tools that people develop through practice. Skill ability is not dichotomous; instead, people's skill ability can be plotted along a wide continuum. People's abilities on these techniques are highly variable; that is, some people have little ability to use a particular skill while other people have enormous ability. There is always room for more improvement through practice. Without practice, skills atrophy.

The skills most relevant to media literacy are analysis, evaluation, grouping, induction, deduction, synthesis, and abstraction. These skills are rarely used in an automatic fashion; instead, they require conscious effort, even when a person has a high ability on them.

To illustrate this distinction between competency and skills, think of reading as it is taught in elementary school. Children learn to recognize symbols that are words. They learn how to vocalize those symbols and how to fit those symbols together into sentences. These are competencies. By the time people have reached secondary grades, it is assumed that they have reading competency, yet they still practice reading. However, at these more advanced grades, reading is regarded less as a competency and more as a skill. Students focus on how to get more meaning out of paragraphs and stories. For example, when teachers ask students to read aloud in elementary school, it is to check students' competencies at word recognition and pronunciation. But when teachers ask students to read aloud in high school, it is to check students' skill at reading for meaning and expression.

This cognitive theory of media literacy is much more concerned with addressing improvement of skills rather than the attainment of competencies. While the percentage of adults in this country who cannot read seems very high at 20%, and this is an important problem to address, this theory is concerned more with the other 80% who have this competency but who struggle with meaning construction. This theory relies on competencies but uses those more as a foundation for a theory that focuses on skills. The theory is much more concerned with people's skills, because skills are the tools we use to construct our knowledge structures. Skill development is what really can make a large difference in a person moving from low to high media literacy. People who have weak skills will not be able to do much with the information they encounter. They will ignore good information and fixate on inaccurate or bad information. They will organize information poorly, thus creating weak and faulty knowledge structures. In the worst case, people with weak skills will try to avoid thinking about information altogether and become passive; the active information providers, such as advertisers and entertainers, will become the constructors of people's knowledge structures and will take over control of how people see the world.

III. Need for a New Paradigm

Thinking about the purpose of media literacy has changed over time. For example, Masterman (1998) has observed that there are three "historical paradigms in media education" (p. vii). The first of these regarded the mass media as a disease and argued that people, especially children, needed to be inoculated against damaging effects. The disease was the corruption of language and the constant appeals to low-level satisfactions; this was a direct threat to higher level culture with its authentic values as a higher art form. People needed to be protected against the mass media.

Then, in the 1960s, there was a shift to a belief that not all mass media were bad; that is, there was a range of content within any medium. The purpose of media education was, therefore, to educate people to make good choices, that is, to discriminate between the good and the bad film or between content that had integrity and that which was merely commercial and exploitive. This was the popular arts paradigm.

In the 1970s, there was a shift to semiotics with its focus on representation. People needed to be taught to read critically, this paradigm reasoned, so that they would not accept the false consciousness presented by the media. However, the false consciousness was not imposed by the media industries, as Marxists claimed; this paradigm favored the explanation by Gramsci that dominance of the ideology was achieved through consent of the populace. The key, then, is not to do away with the power elite but instead to educate the populace to encounter the media critically.

With this cognitive theory of media literacy, I argue that it is time for a fourth paradigm. We need another shift of perspective on why it is important to be media literate. I make this argument, because I feel we need to move beyond the tradition of critical or cultural studies where the writers make strong arguments either (a) that the media have constructed a culture that is harmful to its members or (b) that the media foster a false consciousness. While many of these writings present compelling arguments and raise serious issues for all media scholars to ponder, the arguments stop short of being fully convincing unless the reader believes that there is a standard for truth. Without such a standard, how can we accept the argument that there is a "false" consciousness or that the negative effects that those writers point out are negative for people beyond themselves?

I am not arguing that there are no negative effects. There is potential for hundreds of effects, all of which could be negative. But the valence is for the person to interpret. What I regard as a negative effect to my life may be the most valuable positive effect to you. Therefore, in this book, my purpose is to illuminate the issues and provide the beginning of knowledge structures to help readers construct a higher degree of understanding in their own lives and leave the interpretations up to those individuals. Thus, the most fundamental guiding principle underlying my perspective is that individuals should be empowered to make their own choices and interpretations. If people end up making the same choices as they would have without developing their skills and knowledge structures, then the choices are informed ones, and that is better than choices purely programmed by the media and outside of the consumer's awareness. Also, if an individual's interpretations of meaning in the messages are the same as what the media present, then those interpretations are informed ones, and they are better than interpretations programmed by the media. The key lies not so much with the choices and interpretations but with who makes them. Media-literate people make their own choices and interpretations. They do this by first recognizing a wide range of choices; then, they use their personal, elaborated knowledge structures for context to make decisions among the options and select the option that best meets their own goals. Nonliterate people have no choice but to allow the media to make them, because they have few options and the options they do have are given to them by the media. It's rather like getting up in the morning and finding that your significant other has given you two choices of what to wear to the office: a clown suit or a mermaid outfit. It's a choice, in the literal sense of the term, but not a real choice. The media give us choices, but not nearly the range of options that we need to have to make the best choice, given our goals.

In this book, I hope to influence one more shift in thinking. I accept the premise that the locus for change is the individual and that people need to be educated to read the media better. However, I challenge the argument that the reason people need to be critical readers is to recognize the ideology of the media so they can reject it. I argue that rejection of the ideology is not the goal; the goal, instead, should be to allow people to appreciate parts of the ideology that are functional for them and create new perspectives where the ideology is not functional for them. That is, the choice should be up to the individual. Mindlessly rejecting the media ideology *in toto* is not much better than mindlessly accepting it *in toto*.

I do not believe there is a "false" ideology because to believe that, I would have to also believe that there is a "true" ideology. I accept no basis for such a claim. So the media's ideology is what it is; it is simply a construction by institutions to create practices that result in cultural products that best serve the particular needs of those institutions. There is nothing false about it in the sense that there is a superior place humankind can stand and view the truth. It is much more complex and interesting than that.

Individuals who are not media literate must accept the media's messages as they are presented and fit the round pegs of the media's messages into the square holes of their own lives. People who are media literate know the shape of their lives (that is, the space they want to fill), and they know how to make their own meaning from the images provided by the media (that is, whittle away certain elements and amplify others) so that their product fits their space. Of course, learning how to do this entails, in part, learning to be critical of the media. But the critical exercise is not a rhetorical exercise in recognizing the media ideology, then rejecting it. Instead, the critical exercise is actively using skills as tools on the raw material in the messages to rearrange elements in those raw materials. For example, one of the ideological elements in the media (especially in their entertainment products and commercial messages) is to present hyperattractive characters based on a highly stylized and narrow conception of attractiveness that focuses on youth and a thin athletic body type, which is impossible to achieve for many people. This has led many young women to engage in eating disorders to try to make themselves more attractive, given this narrow definition of attractiveness. Scholars in the third paradigm would train these women to recognize the media's ideology about body stereotyping and make them critical of this. The women would become angry and reject the ideology and much of the media. My perspective is to get these women to confront their acceptance of this ideology, reject it, replace it with their own goals, then search out the many alternative body types that are presented in the media; they end up in a more functional place for their lives, that is, getting past anger, becoming happy, and using the media to find material to support their own view of the world. This is empowerment to help them live a happy life, not empowerment so they can live an angry life in martyrdom.

IV. Synthesized Definition of Media Literacy

Now that I have defined the foundational terms and made some key distinctions. I can present my core definition of media literacy. This definition is synthesized from what I consider the major ideas in the literature, which was reviewed in the previous chapter.

A. The Umbrella Definition

Media literacy is the set of perspectives from which we expose ourselves to the media and interpret the meaning of the messages we encounter. We build our perspectives from knowledge structures. The knowledge structures form the platforms on which we stand to view the multifaceted phenomenon of the media: their business, their content, and their effects on individuals and institutions. The more knowledge structures we have, the more of the media phenomenon we can "see." The more developed our knowledge structures, the more context we will have to help us understand what we see. The more people use these knowledge structures in mindful exposures, the more they will be able to use media exposures to meet their own goals and the more they will be able to avoid high risks for negative effects. Thus, they will be more media literate.

This definition of media literacy can be elaborated under the umbrella by adding two other types of definitions: process definition and product definition. Each of these further illuminates part of the construct of media literacy.

B. The Process Definition

There are two processes to the media literacy construct. One of these is the process of building strong knowledge structures so as to become media literate. The second process is acting in a media-literate manner during exposures to media messages.

How can people construct a strong perspective on the media? The key to doing this is to build a good set of knowledge structures. To build good knowledge structures, people need raw material and tools. The raw material is information, both from the media and from the real world. The tools are skills. There is a set of skills that is generic to all media. By these skills, I do not primarily mean the production skills. The skills of production (writing, photography, acting, directing; editing, sound recording, etc.) can help people become more media literate by adding more information to their knowledge structures. But the production skills are secondary to the more primary skills of analysis, evaluation, grouping, induction, deduction, synthesis, and abstracting. In fact, production skills depend on the use of these seven primary skills.

Both skills and information are important. If we have a great deal of information but weak skills, we will not be able to make much sense of the information. The information will likely be stored in schema, and it may be difficult to access a given bit of information. Skills are needed to sort through information and organize it. On the other hand, if we have strong skills but don't expose ourselves to a range of media messages or real world experiences, our knowledge structures will be limited and unbalanced.

No one is born media literate. Media literacy must be developed, and this development requires effort from each individual. The development also is a long-term process that never ends; that is, no one ever reaches a point of complete media literacy. Skills can always be more highly developed; if they are not continually improved, they will atrophy. Also, knowledge structures are never finished because the media and the real world are constantly changing.

The information in the knowledge structures is not limited to cognitive elements but should also contain emotional, aesthetic, and moral elements. The four types of elements work together such that the combination of any three types helps provide context for the other type.

Each of these four types of information focuses on a different domain of understanding. The cognitive domain refers to factual information: dates, names, definitions, and the like. Some people have few knowledge structures or skills, and this makes development along the cognitive dimension very difficult.

The emotional domain contains information about feelings, such as love, hate, anger, happiness, frustration, and so on. Some people have very little ability to experience an emotion during exposure to the media, whereas others are very sensitive to cues that generate all sorts of feelings in them.

The aesthetic domain contains information about how to produce messages. This information provides people with the basis for making judgments about who are great writers, photographers, actors, dancers, choreographers, singers, musicians, composers, directors, and other kinds of artists. It also helps us make judgments about other products of creative craftsmanship, such as editing, lighting, set designing, costuming, sound recording, layout, and so on. Some of us have a good ear for dialogue or musical composition. Some of us have a good eye for lighting, photographic composition, or movement. The more information we have from this domain, the finer discriminations we can make between a great actress and a very good one; between a great song that will endure and a currently popular "flash in the pan"; between a film director's best and very best work; between art and artificiality. This appreciation skill is important to some scholars (Messaris, 1994; Silverblatt, 1995; Wulff, 1997). For example, Messaris (1994) argues that viewers who are visually literate should have an awareness of artistry and visual manipulation. By this, he means they should be aware of the processes by which meaning is created through the visual media. What is expected of sophisticated viewers is some degree of self-consciousness about their role as interpreters. This includes the ability to detect artifice (in staged behavior and editing) and to spot authorial presence (style of the producer/director).

The moral domain contains information about values. Moral information provides us with the basis for making judgments about right and wrong. When we see characters make decisions in a story, we judge them on a moral dimension, that is, the characters' goodness or evilness. The more detailed and refined our moral information is, the more deeply we can perceive the values underlying messages in the media and the more sophisticated and reasoned are our judgments about those values. Highly media literate people can perceive moral themes well.

Strong knowledge structures contain information from all four of these domains. If one type of information is missing, the knowledge structure is less elaborate than it could be. For example, people who have a knowledge structure without any emotional information are able to be highly analytical when they watch a movie and may be able to quote lots of facts about the history of the movie's genre, the director's point of view, and the underlying theme. But if they cannot evoke an emotional reaction, they are simply going through a dry, academic exercise.

The second process is acting in a media literate manner during exposures to media messages. A person who has a strong perspective on the media phenomenon has high potential to act in a media-literate manner. The set of knowledge structures by itself does not indicate media literacy; the person must actively and mindfully use the information in those knowledge structures during exposures to media messages. Thus, people who are more highly media literate spend less exposure time in automatic processing of messages. They are more consciously aware of their goals for the exposure and are consciously making decisions about filtering and meaning construction. This is not to say that highly media-literate people do not spend considerable time in automatic processing; they do. However, when they are in the state of automaticity, they are being governed by automatic routines that they have had a hand in forming rather than being governed by routines conditioned almost exclusively by the media.

The process of media literacy is so important, because it is not a categorical construct. Media literacy is not a category where either you are in the category or you are not. Media literacy is best regarded as a continuum—like a thermometer—where there are degrees. We all occupy some position on the media literacy continuum. There is no point below which we could say that someone has no literacy, and there is no point at the high end where we can say that someone is fully literate—there is always room for improvement. Media literacy is a constant process.

People are positioned along that continuum based on the strength of their overall perspective on the media. The strength of a person's perspective is based on the number and quality of knowledge structures, and the quality of knowledge structures is based on the level of a person's skills and experiences. Because people vary substantially on skills and experiences, they will vary on the number and quality of their knowledge structures. Hence, there will be great variation in media literacy across people.

People operating at lower levels of media literacy have weak and limited perspectives on the media. They have smaller, more superficial, and less organized knowledge structures, which provide an inadequate perspective to use in interpreting the meaning of a media message. These people are also habitually reluctant or unwilling to use their skills, which remain under-developed and therefore more difficult to employ successfully.

C. The Purpose Definition

The purpose of becoming more media literate is to gain greater control over one's exposures and to construct one's own meaning from the messages in those exposures. When people do this, they are in control of determining what is important in life and setting expectations for experiences in those important areas. If they do not do this for themselves, the flood of media messages will do this for them in the default condition. The media will set the agenda and tell people what to think about. The media will define beauty, success, and happiness. The media will set impossible standards for the way we should live our lives, the appearance of our bodies, the velocity of success in careers, the value of material goods, and the intensity of relationships.

There is a big payoff to being media literate. It is important that this payoff be large, because a great deal of effort is required to build a strong perspective and to apply it continually during media exposures. The payoff is conceptualized much more in terms of accuracy rather than efficiency. Accuracy is defined here not it terms of how closely the reported facts match a standard of truth; instead, accuracy is defined in terms of how often individuals access messages that match their goals for information and entertainment as well as how often individuals are able to construct meaning to match goals for their lives.

Efficiency is a secondary purpose. Efficiency becomes important only after the more primary purpose of accuracy has been achieved. For example, let's say Harry and Bob both read a news story and both get little information from it; that little information is inaccurate. Harry is able to read the story in 5 minutes, and Bob takes 10 minutes. We can't conclude that Harry is twice as literate as Bob; instead, neither are very media literate because neither has gotten much value (accuracy) from the exposure of reading the news story. Now, let's say that Ann and Margie were active readers of the same news story (continually analyzing it and evaluating the claims), drew a good deal of information from their exposure, and incorporated it (through grouping, induction, and deduction) into their existing knowledge structures on the topic. Ann took 5 minutes to read the story, and Margie took 10 minutes. In this later scenario, we can say that Ann is a bit more media literate than Margie, but the real distinction is that both Ann and Margie are far more media literate than are Harry and Bob. Efficiency should never be regarded as the primary criterion of the purpose is media literacy.

Once the criterion of accuracy is achieved, then efficiency becomes an important consideration. Efficiency is not something that can be achieved well in the short term; instead it should be a long-term purpose. Highly developed knowledge structures and highly developed primary skills give the person high potential for efficiency.

V. Summary

This chapter defines the constructs used in this cognitive theory of media literacy. The foundational terms were defined as constructs with special definitions to distinguish them from their primitive term status in everyday language. Then, some of these terms, along with other key terms, were defined through seven contrasts. First, there is an important difference between fully specified and partially specified problems. Media literacy deals with both types of problems, but the more challenging of the two is the task of dealing with partially specified problems. Second, there is a difference between meaning matching and meaning construction. Meaning matching is a relatively automatic task that relies on symbol recognition and matching of a memorized definition to that symbol. Meaning construction builds on meaning matching and is, therefore, a more involved task. Meaning construction requires the use of many more skills and a conscious locus to guide it. Third, exposure is different than attention. Exposure occurs when a person is in physical proximity to a media message, whereas attention occurs only when a person is conscious and aware of the message. Fourth, automaticity was contrasted with mindfulness. Fifth, there is an important difference between information and knowledge. Sixth, there is a difference between schemas and knowledge structures. Schemas are networks of ideas linked together in a person's mind. Knowledge structures are highly organized maps of screened elements. Seventh, this theory relies on a clear difference between competencies and skills.

The chapter builds to a synthesized definition of media literacy. That definition presents media literacy as a perspective from which we expose ourselves to the media and interpret the meaning of the messages we encounter. We build our perspective from knowledge structures. It is not a natural state; instead it must be developed. It is not a category; there are degrees of media literacy. It is multidimensional with development taking place cognitively, emotionally, aesthetically, and morally. The purpose of developing media literacy is to give the person greater control of exposures and the construction of meaning from the information encountered in those exposures.

CHAPTER 4

The Media Literacy Model

4

The Media Literacy Model

This chapter begins with a list of six axioms that form the foundation supporting this cognitive theory of media literacy. The theory is then illustrated in a model.

I. Major Axioms

This theory rests on a foundation of six axioms. Each of these requires acceptance in order for readers to find the theory useful.

A. Responsibility Axiom

The primary responsibility for increasing media literacy resides with the individual person. Unless the person accepts responsibility for his or her own degree of literacy, there will be no motivation for change.

Institutions, such as government, business, religion, the media, and the family, can provide resources to help—as well as obstacles to hinder—the individual. The institution of education, broadly defined, has a special responsibility to introduce basic knowledge structures and to provide reasons for developing media literacy. But ultimately, it is the responsibility of individuals to adopt the media literacy perspective and to work constantly to increase their level of media literacy.

There are situations where experts can impose interventions on other people—particularly children—and help those people to increase their media literacy without the person first deciding to do this. However, if change is to be meaningful, individuals must believe that it is important to increase their media literacy. If change is to be lasting, individuals must make themselves continually aware of information usage options and the consequences of choosing among those differing options.

B. Effects Axiom

Any theory of media literacy must at its core be a theory about how people are affected by the media. All other concerns flow from this core concern. The concern should include the positive effects as well as the negative ones. A theory based only on avoiding negative effects is reactive only and has nothing to say about where people should go, only where people should not go.

Unless we know a good deal about how the media affect people, it makes little sense to suggest strategies for individuals to follow in their everyday lives to avoid risks of negative effects from media influence. Also, until we know a good deal about the negative effects and the relative contributions of the different factors as they influence those effects, it is foolhardy to propose guidelines for governmental regulations.

C. Interpretation Axiom

Humans are interpretive beings. This is a key feature of the human mind. Central to understanding the individual is appreciating how the human mind works. It is not a simple calculating device. It is far more complicated than any computer in the way it can imagine hypotheticals, can incorporate emotions, can create fantasies, can engage in self-reflection, can take shortcuts, and is prey to mistakes in reasoning. Thus, the following questions require more than simple answers: Why do people expose themselves to certain media messages and ignore others? How do people make sense of media messages? How do people construct their own meaning from media messages? Good answers to these questions are needed to craft a convincing rationale for any set of techniques that would purport to help individuals become more media literate. This theory relies on research from cognitive psychology to answer these questions, then build a rationale for what it means to be media literate and why literacy is so important.

The essential questions are then: Who gets to control the interpretations? That is, are the interpretations to come from outside the individual, to be accepted as truth and memorized? Or are the interpretations to be constructed by the individual? This theory rests on the belief that it is far better for the individual to be in control of the meaning-construction task.

D. Importance of Shared Meaning Axiom

It is too radical a position to call for the individual to construct all interpretations. Instead, individuals need to acquire a significant number of interpretations from outside themselves so they can understand other people and use common symbols to communicate with them. If everyone used a different word for a particular concept (say, tree), then communication of meaning would be impossible. We all have to accept certain links between a concept and its designated symbol (be it a word, graphic, sound, smell, movement, or whatever). This task I refer to as matching meaning, and it is an essential part of the media literacy model.

Being highly literate requires that people are able to perform the tasks of meaning matching and meaning construction. Furthermore, it is essential that people know when a task requires meaning matching and when it calls for meaning construction. Allowing the media to construct meaning for people's goals in life, careers, relationships, emotional responses, and other personal domains is a mistake; people need to exercise their own control over these types of personal, partially specified problems. However, it is also a mistake when people want to construct their own meaning for common terms and images and thus ignore the shared meanings that allow us to engage in basic communication.

E. Power Axiom

Knowledge is power. If people are to take control of their meaning construction, they need particular kinds of knowledge. Without this knowledge, they will not have the ability to make substantial changes in a positive direction. Specifically, people need awareness in five areas: media content, media industries, media effects, real world, and the self. With knowledge in these five areas, people are able to make better decisions about seeking out information, working with that information, and constructing meaning from it that will be useful to serve their own goals.

The knowledge in these structures can provide people with more options for exposure and information processing. When people are clear about their options at each phase in the process, they can make better decisions. Also, people will have a much clearer perspective to help them see the border between the real world and the world manufactured by the media. Knowledge structures provide people with clear maps to help them navigate better in the media world so that they can get to those experiences and information they think are important without becoming distracted by those things that the media present as urgent.

F. Purpose Axiom

The purpose of media literacy is to empower individuals to shift control from the media to themselves. The control defaults to the media when people do not think about their media habits, their exposures, and the consequences of those exposures. Currently, most of that control lies with the media, which have programmed exposure habits and automatic routines for interpreting media messages. By developing more media literacy, people can gradually shift much of that control back to themselves as they become more aware of their options (of exposure, of interpretation, and of effect) and consciously make selections among those options to achieve their personal goals more fully.

How can people accomplish this shift? First, they need to understand the nature of their locus. The locus is what guides their decisions. The more they know about the locus, the more they can use it to achieve their message goals.

II. The Cognitive Model of Media Literacy

The media literacy model (see Figure 4.1) is very different from the default model, which was displayed in Chapter 1. The media literacy model requires much more conscious processing of information and much more preparation for the exposures than does the default model.

The media literacy model emphasizes four major factors. At foundation is the factor of knowledge structures. This factor feeds information into the personal locus, which is where decisions are motivated. The third factor is a

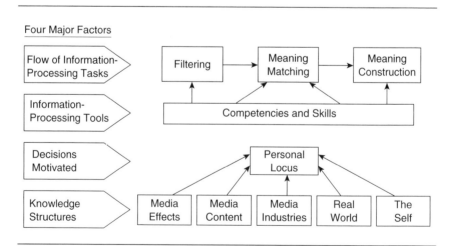

Figure 4.1   The Cognitive Model of Media Literacy

person's set of competencies and skills, which are the information-processing tools. The fourth factor is the flow of information-processing tasks.

The four factors work together interactively in a system. A weakness in one area can suppress an otherwise high level of functioning in the other areas; also, strength within some of these factors is needed to build up the strength in the other factors.

A. Knowledge Structures

The foundation of building media literacy is a set of five strong knowledge structures. The foundational knowledge structures are: media effects, media content, media industries, real world, and the self. With knowledge in these five areas, people are much more aware during the information-processing tasks and are, therefore, more able to make better decisions about seeking out information, working with that information, and constructing meaning from it that will be useful to serve their own goals. The information that makes these kinds of awarenesses possible resides in knowledge structures.

B. Personal Locus

Personal locus is a term that refers to that which governs the information-processing tasks. The personal locus comprises goals and drives. The goals shape the information-processing tasks by determining what gets filtered in and what gets ignored. It also shapes meaning matching and meaning construction. The more people know about this locus and the more they make conscious decisions to shape it, the more they can control the process. The more a person pays conscious attention to his or her locus, the more he or she controls the process of information acquisition and usage.

The more a person engages his or her locus, the more that person will be increasing media literacy. However, being media literate does not mean that the personal locus is always fully engaged and that processing continually takes place at the high end of the continuum. This is an impossible task because no one can maintain that high a degree of concentration continuously. Media literacy is a process not a product. Therefore, becoming more media literate means that a person uses the locus more (thus less time with mindless exposures) and uses it more actively (more time at the higher end of the continuum).

The personal locus operates in two modes: conscious and unconscious. When the locus operates in the conscious mode, the person is aware of options and can exercise his or her will in making decisions. In contrast, when the personal locus operates in the unconscious mode, the decisions are made outside of the person's awareness and control. In both modes, knowledge structures can get formed and elaborated.

The media exert their most powerful effect when the personal locus is operating in the unconscious mode. When the locus is not engaged, people have mindless exposures. That means their minds are on automatic pilot, and their personal locus defaults to the media locus. If they are in an environment where there are audio or visual messages, those messages get into their subconscious unfiltered.

When the personal locus is engaged, the processing is conscious. This means people are aware of the options facing them and make decisions to reach particular goals. The engagement of the locus occurs by degrees; that is, it can be used to a minor degree at one end of the use continuum or to a major degree at the other end. Engaging the locus at the low end of the continuum is characterized by a goal of efficiency; that is, the focus is on putting in minimal effort (although some effort) and reaching a decision quickly. When the goal is more important than mere efficiency, then the locus is engaged more and the amount of processing is higher.

Researchers who design media literacy studies need to focus on people's locus when posing questions such as: Why do some people expose themselves to many messages and many media while others do not? Why do some people expose themselves to "bad" content while others are able to avoid it? Why are some people more affected negatively by the media compared to others?

The personal locus also deals with normative questions such as: How much media *should* people expose themselves to? Which messages *should* people seek out and which messages should they avoid at all costs? Which media effects are good and which are bad? Therefore, the personal locus should be an area of focus for practitioners who want to increase their ability to help people increase their media literacy.

C. Competencies and Skills

After the personal locus provides the plan and the energy, tools are needed to execute the plan. Competencies are the tools that allow us to access simple mental associations. Having competencies does not make one media literate, but lacking these competencies prevents one from being media literate, because this prevents a person from accessing particular kinds of information. For example, people who do not have a basic reading competency cannot access printed material. This will greatly limit what they can build into their knowledge structures; this will also alter the drive states in the locus by making people avoid printed material rather than seek it out.

The more that people use their skills and develop them consciously, the stronger they will become. When the personal locus has strong drive states for using skills, those skills have a much greater chance of developing to stronger levels.

Skills and competencies work together in a continual cyclical process. With certain information-processing tasks, some skills or competencies may be more important than others. For example, with the task of filtering, the skills of analysis and evaluation are most important. With the task of meaning matching, the competencies are most important. With the task of meaning construction, the skills of induction, deduction, grouping, and synthesis are most important. However, the value of the individual skills and competencies varies by particular challenges presented by different types of messages.

D. Information-Processing Tasks

The three information-processing tasks are filtering, meaning matching, and meaning construction (see Table 4.1). These tasks are ordered in a

Table 4.1   Summary of Three Tasks of Information Processing

Filtering Messages	
Task	To make decisions about which messages to filter out (ignore) and which to filter in (pay attention to)
Goal	To attend to only those messages that have the highest utility and avoid all others
Focus	Messages in the environment
Type of problem	Frequently partially specified because the criterion of utility is constantly changing
Meaning Matching	
Task	To use basic competencies to recognize symbols and locate definitions for each
Goal	To efficiently access previously learned meanings
Focus	Symbols in messages
Type of problem	Frequently fully specified
Meaning Construction	
Task	To use skills to move beyond meaning matching and construct meaning for oneself to get more out of a message
Goal	To interpret messages from more than one perspective as a means of identifying the range of meaning options, then choosing one or synthesizing across several
Focus	One's own knowledge structures
Type of problem	Almost always partially specified

sequence of information processing. First, we encounter a message and are faced with the task of deciding whether to filter it out (ignore it) or filter it in (process it). If we decide to filter it in, then we must make sense of it; that is, we must recognize the symbols and match our learned definitions with the symbols. Third, we need to construct the meaning of the message.

The processing of information begins with the task of filtering. How can we make good decisions about filtering messages in a way that, on the one hand, protects us from the negative effects of being overwhelmed or from having our minds shaped by forces outside our control and, on the other hand, helps us take advantage of the positive effects? Furthermore, how can we achieve this in a relatively efficient manner?

Once we have filtered-in messages, we need to determine their meaning. Meaning matching requires basic competencies to recognize elements in the message and access our schema memory to find out what meaning we have learned to associate with that element. This is a relatively automatic task. Increasing media literacy requires that we not stop with this task but that we move on to meaning construction. If we simply accept the surface meaning from the media messages and do not construct meaning for ourselves, we are in danger of negative effects. Some of these effects are relatively minor, but many are more general, profound, and pervasive, and they can change the way we think about reality, truth, and ourselves. Ignoring the problem makes it worse, because the messages will continue to aggressively invade our subconscious and shape our fundamental values as well as the way we think.

Media messages are not always the way they seem. There are often many layers of meanings. The more that people are aware of the layers of meaning in messages, the more they can control the selection of which meanings they want. Constant exposure to media messages influences the way we think about the world and ourselves. It influences our beliefs about crime, education, religion, families, and the world in general. If our exposure is mostly passive, then the mundane details in those messages exert their effect without our awareness. From this massive base of misleading or inaccurate images, we infer our beliefs about the world.

Some people perform these tasks better than others and are, therefore, more media literate than others. Each of these tasks relies on a different set of skills. The more developed a person's set of skills is, the more media literate he or she is. Each task relies on knowledge structures. The more developed a person's knowledge structures are, the more media literate he or she is.

III. Summary

This chapter presents the core of the theory of media literacy by presenting six axioms and a model of media literacy. The six axioms are fundamental beliefs and must be accepted for the theory to make sense. The first axiom is the belief that responsibility for increasing media literacy lies in the individual. Second, people need to be sensitive to the range of media effects. Many of the effects are positive. Third, people are interpretive beings, but fourth, individuals also need to share meaning to communicate. Fifth, knowledge is power. People need to know which knowledge structures will help them most and how to use those knowledge structures. Sixth, the purpose of media literacy is to empower the individual. If the individual does not control the meaning construction task, the media will.

This theory of media literacy is encapsulated in a model that features four major factors: knowledge structures, personal locus, competencies and skills, and the flow of information-processing tasks. Each of these factors works interactively in a system.

The major theme in this theory of media literacy is that processing of information can take place either consciously or unconsciously. With conscious processing, the individual is aware of goals, exercises careful selection of information, and is able to exert a relatively high degree of control over the process of influence. With unconscious processing, the individual is unaware of the schema-driven automatic processing that is taking place and, therefore, is not able to exercise any degree of control over the process of influence. Media literacy requires individuals to spend more time and effort with conscious processing.

Thus, this theory blends normative prescriptions with scientifically derived understandings about how people use information. Scientific understanding without action is a squandering of understanding. Calls for action not grounded in a strong awareness of the environment, how people interact with it, and how it affects people will only lead to prescriptions that may be useless at best and are more likely to make the situation worse.

CHAPTER 5

The Foundational Knowledge Structures

I. Media Content
   A. Content Formulas
   B. Aggregate Figures
   C. Values in the Content

II. Media Industries
   A. Development of Media Industries
   B. Economics
   C. Ownership and Control
   D. Marketing Messages

III. Media Effects
   A. Broad Perspective
      1. Timing of effects
      2. Level of effect
      3. Direct versus indirect effects
      4. Sought versus incidental effects
      5. Valence
   B. Risk
      1. Set-point
      2. Elasticity
   C. Process of Influence
      1. Countervailing influences
      2. Nonlinear relationships
      3. Thresholds
      4. Contingent conditions
      5. Nature of causation
   D. Factors in the Process of Influence
      1. Developmental maturity
      2. Abilities
      3. Drives
      4. Sociological factors
      5. States
      6. Media content

IV. Real World

V. The Self
   A. Personal Knowledge Style
   B. Personal Goals

VI. Summary

5

The Foundational Knowledge Structures

F ive knowledge structures underlie the media literacy perspective. These are: media content, media industries, media effects, real world information, and the self. The more accurate and elaborate knowledge structures people have in these areas, the higher their potential for being media literate. Thus, these knowledge structures provide potential, not a guarantee. The potential must be realized by the personal locus; that is, the person must use this knowledge. When a person's locus is fully engaged, the locus draws information from these knowledge structures and keeps the person aware of options as well as motivated to make good choices based on this information.

The more experience people have, the more context they have to bring to bear on processing new messages. People with the most knowledge learn most from media (Comstock, Chaffee, Katzman, McCombs, & Roberts, 1978; Rice & Wartella, 1981). When people have a great deal of knowledge on a particular topic, they have a strong, well-developed knowledge structure. They are usually motivated to acquire more information on various topics and thus seek out media that will provide them with this information. When they see a new message on the topic, they are able to integrate that new information quickly and efficiently into their existing knowledge structure.

This chapter will illuminate the nature of these five knowledge structures. Space does not permit a thorough articulation of the content of these knowledge structures, but for more detail (still not an inventory) see *Media Literacy* (Potter, 2001).

I. Media Content

People have lots of information about names of TV shows, writers, magazines, names of characters, names of songs, and the like. This information helps them access media messages, and for that reason, this type of information is useful. But this is not the type of information that makes much of a difference to people's level of media literacy. To build a significant knowledge structure about media content, three kinds of information are essential: content formulas, aggregate figures, and values in the content.

A. Content Formulas

There are standard formulas for messages, whether they are news stories, ads, or fictional entertainment. Each of these three types of content has its dominant formula. For example, many news stories follow the inverted pyramid, which presents the most important elements (the who, what, when, where, and why) early in the story, followed by less essential information. Ads typically follow a problem resolution formula. Fictional entertainment stories typically follow a formula of circumstance generation, heightened conflict, climax, and denouement.

A content type's dominant formula can vary. Alternative formulas for news stories include the question-answer format for interviews, the horse race format for campaign coverage, and the anecdote format for human interest stories. For ads, other formulas include the joke-punch line, hard sell, and the mosaic (presenting emotion-evoking images linked with the product).

Knowing the formulas well gives a person the ability to follow the content much more easily. It also provides a standard on which to judge the creativity of the message makers.

B. Aggregate Figures

We can experience the content and the media as individual anecdotal elements—each creative and unique—or we can also be concerned about commonalities and patterns that direct our attention to the big picture.

One way to see the big picture is to construct it for ourselves through the skill of induction. However, when we induce patterns from the media messages for ourselves, the patterns are often faulty, because people are not usually exposing themselves to the full range of messages, nor are they exposing themselves to a sample of messages that could represent all media messages or even all messages within a subset. Therefore, any generalization will be faulty. Also, undertaking an induction of media message patterns is challenging and requires a great deal of effort and knowledge about content analysis.

Fortunately, careful scholars regularly conduct content analyses, so we can save the effort of conducting inductions ourselves and instead learn the aggregate patterns reported by others. It would be useful to have aggregate patterns for a wide range of topics, but unfortunately, many of these have yet to be addressed by scholars, especially patterns in media other than television. However, many of the most important topic areas do have good aggregate figures. These involve the prevalence of certain behaviors in plots (violence and sex) as well as the prevalence of types of characters (gender, age, ethnic background, affluence, careers, and roles) in entertainment programs. There are also aggregate figures available about news, such as length of stories (sound bytes), types of newsmakers, types of news stories (economic, political, feature, sports, etc.), sources, formal features (use of graphics, photographs, talking heads, etc.), and credibility. Also, there are aggregate figures for advertising, such as amount, length, types of products, types of appeals, and product spokespersons.

We need to know the aggregate figures in media content to check our pattern perceptions. For example, we need to know how much violence there really is on television before we can form a useful critical opinion. We need to know whether there are many more males in important roles in the media than there are females. We need to know the patterns of eating, exercise, and other health-related behaviors.

C. Values in the Content

Underlying values are embedded in all messages in the media. We need to be sensitive to what these are. For example, even journalists who claim a high degree of objectivity are presenting a partial and selective picture of the world. Many types of events and people never get covered, and this reveals values about what is important in our culture.

As for advertising, all ads are about consumption. There is something we can buy to solve any problem quickly. Materialism is good. New products are better than old products.

As for entertainment, stories are about conflict and how that conflict is resolved. In our culture, the conflict is usually resolved through competition and often through aggressive, even violent means. Also, stories in the mass media simplify life. Characters are divided cleanly into the good characters and the bad characters; very few are gray. Most issues are presented as having only two sides. In addition, stories focus on the exciting. They truncate time to show only the most interesting events in a story. Thus, the underlying themes of entertainment are: Life should be very exciting, it is led at a fast pace, it presents lots of conflict situations, and you need to be strong and fight hard to win.

II. Media Industries

People generally have poorly developed knowledge structures about the media industries. They may know the names of different newspapers, magazines, TV stations, and film companies, but they know little about who owns them, how they operate, how they interact in the industry, or how they market their messages. The more elaborate people's knowledge structures about the media industries are, the more they will understand why certain content is produced and why the people in the industries make the decisions they do. Four areas of knowledge are especially important: development of media industries, economics, ownership and control, and marketing messages.

A. Development of Media Industries

People need to understand where the media come from and how they evolve. This helps them appreciate the forces that motivate decisions about content and marketing. It also helps them better understand the current nature of each vehicle and what the future is likely to offer. With good projections for the future, people can prepare themselves to avoid certain media or vehicles and shift their resources of time and money to other media they feel are moving in a direction more compatible with their personal goals.

B. Economics

The primary goal of mass media organizations is to maximize shareholder wealth. They achieve this by increasing their business efficiency, that is, by making decisions that will maximize revenue and at the same time minimize costs of doing business.

Media companies increase revenue in two ways. First, they seek to produce a wide variety of vehicles, each with its own target audience, each with a special set of messages of high potential interest to that target audience, and each with its own revenue stream. The more revenue streams, the more total revenue possible. Second, media companies seek ways to maximize the availability of each vehicle to audiences. Thus, they develop means to disseminate their message to broad audiences (not one person or a named set of people such as one's friends) in a way that it is available to all those audience members at the same time. Not everyone may access the message at the same time, but it is available for access.

Keeping costs down is a major challenge, because talent is in short supply and the media compete aggressively for the small pool of talent, thus driving costs up. One potential area for keeping costs down is to reduce the cost of potential failures. Media companies do this in three ways. First, they conduct a great deal of research to monitor what the public exposes itself to, and they try to emulate those messages. Second, they avoid messages with a negative valence to audiences, that is, messages that the public would find offensive and want to actively avoid. Third, they attempt to condition audiences into habitual exposure patterns.

When most people criticize the media, they typically focus on some form of content they dislike and totally ignore the economics that drive the production and marketing of that content. Thus, their criticism is uninformed and has virtually no chance of changing industry practices.

Media companies are businesses that are guided by the profit motive. As such, they have a strong drive to increase revenues while reducing expenses. Revenues are tied to market demands. If there is no demand for a particular type of message, few companies will undertake the high risk of trying to create a demand. Where demand exists, media companies will continue to provide the demanded messages as long as the demand continues. This is one of the major reasons why the criticism about sex and violence in the media has failed to bring about any substantial reduction in that type of content. The industry responds much more to demand than to criticism.

C. Ownership and Control

Many people criticize the government for allowing media companies to consolidate and grow powerful. Is this a danger? Most people think it is; they are concerned that too many of the media vehicles are in the control of too few people.

This is a complex issue. People who criticize this trend toward consolidation need to analyze carefully the advantages as well as the disadvantages that accrue to the public. For example, the economies of scale available to large companies serve to keep production costs lower, and this can result in lower costs to the public. Also, almost all media companies are publicly held. When these companies make a large profit, that money is passed on to shareholders. This is not to say that there are no negative effects of consolidation and the overwhelming quest to maximize profits; what I am arguing is that there are both advantages and disadvantages to consolidation. People who argue against consolidation without recognizing the advantages are just as uninformed as those people who argue that there are no negative effects from media consolidation and the messages they market.

D. Marketing Messages

To know how to seek out the messages they want, people need to understand how media companies market their content. Most people still use the term *mass communication,* but there has been no mass communication in any real sense of the term for decades. There is no mass audience; instead, marketing is niche oriented. People need to understand which niches they are in, as media marketers view them. They then need to think about which niches they would want to put themselves in and which ones they want to avoid.

III. Media Effects

A strong knowledge structure on media effects includes three features. First, it needs an expanded vision of media effects. Second, people need to understand how the process of influence works. Third, people need to know the factors that go into that process of influence.

A. Broad Perspective

When people have a narrow perspective on media effects, many effects happen to them outside their perspective. This eliminates the potential for them to control those effects. A good perspective on media effects is not limited to the obvious effects that show up immediately on exposure and can be easily linked to media influence. There are many more effects; thus, I provide a five-dimensional perspective to orient people to expand their vision on effects. These dimensions are: timing, level, direct vs. indirect effects, sought vs. incidental effects, and valence.

1. *Timing of effects.* Media effects can be immediate or long term. This distinction focuses on when the effect occurs, not on how long it lasts. An immediate effect is one that happens during exposure to the media message. If it does not happen during the exposure, the opportunity is lost. If the effect does happen, it might only last for a short period of time (such as becoming afraid during a movie), or it might last forever (such as learning the outcome of a presidential election), but it is still an immediate effect because it changed something in the person during the exposure.

Long-term effects show up only after many exposures. No single exposure or single type of message is responsible for the effect. Instead, the pattern of repeated exposure sets up the conditions for a long-term effect. For example, after watching years of crime programs and news reports, many people come to believe that their neighborhoods are high-crime environments. No single exposure or event "caused" this belief; the belief is slowly and gradually constructed over years of exposures until one day it occurs to people that they better buy another set of locks for their doors.

2. *Level of effect.* Most of the concern about the media focuses on behavioral effects. For example, *some believe* that watching violence will lead people to behave aggressively or that watching portrayals of sexual activity will make people engage in illicit sex acts. However, media have demonstrated effects that are cognitive, attitudinal, emotional, physiological, *and* behavioral (for some examples, see Table 5.1).

Table 5.1   Media Effects Template

Type	Immediate	Long Term
Cognitive	Temporary learning	Hypermnesia Generalization Exposing secrets Framing of life
Attitudinal	Opinion creation Opinion change	Sleeper effect Reinforcement Internalization
Emotional	Temporary reaction	Sensitization
Physiological	Temporary arousal	Increased tolerance
Behavioral	Imitation Activation	Habit formation Disinhibition Altered behavioral patterns
Societal		Moving mean of society Institutional change

3. *Direct versus indirect effects.* The five levels just listed deal with types of effects in individuals. Those effects are generally regarded as direct. Individuals can also be influenced indirectly, however, when the media exert their influence on large-scale structures such as institutions. When institutions change as an effect of media influence, then the people who participate in

those institutions experience the changes; in this way, the media exert an indirect effect on those people. For example, media portrayals of crime and violence in the news and in entertainment programs could, over time, exert an influence on the criminal justice system so that law enforcement officials are given greater latitude to access individuals' private records, such as Internet usage, library materials used, medical records, and so on. Thus, this loss of privacy would not be a direct effect of the media on the individual; instead, the media influence gradually created a change in law enforcement practices that eventually had an effect on the individual.

4. *Sought versus incidental effects.* People often seek out effects in ways that are easy to observe and to attribute to the media. For example, people read the morning paper to learn about which sports teams won their games yesterday. However, many other effects occur without the person seeking them. These are called incidental effects, because they occur incidental to the motivation of the person seeking exposure.

The sender is not likely to have planned incidental effects. For example, people might watch a highly violent movie to be entertained, that is, excited and pleasantly frightened, and the movie leads to this effect that the person sought. But the movie might also lead to other incidental effects, such as desensitizing the person to the plight of victims of violence and also making the person more fearful that he or she might be a victim of a violent act. The movie's producers did not intend these incidental effects; hence, they think it is unfair when they are criticized for effects that they did not intend to produce.

5. *Valence.* Effects can be constructive or destructive. These are terms that are value laden. Who is to decide what is constructive and destructive? The answer can be approached from two perspectives: the individual and society. From the individual perspective, a person's locus sets the standard. For example, if a person places a high value on a particular kind of information, then finding relevant messages in a book, newspaper, or television show can achieve such a goal and is therefore constructive.

Valence can also be determined by a larger frame than the individual, such as the frame of society. This larger frame is important in two situations. First, the distinction is important when there is a conflict between the individual and society. For example, let's say a person wants to be a master criminal, and so he or she seeks out messages on the Internet, books, and movies to gain information about crimes and how to commit them. In this case, finding such information is positive for the individual but negative from the point of view of society.

A second reason why the distinction between the individual's and society's perspectives on valence is important is that individuals often lack a strong locus to guide judgments about value. For example, when people sit down in front of the television after a hard day at work and want to escape their problems, they are not consciously considering programming, personal goals, drives, and so on. Instead, they simply want an escape experience. But in that flow of television messages, there are all kinds of programmers with their own locus, largely advertisers trying to convince viewers that they have problems that are more serious than people believe them to be—problems such as headaches, allergies, depression, or minor health problems that advertisers want to sell drugs to remedy. This type of message repeated over years leads the general population to believe that they should never feel discomfort and that drugs are good. Also, advertisers often market products that people like but that are not good for society at large: fuel inefficient and polluting cars, guns, boom boxes, and the like.

B. Risk

Once people have a broad perspective on the range of media effects, the important question is: What is my risk for manifesting these effects? The word *risk* refers to positive as well as negative effects. Risk refers to the probability of an effect occurring, and it is used in favor of the word *probability* because it is less quantitative. At the current level of precision in research findings about media effects, we do not have quantitative estimators, but it is not an exaggeration to say that we have a fairly good idea of the factors that go into increasing the risk of many of the effects occurring.

1. *Set-point.* Each effect has its own continuum of influence. On the continuum of influence for each effect, there is a natural point where our risk is normally located. I call this the risk set-point. For example, on the disinhibition influence continuum, a person who is continually exposed to many media messages of violence where the perpetrators are glamorized and the consequences to the victims are sanitized will typically have a risk set-point nearer the manifestation point (where the effect is observed) than will another person who avoids all such messages in the media. Also, a person who has been raised to be highly aggressive, who has low empathy, and who is frustrated is also likely to have a risk set-point nearer the manifestation point than a person who is raised according to the Golden Rule, has high trait empathy, and is rarely frustrated. People's risk set-points are determined by a combination of their traits, typical lifestyle situations, and patterns of media exposure.

A person's set-point on any influence continuum has two properties: position and elasticity. The position is where the set-point is located along the continuum. If the set-point is close to the manifestation pole, then the risk of a person exhibiting the effect is high. The position is determined by traits and long-term conditioning from the media.

Typically, people's risk set-points are fairly far away from behavioral manifestations; that is, it would take a media message with many (or unusually strong) characteristics to push a person all the way up to a behavioral act. In contrast, on cognitive effects, people's risk set-points are fairly close to a manifestation. Thus, some process lines are fairly long and require many factors to move a person all the way to the manifestation, whereas other process lines are fairly short, and the effects require only a factor or two to achieve a manifestation.

2. *Elasticity.* Elasticity refers to the width of the band of probability around the set-point. Movement within the band of elasticity is influenced by current dispositions and states of the person and the present media messages being exposed. If the elasticity is small, then the long-term stable factors (traits and typical story formula) are dominant; but if the elasticity is wide, then the immediate factors (dispositions and idiosyncratic factors in the portrayals) are dominant.

This conceptualization of risk set-point, with the related ideas of positioning and elasticity, are primarily speculation even though it is based on findings from the research literature. At this time, researchers are far from providing estimates of risk as precise as my illustrations indicate. There have been some attempts to construct risk scales (Wilson et al., 2002), but this is an enormously difficult task, which is hampered by the limitations in the effects research we have to date (Potter, 1997). While I believe that this is a fruitful and important direction for empirical research, at the present time this conceptualization is of value primarily as a metaphor for people to use when considering which neighborhoods of risk they may inhabit in psychological space. When people are aware of the factors that go into the determination of a risk set-point, they can better assess the impact of different types of messages in bringing about a manifested effect.

C. Process of Influence

Think of the process of influence as a continuum (Figure 5.1). At one end of the continuum, there is virtually no chance that an effect will be manifested. At the other end of the continuum, there is a certainty that the effect

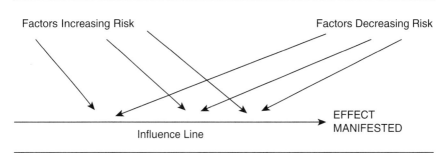

Figure 5.1   Process of Influence

will occur. Thinking of effects as a continuum frees us from categorical thinking, that is, of regarding an effect as either being present or not.

I argue that a continuous process of influence is constantly moving us back and forth along the continuum. Some factors increase risk, that is, move us toward a manifestation, while other factors decrease risk by moving us away from the manifestation point. The movement itself along the continuum is an effect; no outward manifestation is required for an effect to have occurred. Thus, effects are constantly occurring as a result of our unfolding experiences with the media.

The more we know about where we are along the continuum and those factors that move us in the direction we want to go, the more we can control the effects process and the more media literate we are. Such control will allow us to reduce the probability of a negative effect occurring well before it has a chance to manifest itself. Also, such control will allow us to accelerate the manifestation of a positive effect and, if it is a long-term effect, to take comfort in the fact that we are moving toward such an effect even though we have not yet manifested it. Because the purpose of media literacy is to empower people to control effects, it is far better for people to regard effects as movements along a continuum than to see effects as a binary either-or manifestation.

When thinking about how factors increase or decrease our risk for manifesting a negative effect, we need to think beyond a simple additive process. Factors differ in terms of *how* they move the risk point. For purposes of illustration I will mention five here: countervailing influences, nonlinear relationships, thresholds, contingent conditions, and causation.

1. *Countervailing influences.* A given factor might serve to reduce the risk point on a continuum for one particular effect while at the same time

increasing the risk point on the continuum for another particular effect. Thus, the factor is a countervailing influence. One example of a countervailing effect is exposure to television violence. Some theorists argue that exposure to high amounts of explicit violence is bad, because it can trigger a learning effect. Other theorists argue that exposure to high amounts of explicit violence might be good, because it can sensitize people to the brutal nature of violence and therefore make people more sympathetic to its victims and less likely to perpetrate violence themselves. The two effects of disinhibition and sensitization may be happening simultaneously, thus canceling each other out so that on the surface no clear manifestation appears.

Another example of this is children's creativity and daydreaming. Some people argue that TV stimulates daydreaming, because programs are so exciting that viewers will want to relive many of the portrayals they see on TV. Other people argue that TV reduces daydreaming and imagination, because programs have such rapid pacing that they leave children no time to stop and reflect or daydream. Television's ready-made images don't engage the imagination like a book would, they say. Also, TV presents so many fantasies that viewers can access with very little effort that people lose their motivation to create their own daydreams, it might be argued.

Does television exert these two countervailing influences on children's imaginations? Valkenburg and Van der Voort (1995), in a Dutch study of elementary school age children, examined the effect of television viewing on daydreaming. They found an important interaction between the type of daydreaming and the type of TV program children watched. There is more than one type of daydreaming: positive-intense (characterized by vivid, pleasant, and childlike daydreams), aggressive-heroic (action characters acting violently), and dysphoric (escapist). A positive-intense daydreaming style was found to be stimulated by watching nonviolent children's programs and to be inhibited by watching violent dramatic programs. An aggressive-heroic daydreaming style was stimulated by watching violent dramatic programs and inhibited by watching nonviolent programs.

2. *Nonlinear relationships.* The effects process is rarely linear. A linear process is in evidence when one unit of input is associated with one unit of output. Most things in life are nonlinear. This is especially the case with media literacy, where development needs to be conceptualized in a learning curve-style, nonlinear fashion. People cannot expect to receive one unit of gain in media literacy in return for one unit of effort in developing their skills and knowledge structures. Instead, there is a long "dues-paying phase" where the number of units of effort will exceed the number of units of return. Eventually, once a person's skills reach a relatively strong point, the effort to use the skills will be reduced relative to the return.

3. *Thresholds.* Some effects do not show up until media exposure exceeds a certain point. For example, viewing television generally does not have a negative influence on academic performance until it reaches about 30 hours per week and really begins cutting into study time (Potter, 1987). So if Jane increases her television viewing time from 10 hours to 20 hours per week, she is not likely to show a decrease in academic performance. However, if Bob increases his viewing from 30 to 35 hours per week, his grades are likely to drop. Without an understanding of thresholds, the pattern in this example might not seem possible. It does not seem fair that Jane can increase her TV viewing by 10 hours and experience no negative effect on her grades, but Bob increases his TV viewing time only half as much and his grades go down. This pattern does not make sense unless we understand what it means to cross a threshold. This is why it is so important to understand that the effects process is a continuum. It matters where you are on that continuum. If your risk set-point is close to the manifestation level, a small change in your media exposure may be enough to push you over the threshold, while someone else experiences far more exposures and never manifests the negative effect you suffer.

4. *Contingent conditions.* When we expose ourselves to the media, we bring into play our own motives, expectations, and emotions. Each of these can contribute to or take away from the effect. Also, as we interpret the meaning of messages, our skills come into play. For example, if Greg watches a violent fight on television and sees that the perpetrator was attractive and rewarded, he is likely to begin behaving aggressively. Here, the violent message leads to aggressiveness. If Cindy has poor attention skills as she watches the same violence, she might not understand the meaning of the violence and become confused, not aggressive. The violence in this case leads to confusion. Marcia watches the same violent message but laughs at it, because she thinks it is farcical and unrealistic. In this case, the violence leads to laughter. From these three examples, can we say that violent messages lead to aggressive behavior? In general, there is no consistent pattern. The answer depends on the message and the person. When we use an approach that takes all these simultaneous factors into consideration, we discover that *under certain conditions,* violent messages can cause aggressive behavior. In short, the effect is contingent on certain conditions; it cannot be generalized to all people and all conditions.

5. *Nature of causation.* When we think of attributing effects to the media, we raise the issue of causation. After all, if the media do not cause the effect, how can we say that the media have had an influence? However, there are several ways of thinking about causation. One way is to think about

whether the media determine an effect. Another way is to think about whether the media influence the probability of an effect. Given the nature of social science research, it is far better to think the second way.

Causation has a special meaning for social scientists. If an argument for a causal relationship is to be convincing, it must demonstrate three conditions. First, there must be a relationship between the hypothesized cause and the observed effect. Second, the cause must always precede the effect in time. Third, all alternative causes for the effect must be eliminated.

The problem with making a strong case for the media causing certain effects lies with the second and third conditions. To illustrate, let's consider the hypothesis that television violence causes aggressive behavior among viewers. Because a great deal of research has been conducted to test this hypothesis, researchers are generally able to meet the first condition: showing that there is a relationship between exposure to violence and a person being more likely to exhibit aggressive attitudes and even behaviors. However, researchers have a great deal of difficulty meeting the remaining two conditions. Except for short-term experiments, it is very difficult to argue convincingly that the viewing of TV violence precedes a person's aggression. Aggressive behavior (which is the presumed effect) often precedes the TV viewing (which is the presumed cause). Aggressive people often seek out violent content in programming. Viewing the content, then, reinforces their aggressiveness, which leads them to watch more violence. At best, the relationship is reciprocal where each of the two factors is (to a certain extent) the cause of the other.

The requirement of ruling out alternative explanations is also a problem for social scientists. A person's aggressive behavior could have been triggered by nonmedia factors such as a history of frustration, trait aggressiveness, lack of conditioning to avoid aggressiveness, the need to defend oneself with extreme measures, and so on.

If we can get beyond the simple thinking of looking for one determinant of a negative effect and can think more broadly in terms of combinations of factors working in interaction to cause an effect, we are thinking probabilistically. As we have seen above, deterministic causation seeks to explain influences in a simple manner; that is, the argument is that one thing (the media) caused the effect (aggressive behavior). At times, many of these influences may all act in unison to push someone in a particular direction. When this happens, none of these individual influences can be regarded as causing or determining the outcome by themselves. Instead, each of the factors contributes its own special push; that is, each increases the probability of an effect.

Media effects are almost always probabilistic, not deterministic. There are many factors about the audiences, the messages, and the environment that increase the probability that an effect will manifest itself.

D. Factors in the Process of Influence

Almost an infinite number of factors could conceivably exert some influence on the effects process. However, six groups of factors should command most of our attention. These six factors are: developmental maturity, abilities, drives, sociological factors, states, and media content.

The relative importance of each of those individual influences changes according to the effect. This point emerges clearly when reading reviews of the effects literature on violent television content (Bushman & Huesmann, 2001), horror films (Cantor, 2001), sexual content (Malamuth & Impett, 2001), prosocial content (Mares & Woodward, 2001), advertising (Kunkel, 2001), and popular music (Roberts & Christenson, 2001).

The following discussion is by no means an inventory of all factors. It is far too early in the history of media effects research to have achieved such a goal. It is hoped that this list can serve as an organizer of the information that exists at our current plateau of knowledge and that it will suggest an agenda for future media effects research.

1. *Developmental maturity*. This factor is especially important during childhood, and this is why children are often treated as a special group when it comes to the media. Our capacities increase from infancy through adolescence. This is obvious physically; that is, as we age from infancy, we are able to run faster, jump higher, and lift heavier objects.

We also mature cognitively, emotionally, and morally. When we are very young, our minds, emotions, and moral reasoning are beginning to develop and thus have a lower ceiling of capacity than when these characteristics are more fully developed.

2. *Abilities*. Developmental maturity defines potentialities; that is, at a given age, there are limits to what a person can understand, feel, and reason morally. In this section, I deal with abilities, which are more likely to be under a person's control; when people use their abilities well, they can achieve their potential.

There is evidence that certain people are cognitively developed to a level where they might achieve certain things, but they do not exercise their abilities to achieve that potential. For example, Piaget's theory says that children are fully developed cognitively and therefore are capable of adult thinking (formal operations) at age 12. However, King (1986) conducted a review of the published literature that tested the formal reasoning abilities of adults and concluded that "a rather large proportion of adults do not evidence formal thinking, even among those who have been enrolled in college" (p. 6). This conclusion holds up over the 25 studies she analyzed, including a variety of tests of formal reasoning ability, and over a variety of samples of adults 18 to 79 years old. In one third of the samples, less than 30% of the respondents exhibited reasoning at the fully formal level, and in almost all samples, no more than 70% of the adults were found to be fully functioning at the formal level.

Ability to reason morally is not always shown to be more advanced with age. For example, Van der Voort (1986) found no evidence that children judge violent behavior more critically in a moral sense as they age. He found no reduction in the approval of "the good guy's" behavior, and as children aged, they were even more likely to approve of the violent actions of "the bad guys." So while children acquire additional cognitive abilities with age, they do not necessarily acquire additional moral insights. There is a range of moral development among people of any given age. Also, older children do not automatically have higher moral development than younger children.

3. *Drives.* Drives energize action. They are shaped by motivations. Some motivations are relatively enduring whereas others are temporary. For example, when people have a conscious need for a particular kind of information, they will actively seek out this type of information in the media, and the chance of their learning from this experience is high. People who are better educated with higher intelligence are more motivated and have a stronger drive to seek out information from the media (Roberts, 1973). These people select the information that has the greatest utility to them.

4. *Sociological factors.* The effects of the mass media are moderated by sociological factors such as conditioning by society and its institutions. If people hear a fact that is counter to their political and religious beliefs, they are likely to discount the fact and forget it or to remember it as an example of a falsehood. Thus, the degree to which people are socialized by certain institutions influences the degree to which the media can have an effect (Comstock, 1980; Murray, 1980).

Another sociological factor is interpersonal networks. People with strong interpersonal ties will use them to filter media messages (Comstock, 1980; Liebert & Schwartzberg, 1977). The more a person identifies with a peer group and the more cohesive that group is, the more the person will be influenced by the group and the less effect the media will have.

5. *States.* A state is a drive or emotional reaction that occurs in response to some temporary stimulus. It is relatively short-lived. Often, something will

happen in our lives that will cause us to feel angry or frustrated. This state can interact with media content and lead to certain effects. For example, someone who is frustrated and then views violence will be much more likely to behave aggressively than if only one of these conditions is present.

The media frequently generate states. Perhaps the most important state is arousal. When viewers are aroused, their attention is more concentrated, and the experience is more vivid for them. They will remember the portrayals more vividly and will be more likely to act while aroused (Comstock et al., 1978; Zillmann, 1991).

Certain production techniques tend to arouse viewers. These techniques include fast cuts, quick motion within a frame, loud music, and sound effects. Also, certain narrative conventions (such as suspense, fear, life-threatening violence, and erotica) can lead to arousal.

Identification with particular characters is also a key factor in the effects process, because people will pay more attention to those characters with whom they identify. We become involved in the media-depicted events through a psychological relationship with the characters in a two-step process. First, we make a judgment about how much we are attracted to the character and how much the character is like us—or how we would like to be. Second, we engage in an "as if" experience in which we imagine ourselves in the role of the character. Viewers form strong attachments to certain characters, depending on what those characters do and say (Hoffner & Cantor, 1991). The stronger the attachment is, the stronger the probability of an effect (Bandura, 1986, 1994).

6. *Media content.* The content of the messages matters a great deal. For example, people who expose themselves to news are likely to learn about current events whereas people who expose themselves to soap operas will learn what the characters have done that day. Both types of content result in learning, but the type of learning is different.

Content differences also influence long-term effects. People who watch a lot of television (regardless of the particular shows) have been found to develop a belief that the world is a mean and violent place, because there is so much crime and violence across the television landscape (Gerbner, Gross, Signorielli, Morgan, & Jackson-Beeck, 1979). This is especially true for people who watch mostly crime and action/adventure programs (Potter, 1991). People who watch only prosocial programming, such as *Misterogers Neighborhood, Sesame Street*, and similar programs, are likely to experience a different effect.

When the media present a relatively constant picture of a social world, their effect is more powerful because all the content is pointing to the same type of effect. When the media present messages that are the same as those presented by institutions such as family, education, religion, and the legal system, then all those messages reinforce one another. When there are differences across messages, the media messages are often regarded as the most important. This is especially true for people who spend more time with the media than other institutions and for people who like, trust, or are aroused more by the media messages than messages from other sources.

The context of portrayals is also influential. People learn social lessons by watching what happens to people and characters they observe in the media. For example, if a character's behavior is portrayed as being successful and rewarded, the viewer will learn that behavior was good and useful. If the behavior is punished, the viewer will learn that the behavior is bad and should not be tried (Bandura, 1994). Also influential are characters who are attractive and who perform actions that appear justified.

IV. Real World

People need a strong knowledge structure of information gained from real-world (in contrast to media) sources. For many experiences, the media provide relatively accurate information; this is the case with in-depth news reporting. Also, with many topics, the media provide the only source of information. For example, very few people know what the President, Cabinet members, and Congress people do all day without the coverage from national news organizations.

The media, however, also present distorted pictures of the real world. When people use that distorted information as a basis for their own decisions about how to function in the real world, they can increase their risk for negative effects.

If a person's knowledge structure is composed primarily of information only from the media, then this structure may be dominated by media-stimulated generalizations and internalizations from the media world. With many topics, we have no choice but to rely primarily on media information. This is what makes the media so powerful a socializing influence: We cannot check out the media information by comparing it to information from other sources such as real life. For example, almost no one knows what it feels like to be a professional athlete. We are given some insights about what the life of a professional athlete might be like, but almost no one has an opportunity to check those insights out for themselves. This is true for almost all content of news. The same is true for much fictional programming. Viewers do not know what it feels like to be a detective, an emergency room doctor, a press secretary, or many other characters portrayed on TV. Because viewers do not have an opportunity to check it out in real life, it is impossible to prove the messages false or inaccurate. When people are asked if TV entertainment is credible and a reasonable representation of the way people live, most people say yes. As people increase their amount of viewing, their perception of the reality of TV entertainment programs increases. This is especially true among children and those who have the least amount or variety of real world experiences.

But much of the information from the media does not reflect the real world very well (Potter 2001). Analyses of the content of the television world of fiction repeatedly show that the patterns there are different than those in the real world in terms of gender and ethnic make-up (Greenberg, Edison, Korzenny, Fernandez-Collado, & Atkin, 1980), acts of violence (Gerbner, Gross, Signorielli, & Morgan, 1980; Potter 1999), sexual activity (Kunkel et al., 1999; Sapolsky & Tabarlet, 1990), use of drugs and alcohol (Hartman, 1999), portrayals of families (Douglas & Olsen, 1996), portrayals of government employees (Aversa, 1999), and even values (Comstock, 1989; Potter, 1990). This is the case not only with fiction but also with news. A great many important happenings are not covered by the news (Jensen, 1997). National news overemphasizes only parts of this country (Graber, 1988) and only occurrences that follow a certain formula (Fishman, 1980). Also, news coverage focuses on high-profile examples and ignores the larger context surrounding the issue (Bagdikian, 1992; Parenti, 1986). Thus, it is important that people increase their nonmedia sources of information.

V. The Self

People need a strong knowledge structure about their own self to be media literate. Unless they have a good self-awareness, they will not know their own goals for life, their own strengths and weaknesses, and their own knowledge style. Without awareness in these areas, they cannot build a strong personal locus to control the meaning-construction task.

People are constantly developing their personality—the essence of who they are, as psychologists call it. In this construction of self, people use information they get from the media (Grodin & Lindlof, 1996; McDonald & Kim, 2001). People search out stories with characters who serve as models. Caughey (1986) goes so far as to claim that all contact with media is a form of social interaction and that in these interactions, people identify with characters and try to imitate them in some form. At the extreme case, people try to become the characters they use as role models in the media.

Some people look for themselves in the media, and that can be a positive thing if they realize that the media provide suggestions for what lives could be like in certain settings, with certain types of people, and with certain professions. To separate themselves from the media world and have their own unique perspective on the media so they can use the media rather than have the media use them, people need to be clear about their personalities in two areas: their personal knowledge style and their personal goals. This awareness is essential to one's locus.

A. Personal Knowledge Style

People differ in terms of their styles of encountering and using information. These styles are based on a person's basic cognitive, emotional, and moral development in general as well as five factors in particular. This idea is developed in detail in the next chapter.

B. Personal Goals

This includes both a person's immediate goals and long-term goals. Media literacy requires that people have a correspondence between immediate and long-term goals. When this occurs, the person's immediate goals contribute to the achieving of the long-term goals.

Every day, we have goals for information and entertainment. We seek out messages in the media. These immediate goals are based on information needs as well as emotional needs. Some of these goals are conscious, such as wanting to find out what the weather will be like tomorrow or what the definition of a word is. We know what messages we need to find, and we are aware of how to locate those messages. Other goals are unconscious. These are governed either by drive states or habits. With drive states, we may be feeling bored and have a drive for excitement. We are not sure what would excite us or where to look specifically, so we automatically search the radio or flip through magazines until something gets our attention.

Longer term goals deal more with the core of who we are, who we think we are, and what we want to become. They are more fundamental than the immediate goals and influence those immediate goals. The long-term goals are focused more on career and relationship matters.

VI. Summary

To provide a strong foundation for media literacy, people need strong knowledge structures in five areas: media content, media industries, media effects, real-world knowledge, and the self. These knowledge structures feed the locus (see next chapter) with information and give people more options for exposures and meaning construction.

The more people know about media content formulas, aggregate patterns of characters, happenings, and values, the more they will be able to appreciate the amazing content of the media and the more they will be able to protect themselves from the spurious content. Also, people need to understand the media industries, how they developed, their economic nature, patterns of ownership and control, and how they market their messages.

Awareness of a full range of media effects is essential to media literacy. We live in a media-saturated environment, and the effects are constantly happening to us as they shape our knowledge patterns, attitudes, emotions, and behaviors. Media effects even trigger physiological reactions, such as our heart rate, blood pressure, and other bodily functions. We don't even need to experience a change to see that the media have had an effect on us, because the most prevalent effect is the movement of risk points along a continuum of influence.

The effects process is a complex one. That is why it requires a person of relatively high media literacy to appreciate the situation. People who are at low levels of awareness about the process of influence will likely think in categorical terms; that is, either there is no effect or there is an effect—in which case it is likely too late to do anything about it. Instead, people need to appreciate that there are many factors that move a person's risk set-point along a continuum of risk. The more people can control the positive factors to influence the positioning of the set-point, the more they will be in a position to make media exposures lead to the effects they want and to avoid the effects they do not want. The more aware people are about what factors influence risk, the better they can control the process of influence. They can arrange to include factors for those effects they want, thus increasing the probability that the desired effect will reach manifestation.

Awareness of the real world and self are also important. Without a good set of real-world information, we cannot evaluate the accuracy of many of the media's messages. Also, each of us has a personal information style, which is our general approach to acquiring and processing information. It is a style based on a lifetime of experience with information from the media and nonmedia sources.

A full awareness in these five areas enriches the personal locus, because it gives the person a full range of potentialities. When people understand the messages and the motivations in the industries that produce them, they can understand better the process of influence. They can plan more realistic goals for their exposures. When people recognize the effects that are having a positive influence on them, they can do things to increase those effects. When people recognize when effects are having a negative influence on them, they can do things to decrease those effects.

CHAPTER 6

The Personal Locus

6

The Personal Locus

The most important explanatory construct of degree to which a person is media literate is the personal locus. *Personal locus* is a term that refers to the place in a person's mind where decisions get made about information-processing tasks. It occupies a central position in the media literacy model by drawing information from the five foundational knowledge structures, then governing the use of competencies and skills in the information-processing tasks. A strong personal locus will continually drive the person to expend more mental energy in information-processing tasks. The more developed those knowledge structures are, the more options are recognized by the personal locus, the more context people have to choose among those options, and the more emotional energy they have to generate drives. When their personal locus is not engaged, people are in the default model of automaticity.

I. What Is the Personal Locus?

The personal locus is a hypothetical construct that is best understood as having two dimensions: control and consciousness (see Figure 6.1). The vertical axis represents the control dimension; at one pole, the media have total control, and at the other pole, the person has total control. Typically, in everyday life, control is shared; the more control exercised by the person, the higher the media literacy. Higher personal control is a goal of media literacy. Complete personal control can never be achieved. There are too many messages in our culture, so people must rely on default processing to handle the majority of messages.

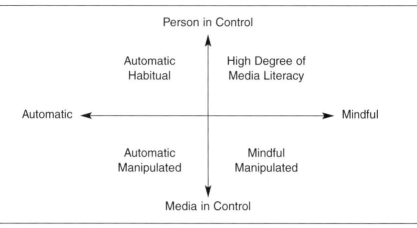

Figure 6.1   Neighborhoods in the Locus

The horizontal axis in Figure 6.1 represents the degree of mindfulness a person has during media exposures. The left side of the figure indicates a state of automatic processing where people employ default routines without thinking about them. As people move from left to right on this dimension, they increase their awareness of what they are doing, the specific goals for exposures, and the options available to them at each step in the information-processing flow. At the right side of the horizontal axis, people have reached mindfulness, which is a self-reflexive state where people are fully aware of the information processing they do and achieve a meta-perspective on it as they watch themselves make decisions while consciously monitoring what they are doing as they are doing it.

In this theory, both control and consciousness are conceived of as drives. The more a person is energized to control, the more the person is moving up the vertical axis. The more a person is energized to be aware, the more the person is moving to the right on the horizontal axis. Most often these drives are states that are triggered by a particular need to respond to a certain type of message.

There is considerable variation among people in terms of how often they are in these drive states. People who are frequently in high drive states for control and awareness can be regarded as having a drive trait; that is, their baseline of energy is much higher than the baseline of other people. Ultimately, the goal of media literacy treatments is to put people into high drive states for control and awareness, then make the experience rewarding so the person feels that the expenditure of effort was more than paid back; thus the experience is reinforcing. Through a sequence of these treatments and received rewards, the person conditions a drive trait.

There are times in everyone's lives when they have a high drive state to seek out and process information. For example, when preparing to make a major purchase like an automobile, people will seek out certain kinds of ads in newspapers, radio, television, and the Internet. They will analyze the information in those claims carefully, looking for the elements they want most in an automobile. They will group vehicles into categories by price, performance, features, and lifestyles. They will compare the "apples and oranges" across the different features and prices and make a careful, reasoned judgment about which automobile to buy. Driving all this mental effort is the emotional commitment to make the best decisions.

Some people often find themselves in this drive state for high control over media exposures and decisions. They feel that many tasks in their lives require large amounts of relevant and accurate information. Because they are in this drive state so often, they are likely to be conditioned to stay in it, even when the decisions are not as important; that is, they may have developed a high drive *trait* for information. In contrast, other people rarely find themselves in a high drive state for information, and when they do, the reward is rarely large enough to convince them that the effort was worth it, so over time they may become conditioned to a low drive trait for information.

A person's drive for information can be regarded both as a state and a trait. As a state, drives for information arise quickly and can often be satisfied within a matter of minutes. These changes are relatively minor and are determined by a person's mood, situation, location, time of day, and other temporary factors. For example, a person might want weather and traffic information in the morning, stock prices at work, advertising coupons at lunch, then escapist entertainment after a long day at work. Some of these needs are for something specific (like weather in a specific location at a specific time), or while other needs are more general: some kind of entertainment to enable escape from the stress of the day.

Drive states are constantly in flux, but a base-level drive for media messages can be regarded more as a trait. The states fluctuate around the baseline trait drives. Even people with low trait-like drives for information will periodically experience a strong need for a particular kind of information. Conversely, people with very high trait drives for information will periodically experience fatigue or information overload as a state.

The more people know about their locus, the more they can make conscious decisions to shape it. People need to commit to the importance of getting enough accurate information to make major decisions and experience the emotional reward for this effort. The more often they can experience this, the greater the likelihood they will develop a trait drive. Once they have achieved this trait-like drive, they will have more emotional energy continually available.

The more researchers understand a person's locus, the more they should be able to predict the person's level of media literacy and thereby explain the effects the person will experience. Studying the locus focuses research at the decision-making point for exposure and meaning construction. The locus holds answers to research questions such as why do people choose to switch from automatic processing to conscious processing.

II. Neighborhoods in the Personal Locus

Although both axes are continua, it is possible to talk about the spaces they suggest as four neighborhoods. I've labeled these neighborhoods as: automatic-habitual, automatic-manipulated, mindful-manipulated, and high degree of literacy (Figure 6.1).

A. Automatic-Manipulated Neighborhood

Most people operate a good deal of time in the Automatic-Manipulated neighborhood, as they react to the overwhelming number of messages from the media and the truly daunting task of processing all those messages. Most people most of the time do not want to expend the effort to become aware of all the effects of the media or how those effects work on them. They would rather ignore this information. Also, during exposures, they would rather float along on automatic pilot until something captures their attention; this means that the decision to pay attention is made by triggers in the media message, not by the person. In other words, people allow the media to condition them with certain triggers and depend on those triggers to snap them out of the screening-out state of filtering. Thus, in this neighborhood, people are at highest risk of negative effects, because those effects occur largely without their control and most often even outside their awareness.

B. Automatic-Habitual Neighborhood

The Automatic-Habitual neighborhood differs from the Automatic-Manipulated neighborhood in the sense that people have a higher drive to control their exposures and meaning construction, but they exercise this control with automatic processes. They build those processes themselves, rather than let the media condition them. Thus, this neighborhood is a more media literate one than the Automatic-Manipulated one.

Another characteristic of people in this neighborhood is that their high drive for personal control over filtering and meaning-construction decisions is undirected, because their foundational knowledge structures lack information about media content, industries, and effects, as well as their own personal goals and skills. Thus, people in this neighborhood are not aware of all their options, or they don't know how to make good decisions among the options. Also, it may be that this missing information is emotional, and people do not have the emotional drive energy to maintain a high degree of awareness during exposures.

C. Mindful-Manipulated Neighborhood

When people have a high drive for awareness during exposures, they pay a good deal of attention to the messages and criticize them. However, because of significant gaps in their essential knowledge structures, their criticism is often faulty. They do not understand how the media are controlling them, so they do not know how to avoid this condition. They do not know what the alternatives are to their habitual exposures. They do not perceive much of a range of options. These are people who constantly watch television, while complaining that there is nothing they like on television; they do not enjoy reading books, because they feel there are no good authors; they can't enjoy listening to CDs, because they believe none of today's music is any good. These people feel manipulated by the media, but they don't know what to do about it. They do not know enough to empower themselves to take steps to change the things that bother them so much.

D. High Degree of Media Literacy Neighborhood

When people work their way into the High Degree of Media Literacy neighborhood, they are much more in control of their exposures and how those messages affect them. Because they are aware and empowered, they can deal with the normative questions much more effectively. These are questions such as: How much media *should* I expose myself to? Which messages *should* I seek out, and which messages *should* I avoid at all costs? Which media effects are good and which are bad? The answers to these normative questions ultimately come down to what a person believes the answers should be. That is, those messages and effects that have utility to the person will be the positive ones, and those that do not will be negative. People then should do those things that achieve their personal goals.

Some general guidelines are available at the societal level for answering these normative questions. These guidelines array messages on a long continuum of good to bad. At the good end are those messages that strengthen society and its goals; these messages are usually taught in formal educational institutions: messages about how the government works and how individuals can be citizens to make government better. At the bad end are messages of hate, obscenity, and slander, as well as lessons about how to commit crimes. For the wide latitude of messages in the middle, individuals are left to determine how useful those messages are to their own lives. As for media literacy, people need to know how to construct personal goals for information to help them sort through all the messages in the middle. They also need to know how to evaluate the information at the poles to determine the validity of the goals of society. When people find the goals of society valid, they can internalize those goals knowing there is congruence between society and their own goals. This sorting is done mindfully, not accepted mindlessly. Where people find a difference between their own personal goals and those of society, they need to understand the risks of diverging from society's goals.

III. Shaping the Personal Locus

To achieve higher media literacy, people first need to work on their personal locus; then, the personal locus will help them over time to increase their literacy. To move into the media literacy neighborhood, people need to increase the drive for personal control and the degree of awareness during exposures. But how does one do these things? In this section, I provide four areas in which a person can work. This work will help transform the personal locus.

A. Understanding Drives

This task is essentially an emotional one, that is, building commitment to the importance of personally controlling one's exposures as well as increasing one's awareness during those exposures. To start, people must believe this is important enough to invest energy. That belief must have an emotional component to provide the energy for a drive.

A strategy for increasing drive can begin with giving people dozens of reasons why personal control is important. Because this is an appeal to cognitions, simply providing reasons will not be effective. People need to become emotionally committed to this idea. They need to experience an emotion— the stronger the better. The emotion can be a negative one, such as anger at the media for manipulating them. Or the emotion can be a positive one, such as pride for improving themselves or the need to achieve.

Another way to increase drive is through operant conditioning, that is, to find a person in a drive state (for control and awareness) and reinforce it. There are several natural drive states with the media. I will illuminate four of these: pleasure, economics, uncertainty, and inertia. If we know the relative importance of each of these principles to a person, we can more accurately predict the level of their drive for media messages in general and even for particular kinds of content.

1. *Pleasure principle.* Perhaps the most fundamental principle is the pleasure principle. This principle states that people seek out experiences they expect to find pleasant and seek to avoid experiences they expect to find unpleasant. The more they expect an experience to be pleasant, the stronger the drive to seek out that experience. When people have a history with a particular kind of experience, their expectations will be conditioned by those experiences.

Pleasure at its base is a simple physiological or emotional reaction. It requires no analysis and little effort to label. People who have had wide experience usually have known more varied forms of pleasure, moving into the cognitive, aesthetic, and moral realms. For example, people who have watched many movies with a critical eye are likely to have a much more elaborated knowledge structure about the aesthetics of film and are, therefore, able to perceive many more things in a film that could stimulate pleasurable reactions.

People at lower levels of media literacy regard pleasure in a simple and limited manner, but people at higher levels of media literacy are capable of experiencing pleasure in many different forms. However, pleasure is still something that everyone seeks; the differences across people are attributed more to their abilities in finding things in messages that can evoke pleasure.

2. *Economic principle.* People are driven to achieve value in return for the expenditure of their resources. Thus, when seeking a rewarding goal, people will continue to expend energy and other resources in the pursuit of that goal as long as they believe that the reward is at least equal to the effort. The value of a goal, therefore, lies in the favorable comparison of perceived reward and perceived effort.

3. *Uncertainty principle.* With partially specified problems, people face uncertainty—uncertainty about what the task really is, uncertainty about how to get started, and uncertainty about what a reasonable solution is. All this uncertainty creates a drive. If people label the drive negatively—for example, as frustration—they will solve the uncertainty situation by rejecting the task and taking as many shortcuts as possible to get past the task efficiently. However, if people label the drive positively—for example, as a stimulating challenge—they will use the drive energy to address the task and work until they have met the challenge. Therefore, the key to using the

uncertainty principle to increase media literacy is to get people to approach partially specified problems in a positive manner. Also, it helps if the initial problems are relatively simple so that people can easily solve them and build their confidence through successes. This conditioning will help them approach each successive problem in a positive manner.

4. *Inertia principle.* People are not always goal directed. Of course, if one looks hard enough and is willing to infer motives, one can usually attribute a goal to almost any behavior. But much of the time, especially with mundane behaviors, people are not aware of their behavior. They simply act out of habit. It is easier to continue with a habit than it is to break it. So with media literacy, it is important to get people started with good habits early.

B. Understanding Personal Knowledge Style

People differ in terms of their styles of encountering and using information. Some cognitive psychologists have argued that there are primarily three approaches to information (Lau, 1986; Taylor, 1981). These were consistency seekers, naive scientists, and cognitive misers. One group of scholars regarded people as consistency seekers, because they are motivated to minimize inconsistencies by revising an element of a belief system such as an attitude to permit cognitive consistency and thus eliminate dissonance. Another group of scholars regarded people as naive scientists who try to solve problems rationally by deducing answers from careful analysis. The third group of scholars regarded people as cognitive misers who are motivated to economize in the processing of information. It is likely that all of us have elements of all three styles, and we switch depending on the demands of the situation.

Let's move beyond these three types and look at this in a more elaborated manner, focusing on the abilities people use when encountering information. In this theory, I suggest we consider a person's knowledge style. A person's knowledge style is composed of a person's basic cognitive, emotional, and moral development in general as well as five factors in particular: type of intelligence, field dependency, tolerance for ambiguity, conceptual differentiation, and reflection-impulsivity. The combination of these trait abilities determines the degree to which a person is naturally media literate. Those who are not naturally media literate will have to work harder.

1. *Type of intelligence.* Research has shown that there are generally two types of intelligence and that these change as adults age. One type of intelligence is called crystalline, which is the ability to memorize facts. With most adults, crystallized intelligence seems to increase throughout the life

span, although at a decreasing rate in later years (Sternberg & Berg, 1987). This means that as adults get older, they do better on tests requiring factual knowledge of their world, such as vocabulary and general information. In general, older people can more easily add new information to existing knowledge structures and more easily retrieve that information from those knowledge structures they use most often.

The other type of intelligence is fluid, which is the ability to be creative and see patterns in complex sets of facts. Fluid intelligence increases in early adulthood but then decreases. This means that there is a decrease in our ability to use abstract symbols, manipulate words and numbers, recognize analogies, and complete number series.

The implication of this difference in the development of the two types of intelligence has a direct application to media literacy, where we need to develop both. Highly developed crystalline intelligence gives us the facility to absorb the images, definitions, opinions, and agendas of others; thus, we continue to expand our competencies, and this makes us better at meaning matching. Highly developed fluid intelligence gives us the facility to challenge what we see on the surface, to look deeper and broader, and to recognize new patterns; thus, we continue to develop our skills, and this makes us better at meaning construction.

2. *Field dependency.* Field dependency is a continuum along which people are arrayed according to their ability to distinguish between signal and noise in any message. Noise is the chaos of symbols and images; signal is the information that emerges from that chaos. People who are highly field-dependent get stuck in the field of chaos, seeing all the details but missing the big picture, which is the signal. Field-independent people are able to sort quickly through the field to identify the elements of importance and ignore the distracting elements (Witkin & Goodenough, 1977).

For example, when watching a story during a television news show, field-independent people will be able to identify the key information: the who, what, when, where, and why of the story. They will quickly sort through what is said, the graphics, and the visuals to focus on the essence of the event being covered. People who are field-dependent will perceive the same key elements in the story but also pay attention to how the news anchor is dressed, the hair, the makeup, the color of the graphics, the background people walking around the scene, and so on. To the field-dependent person, all of these elements are of equal importance, so they are as likely to remember the trivia as they are to remember the main point of the story.

We live in a culture that is highly saturated with media messages. Much of this is noise; that is, it does not provide us with the information or emotional reactions we want. The sheer bulk of all the information makes it more difficult to sort the important from the trivial, so many of us do not bother to sort. Instead, we default to a passive state as we float along in this stream of messages. Developing media literacy requires that we take a more active role and consciously sort, thus becoming more field-independent.

3. *Tolerance for ambiguity.* Every day, we encounter people and situations that are unfamiliar to us. To prepare ourselves for such situations, we have developed sets of expectations. What do we do when our expectations are not met and we are surprised? People who have a low tolerance for ambiguity choose to ignore those messages that do not meet their expectations and hence appear confusing to them. In contrast, those people who are willing to follow situations into unfamiliar territory that go beyond their preconceptions have a high tolerance for ambiguity. A little confusion does not stop them; instead, it motivates them to search harder for clarity.

During media exposures, people with a low tolerance tend to encounter messages on the surface. If the surface meaning fits their preconceptions, it is filed away and becomes a confirmation (or reinforcement) of those pre-conceptions. If the surface meaning does not meet a person's preconceptions, the message is ignored. In short, there is no analysis.

People with a high tolerance for ambiguity do not have a barrier to analysis. They are willing to break any message down into components and make comparisons and evaluations in a quest to understand the nature of the message and why their own expectations were wrong. People who consistently attempt to verify their observations and judgments are called scanners because they are perpetually looking for more information (Gardner, 1968).

4. *Conceptual differentiation.* People who classify objects into a large number of mutually exclusive categories exhibit a high degree of conceptual differentiation (Gardner, 1968). In contrast, people who use a small number of categories have a low degree of conceptual differentiation.

Related to the number of categories is category width (Bruner, Goodnow, & Austin, 1956). People who use few categories of classification usually have broad categories so as to contain all types of messages. For example, if a person has only three categories for all media messages (news, ads, and entertainment), then each of these categories must contain a wide variety of things. In contrast, someone who has a great many categories would be divi-ding media messages into thinner slices (breaking news, feature news, docu-mentary, commercial ads, public service announcements, action/adventure shows, sitcoms, game shows, talk shows, cartoons, and reality shows).

When we encounter a new message, we must categorize it by using a leveling or a sharpening strategy. With the leveling strategy, we look for similarities between the new message and previous messages we have stored away as examples in our categories. We look for the best fit between the new message and one of our remembered messages. We will never find a perfect fit; that is, the new message always has slightly different characteristics than our category calls for, but we tend to ignore those differences. In contrast, the sharpening strategy focuses on differences and tries to maintain a high degree of separation between the new message and older messages (Pritchard, 1975). To illustrate this, let's say two people are comparing this year's Super Bowl with last year's Super Bowl. A leveler would argue that the two games were similar and point out all the things the two had in common. The sharpener would disagree and point out all the things that were different about the two games. Levelers tend to have fewer categories so that many things can fit into the same category, while sharpeners have many, many categories. In our example, the first person would likely have only one category for Super Bowls, feeling that all the Super Bowls are the same. A sharpener might have a different category for every Super Bowl, treating each one as unique.

5. *Reflective-impulsive.* This refers to how quickly people make decisions about messages and about how accurate those decisions are (Kagan, Rosman, Day, Albert, & Phillips, 1964). People who take a long time and make lots of errors are regarded as slow and inaccurate. This is the worst combination. Those who are quick and make few errors are fast and accurate. This is the best combination.

Typically, there is a trade-off between speed and accuracy, so we are usually either reflective or impulsive. Those who take a long time and make few errors are reflective, and those who are quick and make many errors are impulsive.

Now let's take a look at all five cognitive style characteristics together. A weak knowledge style is when a person:

- Is weak on crystalline and fluid intelligence
- Is field dependent
- Has low tolerance for ambiguity
- Has weak conceptual differentiation
- Is highly impulsive

People with the above combination of characteristics are likely to be weak on media literacy and will spend most of their lives in the default model of information processing. For them, the natural abilities they need to develop media literacy are so weak that the costs for mindful information processing are very high. The challenge in helping them increase their media literacy is primarily an emotional one, that is, in increasing their drives to such a degree that they have the mental energy to work through their weaknesses.

C. Transforming Schema Into Knowledge Structures

Typically, people use schemas when processing information from the media. Most of this processing is automatic, and schemas provide the simple associations that guide this processing. As long as people's goals are efficiency driven, then the use of schemas is functional. But when the goals are accuracy driven, the simple associations provided by schema are not sufficient. People need more context and depth; thus, they need to draw from knowledge structures.

Even when people's goals are efficiency driven, schemas can create problems. For example, with efficiency, we sometimes pick the wrong schema; that is, when we are confronted with a task, we usually access the easiest schema, and if it seems to work, we use it, even if it is not the best one to use. Also, if we cannot find a schema that fits, we pick the one that fits the closest and use it.

Given the massive amount of information flooding our culture, we need to be guided by efficiency goals, and therefore, we need to use simple schemas as shortcuts. Also, if our thinking skills are not very good, then we typically use the efficiency goal exclusively. The accuracy goal requires more thinking from us as we reformulate a schema by carefully grafting in new information and pruning away inaccurate facts and images.

While we may save time in using the efficiency goal, the danger is that we are too quick in (a) throwing away important information, (b) giving up on searching for elements in an experience, (c) selecting peripheral rather than important information to incorporate into schema, (d) putting an element in the wrong schema, and (e) putting an element in the correct schema but in the wrong place, such as linking it with the wrong elements. All of these lead to inaccuracies. If we continue adding to these inaccuracies over and over, our schema will be superficial and composed of lots of inaccurate information. When we rely on schema like these, we will find ourselves arguing for some myths or bad opinions—absolutely convinced that we are right—then get frustrated that we cannot make others realize that *they* are wrong. It can be a big problem if we do not periodically compare our schema to accurate information and rework our schema to remove the old, misleading, and biased information.

It is unrealistic to expect people to develop well-formed knowledge structures on every topic they will encounter in the media or in life. Instead, people often need to use simple schema. However, there are times when it is far superior to use knowledge structures. The earlier people can see the value of this, the more they can do to build knowledge structures in key areas.

Media literacy requires the transformation of many of our informal schema into formal knowledge structures. When people do this, they are analyzing and evaluating what they have in their memories. They are cleaning out faulty information, which either is inaccurate or has gone out of date. They organize the valuable information in structured patterns that make sense from a context point of view, not just an associative point of view. Organization based on association allows for faulty habits to be reified. For example, if a person thinks 6 times 6 equals 35 and has made that faulty association several times, then the association is relatively strong and will automatically be made the next time the person sees 6 times 6. Or if a person thinks a tomato is a vegetable because it is usually served with other vegetables, then the association is strong and will continue to be made, even though the tomato has important characteristics in common with fruit and should be so catalogued. These examples are admittedly minor ones; there are not huge consequences for being wrong. But what I am illustrating with these simple examples is that sometimes errors are made and associations get established, repeated, then reified. When the only structure is an association among nodes, then there is no basis within this system for spotting errors and making corrections.

Knowledge structures provide a much better context for tasks requiring the skills of grouping, induction, deduction, synthesis, and abstraction. With a better context, people can use their skills more successfully and with more confidence. Their skills will grow stronger. This will also result in the construction of better knowledge structures, which in turn will provide better contexts for further meaning construction. Also, the higher organizational power of knowledge structures (compared to schema) will result in quicker and more confident information cataloguing and hence allow for more efficient information retrieval later.

D. Increasing Personal Responsibility

People like to criticize the media and blame them for all sorts of negative behaviors and trends in society. Is the problem primarily lack of government regulation? Or is it primarily the failure of parents to raise their children strictly enough? Or is it a problem of message producers not being responsible? Or is it a problem because researchers have not yet been able to determine all the details about how people are affected by the media? Of course, all of these factors—regulators, parents, producers, researchers—contribute to a problem of negative effects from the media, and if any of these factors was altered, the degree of risk of harm from potential negative effects would likely be changed.

Missing from most lists of blame are people themselves. This is a serious oversight, because people are part of the blame complex. Furthermore, people are the one element in any blame complex that can be changed most easily. When people decide to change, the alterations that accrue are usually more lasting. For example, regulators can force people to do things, but it is always better if people decide to do those things for themselves: that is, if those things can be shown to be in their best interests. Then, people will do those things not because of regulations but because they believe they are better off when they do those things. Thus, for example, people who believe that wearing seat belts in vehicles will make them safer will be likely to develop the seat belt-wearing habit more than people who feel they are being forced to wear seat belts because of some law.

When individuals change, they notice an immediate alteration in their personal locus and hence in their level of media literacy. If no one else changes, the one person who changed still reaps many benefits. But if many individuals change, then larger scale changes will also come about. For example, producers of media content are following the demands of their markets. If enough people demanded a different form of message, some marketers would provide those messages.

For a lasting solution to the problem of negative media effects, individuals need to first change their behavior. This is hard to do, because much of their current behavior is habitual. Changing habits is difficult, especially when those habits are functional, that is, deliver some desired outcome. To show that other outcomes are better than the current ones, people need to be made aware of the risks they currently face and the alternative opportunities they could realize. This requires education.

It is the responsibility of the educational institution to introduce basic knowledge structures and to provide reasons for developing media literacy. Many people believe that education is the key, that is, making people better consumers of messages in our information-saturated society. This has many advantages, such as not threatening the First Amendment, thus preserving the maximum freedom for message senders and receivers. Education is oriented toward helping people make better decisions, and this could change the market for messages so that there truly is a wider range and better balance. Education also has the advantage of putting the locus of the solution on individuals because the need for different kinds of information varies across individuals and that diversity should be preserved.

We cannot simply reprogram people. The human brain is not like a computer. Writing in *How the Mind Works*, Steven Pinker (1997) argues,

> Computers are serial, doing one thing at a time; brains are parallel, doing millions of things at once. Computers are fast; brains are slow. Computer parts are reliable; brain parts are noisy. Computers have a limited number of connections; brains have trillions. Computers are assembled according to a blueprint; brains must assemble themselves. (p. 26)

Pinker argues that the mind is not a single organ but a system of organs that have psychological faculties or mental modules.

The human mind is complex. Also, humans exhibit profound differences in interests, beliefs, behavior patterns, and so on. Rather than relying on the stick of regulation to force change, I prefer to believe that the carrot of higher insight will motivate people to make changes that they see are in their best interests.

Factors outside the individual can provide resources to help or hinder an individual's development of media literacy. These factors—such as regulations, producers, and programmers—should not be relied on either to stimulate media literacy in the individual or to provide a safety net that prevents nonliterate people from experiencing risks from negative effects. These factors have their own agenda. With media businesses, the goal is money. The businesses will accept the risk of developing services when they think they can generate revenue. Businesses will also develop services when they believe that individuals will give them attention, so that businesses can rent that attention to advertisers. Thus, businesses respond to market opportunities and are willing to accept risks only when they believe there is a good chance of generating revenues large enough to compensate them for their efforts.

With regulators, the goal is public favor. Creating new regulations that change existing behaviors and business practices puts regulators at risk of losing public favor. But if the benefits of increased public favor from one group are greater than the risks of losing public favor among another group, then regulators will take the risk. For the individual, the most empowering agenda is the person's own agenda. People have full control—if they take it—over creating and executing this agenda. But they need to begin by taking more responsibility.

IV. Functions of the Personal Locus

When people have a strong set of foundational knowledge structures, their personal locus can perform three functions well. First, the locus makes the person aware of more options in any problem-solving situation. More elaborated knowledge structures present people with more options for media messages and for the construction of meaning from those messages. People who are aware of what is on 100 cable channels will have more options for viewing than a person who has awareness limited to three channels. A person who is only aware of the news magazines, *Time, Newsweek,* and *US News & World Report,* will be more limited than other people who know about a dozen liberal magazines, another dozen conservative magazines, and several score of magazines of all kinds of other political persuasions. A person who has a well-developed knowledge structure on a particular topic will have more options for construction of meaning.

A second function for the personal locus is the drawing of criteria from the knowledge structures to help the person make better choices among options. Better-developed knowledge structures can provide standards for evaluating alternatives. Without such standards, it is not possible to make reasoned evaluations.

The full range of available information makes the task seem easier and more likely to succeed, introducing the third factor: shaping drives in a positive direction. Well-developed knowledge structures include emotional elements. Some of these are attractive elements, that is, memories of good exposures that serve to reinforce that experience. This sets up a positive drive to seek out that type of message again. Some of the emotions are negative; that is, people may feel frustration, because new information does not fit with their existing information. Thus, they are in a state of dissonance, and they have a drive to reduce the dissonance.

V. Summary

The most important explanatory construct of the degree to which a person is media literate is personal locus. *Personal locus* is a term that refers to that which governs exposures to messages and the processing of information from those messages. Drive for control and drive for awareness are what bring energy to the locus. Drives are generated and shaped by four principles: pleasure, economic gain, uncertainty, and inertia.

People who want to improve their level of media literacy need to become committed to increasing their drives for personal control and awareness during exposures. To do this, they need to reshape their personal locus. Personal locus is reshaped through increasing understanding about drives, understanding about one's personal knowledge style, and personal responsibility for one's own media literacy.

When a person has a strong foundation of knowledge structures, the information flows into the personal locus and allows it to perform well in three areas. First, the personal locus can make people more aware of a wide range of options. Second, the personal locus can help people pick the best option for their purposes, thus increasing personal control. Third, the experience of the first two areas helps shape drives in a positive direction, thus ensuring a high level of energy to help people through the more difficult media literacy tasks.

Personal Locus
Propositions and Research Questions

Propositions for Practices

1. To increase media literacy, one must increase:
   (a) drive states for control over information-processing decisions
   (b) drive states for awareness

2. Interventions need to do the previous (Proposition #1), then make it rewarding so that the effort is linked with value that is greater than the effort.

3. The long-term goal of interventions is to strengthen the locus by turning positive drive states into positive drive traits.

Propositions for Research

1. Locus drive states can be conditioned to become locus drive traits.

2. Conditioning is successful when people are shown that the costs to them (mental effort to delineate goals, search for information, apply skills, deal with uncertainty, and reach a conclusion) are smaller than the payoffs (rewards in the form of satisfaction of a job well done, surprise at seeing more or different things, or stronger emotional reaction).

Research Questions

1. *Conceptual*
   How do people make decisions about the costs involved in media exposures and information processing?

   How do people make decisions about the value that accrues from media exposures and information processing?

   How can value of information processing be increased to a point to overcome resistance by people who have a weak knowledge style?

2. *Measurement*
   How can personal locus drive states and traits be measured in a quantitative manner so that their change can be monitored after interventions?

   How can people be measured to determine their personal locus neighborhood?

3. *Treatments*
   What media materials work best in creating positive personal locus drive states?

   What are the characteristics of these materials that make the costs low (for increasing person control and awareness) and the value high?

   How can high value for interventions be maintained over time so that people can be conditioned to expend more effort during all stages of information processing?

CHAPTER 7

Competencies and Skills of Media Literacy

7

Competencies and
Skills of Media Literacy

This theory makes an important distinction between competencies and skills, as readers will recall from Chapter 3. Competencies are the abilities people have acquired to help them recognize elements in messages and to associate denoted meaning with those elements. Competencies are learned early in life, then applied automatically. Skills, in contrast, are tools that people use to address the less fully specified problems of information processing, especially filtering and meaning construction. Media literacy relies on the skills of analysis, evaluation, grouping, induction, deduction, synthesis, and abstraction.

This chapter first defines competencies in more detail and shows how competencies are integral to media literacy as a foundation. A person cannot be media literate without these competencies, but having all these competencies does not guarantee literacy; the competencies only open up the potentialities for media literacy.

The great elasticity in media literacy is with the skills: There is a large difference between those people who are strong on this set of skills and continually use them well compared to those people who are weak on these skills and continually use them in a faulty manner. People who have highly developed skills have the tools to create and maintain elaborate knowledge structures of accurate and useful information. This information is easily used by the personal locus, which drives more mindful processing of information.

The more people know about the skills required to be media literate, the more they can control their development. Therefore, it is important that people are aware of what these skills are and what their levels of ability are on them.

I. Basic Competencies of Media Literacy

Competencies are developed throughout childhood as people learn basic levels of listening, speaking, reading, writing, and viewing. Some of these competencies are necessary in creating exposures (such as manipulating a remote control device, turning on a TV, accessing an Internet site, etc.) whereas others are necessary during the exposure (such as listening, reading, and viewing). Regardless of whether the competency generates or maintains an exposure, there are certain generic qualities to them. One of these qualities is that competencies are relatively simple to learn; they don't require much practice. Once people have acquired a competency, they are able to perform it fully; that is, there is little room for improvement. Competencies are categorical—either people have the ability to do something, or they do not.

Media literacy includes three kinds of competencies. They are the recognition of referents, the recognition of patterns, and the matching of meanings to referents. I use the term *referent* as others might use the term *symbol*, to refer to units in messages that signal meaning. However, I avoid the term *symbol* because there are huge literatures with fine discriminations made about symbols and signs, the signified and signifiers. Although that work is important, it is too complex in its discriminations to serve a purpose here useful enough to warrant the introduction of that degree of complexity.

A. Recognizing Referents

With the message-encountering competencies, the recognition of referents is primarily a task of unitizing. For example, when listening to a continuous flow of sounds and pauses, people must have the ability to separate the sounds into units. People must know how to figure out which pauses are significant and which are not and which sounds go together, that is, where the breaks between referents come. In reading, people must know how to determine which letters go together to form words and which words are united as being in the same thought.

Some referents are words, so we need to know what is a word compared to a letter, a sentence, a line of type, and so on. Some referents are elements in pictures, so we need to be able to recognize form, dimension, and perspective. Some referents are audio, so we need to be able to recognize voice, music, and sound effects. Some referents are movements on a screen; we need to be able to recognize a cut, dissolve, pan, zoom in, and so on.

It is easy to take this competency for granted, because we have been using it so automatically and so well for so many years. But as children, we had to learn this competency. Very young children watch television in an exploratory mode, because they do not have a strong command of referents and conventions. They attend primarily to perceptually salient formal features (such as loud sounds, unique voices, special effects, etc.) and struggle to figure out what they mean. With cognitive development and additional experience, children are better able to recognize referents.

With newspapers, young children look at the front page and "see" the same thing as an adult, but they cannot extract many elements. They recognize that certain things are pictures, but they aren't able to extract any of the words or graphics; that is, they cannot distinguish the boundaries of the referents there. With radio, children "hear" the sounds but cannot recognize the boundaries between the songs, jingles, stingers, happy chat, serious news, and ads.

B. Recognizing Patterns

The individual referents are the micro-units in a message: a word in a sentence, a figure in a photograph, a note in a melody. When many referents occur together, which is almost always the case, we need to see connections among the individual elements. Words form sentences, then paragraphs, chapters, and books. A visual shape is part of the overall composition of a photograph. A musical note played against other notes can be part of a chord; and when the note is played as part of a sequence of notes, it can form a pattern of a melody.

Some patterns are rather simple. For example with print, the letter is the basic referent unit. These letters are not arranged randomly; instead, the author arranges the letters into words. Learning to read means attaining the competency to recognize that letters form words, that words form sentences, and that sentences form paragraphs, and so on. Readers know the rules of grammar and sentence syntax, which help them recognize these patterns with ease. Also, these relatively simple rules are shared, so that everyone with this competency recognizes the same patterns.

As patterns become more complex, recognizing the pattern is an increasing challenge. However, often, there are enough rules in a person's competency to ensure that the problem is fully specified and that the person will feel confident in recognizing one and only one pattern, which all people confronted with the same task will perceive. For example, let's say a newspaper's front page is lying on a table. This front page contains many referents: individual words arranged in sentences, sentences arranged in stories, stories arranged in columns with headlines and subheads, pictures with cutlines, top matter (name of newspaper, price, weather blurb, etc.), graphics, table of contents, and so on. Despite the large number and many different kinds of referents, most people will automatically recognize the pattern of a newspaper's front page, and if 20 people pass by that table, chances are high that all 20 will recognize the same pattern.

Another example of a complex referent set is a photograph. Messaris (1994) argues that children need to learn to recognize the referent of still images because of their two dimensionality, lack of color, and reduced detail. Building on this competency is the moving image of television and film, where people also need to recognize the interplay of pictures, speech, music, graphics, and special effects. Production techniques can help us identify these patterns, but we must learn how production techniques cluster into patterns. There are formulas for the way a camera frames an object so as to reveal its image as a coherent object, action, or space through the successive presentation of partial views. Beyond the audiovisual language of film and television, we need to develop the competency to follow stories.

People must also be able to spot patterns in narratives. We must be able to link a character's motives with actions; link actions with consequences; understand the unities of time and place; and infer themes. If we cannot make these linkages, we will not be able to see the patterns among the referents.

Referent sets differ enormously in terms of their complexity. The more complex sets are usually more challenging, but once we have learned to recognize the pattern in a referent complex, we have the competency and can continue to recognize that pattern in all future encounters with such a referent set. However, the challenge for media literacy lies not in the degree of complexity of the referents; instead the challenge for media literacy lies in the degree of specification of the problem in the task. If the task is recognizing a pattern and we have a fully specified problem, then people can solve this problem with a competency. However, if the task in recognizing a pattern is only partially specified, then people will not have enough rules to guide them to a full recognition of the pattern; instead, people will need to move beyond competencies and use skills.

This competency of recognizing patterns is closely linked with the previous competency of recognizing referents. As illustrated above, many referents are actually patterns of subordinate referents. For example, a word is really a pattern of letters; a sentence is really a pattern of words; a story is a pattern of characters in actions.

C. Associating Definitions

Once we have unitized the flow into referents, we need to associate meaning with each referent. To do this, we can use even the simplest schema where a referent is one node and a meaning is another node; when these two nodes are linked in a schema, the triggering of one leads to a simple association with the other. We have previously learned these meanings, in the form of denoted definitions. Association of a referent with a previously acquired definition is an easy task relative to the much more difficult task of constructing meaning with few guidelines.

The meanings associated with referents are usually learned from memorization. For example, we memorize the definitions of words and the conventions of grammar and expression to be able to read. From the experience of listening to radio, we know that certain sounds signal the lead-in to news, certain voices convey humor or seriousness, certain sounds convey danger or silliness. With television and film, we learn the meaning of a flashback, an extreme close-up on a character's face, character stereotypes, and what to expect in the unfolding sequence of a detective show. We have learned to connect certain referents with certain meanings.

D. Developing Competencies

The acquiring of these foundational competencies is influenced by our childhood rates of maturation cognitively, emotionally, and morally. For example, when we are very young, our minds are not mature enough to recognize written referents and associate meaning with them. When our minds mature, we reach a point where we have the potential to read, but we must work to deliver on that potential. Try to think back to when you were about 5 years old and first learning how to read. You had to expend a good deal of effort to concentrate on each word and recognize its meaning and how it sounded when pronounced. Then, you needed to work on putting words together into sentences in order to recognize a larger chunk of meaning. The act of reading a page of a book took a long time and was exhausting. Now, after years of practice, you take the competency of reading for granted. Your eyes fly over the words barely "seeing" them. Instead your mind is "seeing" the ideas and images evoked behind the words. The little black lines that form the letters and words are transparent; you see right through them and into the author's meaning.

By early adolescence, we are fairly proficient with all of these foundational competencies and have reached a level of functional literacy; that is, we know how to expose ourselves to all types of media and get information as well as entertainment from them fairly easily. Additional practice continues to improve those competencies until their use becomes automatic. We do not need to think consciously as we apply them.

Once we have acquired these competencies to a point where we are comfortable with them (usually during the early elementary school years), we think we are media literate. We feel very proficient with these competencies. Our media exposures are more efficient—we no longer struggle when reading a newspaper article or following a plot in a TV show or film—but the danger of feeling proficient is that we no longer feel we need to concentrate. This leads to mindless exposure where we accept the surface meanings in the messages. Many people stay on this plateau, practicing these foundational competencies the rest of their lives. People who do this feel a false sense of literacy because exposure comes so easily, and they fall into the mindless processing trap, which limits them to accepting the surface meanings in the messages.

E. Moving Beyond Simple Associations

Earlier in this section, as we talked about associating definitions, I used the example of two nodes being linked where one node was a referent and the second node was a definition. This works well for many referents. In fact, for years, many cognitive psychologists used this as a model for human thinking. For example, it was believed that when readers saw the printed word *dog*, they automatically associated this three-letter combination with a certain type of four-legged furry animal. Thus, the human mind was regarded as a large dictionary of learned definitions. Every time the mind perceived a referent, it would work like a machine to match that referent with its meaning from that mental dictionary. While this model of thinking still holds in many situations, at other times, it is far too simple.

Some referents have more than one associated meaning. For example, *bad* can mean "not good" but it can also mean "very good." *Cool* can mean a low temperature, a chilly demeanor, a laid-back attitude, or "very good." When a referent is associated with several definition nodes, the association cannot be done automatically. Instead, we need to devote some conscious energy to make a decision about which of several (often conflicting) meanings to accept. How do we make such a choice? We must pay more attention to the context of the referent and let the context guide our choice of meaning. For example, when trying to determine the meaning of a particular word in a sentence, we often must understand the meaning of the sentence before we can figure out the meaning of the particular word. The sentence provides the context. The idea conveyed by a sentence has more to it than the simple sum of the meanings of each word. The arrangement of words and the grammar as well as punctuation are important. For example, if two characters are kissing, and one says, "Don't! Stop!" that conveys a different meaning than if the character says, "Don't stop." The way the sentences are arranged into paragraphs and stories conveys more meaning than the simple sum of the ideas conveyed in each sentence. If you read about a mother saying, "You are so smart" to her child, the meaning can change given the overall story. If the mother has just seen her child brag that he can take his bicycle apart and fix it but in the process he destroys it, the mother's comment is sarcastic. But if the mother has just looked at the child's report card and sees all excellent grades, the comment is one of pride and happiness.

Determining the meaning of words, sentences, and stories often requires people to make a choice among meaning options. This does not mean that this is not a fully specified task; it is. What makes it fully specified is that the meaning associations already exist in our minds. For example, Barsalou (1992) estimates that the typical human has a vocabulary of more than 50,000 words; that means they know many meanings and the characteristics for thousands of different kinds of things. While many of those referents may be linked to more than one definitional node, contextual information resides in those nodes, so there is enough guidance in the schema to make the selection of meaning a fully specified problem.

Foundational competencies are essential to media literacy. I do not mean to imply that acquiring these competencies is not a significant accomplishment. The fact that we acquire these competencies when we are so young and that they are acquired by so many people does not mean they are simple competencies. They are fairly complex, as anyone knows who tries to explain the process needed to acquire these competencies (see Chomsky, 1972). However, the acquisition of foundational competencies is only a first step in a process of development toward media literacy. Other challenges require other competencies to develop to relatively high levels of media literacy.

The foundational competencies give us the ability to associate simple meaning from media messages. That meaning rests on the surface of messages and is easy to see. But there are many layers of meaning in media messages. To see the range of meaning and to have the control to select the ones most useful to us, we need to employ skills.

II. The Skills of Media Literacy

The application of skills requires more concentration than the application of competencies, which are more automatic, once learned. When applying skills, there are always options in how they are to be applied, and there is a great deal of elasticity in how well they can be applied. The application of competencies can take place in a relatively passive manner, but skills require active thinking.

The tasks of exposure and information processing are riddled with partially specified problems. Everyone comes to these tasks with different experiences and different goals. Thus, a theory cannot prescribe a list of procedures, because the beginning and ending points of information processing are infinite in number. A list of techniques that might be best for one person might lead another person to great frustration or risk of a negative effect. Therefore, a theory of media literacy can never be specific and prescriptive, but a theory can have great value if it provides a map that outlines a procedure that is generic to any exposure task and information-processing task.

A theory of media literacy cannot be detailed and prescriptive. That is, such a theory cannot present a complete list of specific steps for people to take to develop a high degree of media literacy. If the media literacy problem was what is called "fully specified," then it would be possible to develop such a complete list of steps. But the problem of media literacy is not fully specified; instead, it is partially specified. This means that some parts of the problem have not been—and can never be—specified. Before I lay out what these unspecifiable parts are, I must first outline the seven skills of media literacy and explain how they are used to solve partially specified problems.

There are seven key skills of media literacy (see Table 7.1). These skills are the tools we use to encounter messages and process information. Each of

Table 7.1   The Seven Skills of Media Literacy

Skill	Task
Analysis	Breaking down a message into meaningful elements
Evaluation	Judging the value of an element; the judgment is made by comparing the element to some criterion
Grouping	Determining which elements are alike in some way; determining which elements are different in some way
Induction	Inferring a pattern across a small set of elements, then generalizing the pattern to all elements in the set
Deduction	Using general principles to explain particulars
Synthesis	Assembling elements into a new structure
Abstracting	Creating a brief, clear, and accurate description capturing the essence of a message in a smaller number of words than the message itself

the seven skills is presented separately below; however, we rarely encounter a problem where we use one and only one skill. Most often, skills are used together in various combinations and in different orders.

A. Analysis

Analysis refers to the breaking down of the message into meaningful elements. For example, docudrama messages offer no guidance to audience members trying to separate the elements that are based on actual occurrences, and therefore are informative in the traditional sense, from those elements that are fiction and designed purely for entertainment value. Audience members must break these messages down to determine which are based on fact and which are fictionalized if they are to appreciate accurately the events being portrayed.

Analysis is the most fundamental of the seven skills, because the elements produced by an analysis are the raw materials for the other six skills. With the docudrama example, once people have broken the message into elements, they need to evaluate the elements, group them, look for patterns to make inductions, and so on.

Three kinds of analysis are useful for media literacy: focal plane analysis, component analysis, and outline analysis (for more detail on these, see Potter, 2004). Focal plane analysis is the searching for one fact in a mass of information. A simple example of this is when we search the dictionary for the meaning of a particular word. We do not want to read the entire dictionary; instead, we are concerned only with one word and its definition. We have a knowledge structure that tells us that dictionaries are arranged alphabetically, so we use this information to guide us to our one word and ignore the rest of the dictionary. Another example of a focal plane analysis is when we want to find out what the weather will be today, so we go to the local newspaper and its weather prediction section. We have a knowledge structure that tells us how our newspaper is organized, and we use that information to search for only what we want and ignore the rest.

Component analysis is breaking the message down into its component parts. For example, we can break a news story down into its elements: who, what, when, where, and why. We can break an ad down into its sponsor, product, selling appeal, and so on. Any message can be broken down into different types of components, depending on the need for the analysis. Returning to the news story example, the who, what, when, where, and why are components of the information dimension, but other dimensions could be used for the analysis of a news story. One possible analytical dimension is a structural dimension; we could break the story down into paragraphs, sentences, or words. Another dimension is format elements; we could break the story down into text, photographs, graphics, and headline. Yet another dimension is source; we could break the story down by source of information. There are many possible dimensions for analyzing almost any media message; thus, analysis is almost always a partially specified problem. We have to think about all the dimensions available for an analysis, then select one that is most useful for the need driving the analysis.

Outline analysis is breaking the entire message down into its components and subcomponents. The result is an outline that shows all the components and how they are organized in relation to one another. This begins as a component analysis but becomes more detailed. Because this type of analysis requires a great deal more effort than the other two, it is usually not undertaken unless there is a strong reason for accuracy. For example, if you are planning to make a major purchase such as an automobile, your drive to make the best decision might be high enough to conduct an outline analysis for each automobile you are considering, so you expose yourself to messages about those automobiles in all the media outlets you can access and use that information to construct outlines.

Being good at analysis requires highly developed knowledge structures. The more context you have (about narrative forms, industry motives, message conventions, etc.), the more dimensions you will be able to use in the analysis and the more in-depth the analysis can be.

Analysis is not limited to cognitive elements in messages. It can also be applied to emotional elements, aesthetic elements, and moral elements. Any message can be broken down in many ways. With media literacy, the most important forms of analysis are along these four dimensions. The cognitive analysis will result in facts as elements or other informational elements. The emotional analysis will result in triggers in the message that stimulate different emotions. The aesthetic analysis will result in units of craft or artistic achievement, and the moral analysis will result in value elements.

B. Evaluation

Evaluation is making an assessment of the worth of an element. The assessment is made by comparing the element to some criterion. Usually, the criterion is accuracy or utility. For example, with cognitive information, we identify a fact in a media message and compare it to a fact from some authority, perhaps in our existing knowledge structures, if we trust the accuracy of those facts. If the fact in the message matches the fact in a knowledge structure, we judge the message fact to be accurate. The criterion here is accuracy. However, if we find an element in a media message that does not conform to our existing knowledge structure, we must decide whether to give high value to the new element and therefore change our knowledge structure or to value more highly our existing knowledge structure and disregard the new element. The criterion here is utility; that is, we determine if the new element is more useful to us than the element in our knowledge structure.

As an example, let's say you hear a damaging claim against a political candidate whom you favor. Your existing knowledge structure has a great many positive elements about this candidate. The new claim does not fit into your existing knowledge structure, which is favorably constructed for the candidate. You must decide whether to believe the new claim and incorporate it into your knowledge base, which would require substantial alterations, or to disregard the new claim. You could use several strategies to make the evaluation. You could examine the credibility of the claim, that is, who is the source of the accusation and does it seem plausible. Another strategy is a weighting one. If the claim sits out there by itself with no additional people coming forth to support it, then the claim has little weight, especially compared to the weight of favorable knowledge you already have about the candidate.

People who operate at higher levels of media literacy will often be more careful, reasonable, diligent, and logical when making evaluative judgments. People at lower levels of media literacy will most often feel the effort is not worth it and quickly make a judgment based only on superficial intuition.

Making good evaluations requires the use of knowledge structures with well-developed information in four areas: cognitive, emotional, aesthetic, and moral. The more information a person already has, the easier it is to make judgments about new information. For example, if people use a knowledge structure with only cognitive information, they have the basis for undertaking a logical reasoning process. But what happens when this logical process results in several good judgment alternatives? If we also had some emotional information in that knowledge structure, we could draw on that additional knowledge. Goleman (1995) reminds us that an important part of evaluation is emotions. Unless we factor in how we feel about something, we may become paralyzed and unable to make a judgment. We need to have enough self-awareness about our emotions to determine where our preferences lie. Goleman says that many decisions "cannot be made well through sheer rationality; they require gut feeling, and the emotional wisdom garnered through past experiences" (p. 53).

When we are highly media literate, we use our emotions; we don't ignore them. If we try to ignore them, they can influence us subconsciously. If our emotions stay at the subconscious level, they can still exert influence on our decisions and behaviors, but they do so without us being aware of it. Even without our awareness, decisions are being made, attitudes shaped, and behaviors acted. Goleman (1995) reminds us: "As Freud made clear, much of emotional life is unconscious; feelings that stir within us do not always cross the threshold into awareness" (p. 54). Being media literate requires us to develop greater self-awareness about our emotions so we can use them in the evaluation process.

C. Grouping

The skill of grouping is focused on comparing and contrasting. The task is to determine how elements are similar to one another (comparing) and how elements differ from one another (contrasting). Thus, the elements can be arranged in groups such that all elements in a given group share some commonality while the elements not in that group lack that commonality.

Let's consider an example. Imagine that I show you three objects: a red ball, a pear, and a knife. Then, I ask you which of the three objects is associated most with an apple. You could pick the red ball, saying that both share the same shape and color. Or you could pick the pear, reasoning that both are examples of fruit. Or you could pick the knife, thinking that you use a knife to pare the apple before eating it. Which of these three answers is correct? They all are, because they all have a reasonable association with an apple. Making good comparisons is not a foundational competency; it is not simply memorizing the one best association for every object or concept. Instead, comparisons rely on people's ability to see reasonable connections among objects. The more connections people can see and articulate, the stronger is their skill of comparison. Thus, people are more media literate when they can see a given object from many different perspectives, each of which relates the object to something else.

On what points can we make comparisons/contrasts with the media? One point of comparison is to look across media. How is a message changed as it is freed from the constraints of one medium and becomes subject to the constraints of another? Some elements do not change, but others do.

Another point of comparison is to look across vehicles. Within any medium, there is a variety of vehicles. Making comparisons across vehicles reveals the editorial perspectives, business constraints, and vision of the audience. To see for yourself that not all magazines are alike, compare a nonfiction story in *Newsweek, Cosmopolitan,* and *Soldier of Fortune.*

Other points of comparison are across episodes of a show to see character development or across performances of a particular artist to assess his or her range. There are many possible points of comparison, and not all of them are equally useful. A key to using these advanced skills is to have an agenda to assess a deeper and broader set of meaning in the messages, then apply the skills consciously in working toward that goal.

Grouping is an important skill for incorporating new information into our existing knowledge structures. After we have broken a media message down into its component parts, we need to compare those elements with the elements in our existing knowledge structure. Elements that match are compared; elements that differ are contrasted. If some elements are different, then we can add something new to our knowledge structure. If all of the elements match, then the message adds nothing new to our existing knowledge structures, but that does not mean that our knowledge structure is not changed. The information can reinforce our existing knowledge structures and add weight to them, thus making them more resistant to change later on. Also, people must decide whether their existing groupings continue to make sense or whether the incorporation of the new information requires a new configuration.

On the surface, the grouping skill seems guided by some simple, easy-to-follow rules. While this is true, things can get complicated when we examine how people actually make their classifications. Rarely do people follow the simple rule of looking for all characteristics of the elements and looking for patterns of similarities and differences, because most elements have many, many characteristics and those characteristics do not always fall neatly into discrete categories. Because of this complexity, people look for shortcuts. After years of research on human classification strategies, cognitive psychologists have observed that people generally use one of four models to categorize things: exemplar model, prototype model, classical model, and mixed models (Barsalou, 1992; Fiske & Taylor, 1991).

The exemplar model is used when people represent a category with memories of exemplars that they encounter in everyday experience; for example, the category of "surfer dude" might be represented in memory by a particular person. If you meet a young man who has some of the characteristics of your prototype of surfer dude (perhaps blonde hair and lives at the beach) you might reason that the match of the person's characteristics with your prototype is close and conclude that the person is a surfer dude. The key phrase here is "if the match is close" because it suggests a shortcut; that is, the person need not exhaust all possible characteristics and match them. Also, the person need not find a perfect pattern; if the new person matches a few of the characteristics of the person's model for surfer dude, the new person quickly gets classified as a surfer dude.

With the prototype model, categorizations are guided not by a single example but by a set of characteristics that make up the category, thus a prototype, which is a single, centralized category representation. The category system abstracts properties that are representative of a category's exemplars and integrates them into a category prototype. A prototype for bird would include elements such as small, flies, sings, and so on. When people see something that looks like a bird, they match the qualities they see to the characteristics in the prototype. The goal is to maximize similarity of real-world object to the prototype's characteristics.

The classical model relies on formal rules for category membership. For example, for old maid, the rules are female, human, adult, unmarried. These are individually necessary. Jointly, they are sufficient for the categorization. The classical model requires a clear definition of the category. Barsalou (1992) explains that some categories are relatively easy to define (odd numbers, old maid) while others are much more difficult (chair, games, furniture, tools). A good definition tells people how to categorize objects; that is, it provides enough information so that when a person sees something that might be an example of a particular concept, the definition has enough detail to guide the person to conclude with confidence that this thing is the concept or not.

An explanation about how grouping is done is provided by Smith, Shoben, and Rips (1974), who proposed a feature comparison model. They argued that the meaning of a word or a concept consists of a set of elements called features. There are two types of features: defining features and characteristic features. The defining features are those that must be present in every example of the concept. The characteristic features are usually but necessarily present. For example, think of the concept of bachelor. The defining features are male, adult, unmarried, and human. If a person is a female, she cannot be a bachelor. Infants cannot be bachelors. Married men cannot be bachelors. Dogs cannot be bachelors. There are also other features that are strongly associated with the concept bachelor—young man, lives in his own apartment—but these are not necessary features; therefore, they are characteristic features instead of defining features.

Finally, mixed models use a combination of the other three models. People are conscious of the task and choose elements from the three grouping strategies to achieve their particular goal.

Barsalou (1992) says that taxonomies and partonomies are helpful in organizing knowledge. Taxonomies are organizations of concepts by the type of relationship, which specifies that one concept is a type (or instance) or another. Thus, travel alarm clock is part of a larger category of alarm clock, which is part of a larger category of clock. Partonomies are organizations of concepts by the part relation, which specifies that one concept represents a part of another. Thus carburetor is part of an engine, which is part of a car.

The skill of grouping, like most of the other skills, is highly elastic; that is, it can be used with simple, fully specified problems almost as if it were a competency. It can be used in a quick exemplar manner to achieve efficiency, usually at the expense of accuracy. It can be used in challenging, partially specified problems where people conceptualize a fresh configuration of characteristics to use as a classification criterion to arrive at a highly creative and original set of groups.

D. Induction

The skill of induction is used to infer a pattern across some elements. The pattern is then generalized to explain all possible elements in the set. For example, let's say you go to a movie in which a young child throws a temper tantrum. Then, after the movie as you are walking through the theater lobby, you observe a child crying loudly, because her parents would not buy him or her a box of candy. You find yourself thinking: "All children are so spoiled these days!" You have observed the behavior of only two children, and across these two elements you have inferred a pattern, then generalized it to all children. Induction is the process of observing a few examples, inferring a pattern among those examples, then constructing a general principle that represents that pattern we inferred.

One of the media's more insidious effects is to provide people with several superficial examples and lead people to infer certain patterns about whole classes of people or events. For example, people who read a news story about a criminal who copies an unusual bank robbery depicted in a popular recent movie might conclude that all movies are bad or that certain movies are responsible for the high rate of crime in society. Concluding that all movies are bad because one person copies a particular action in one movie is a faulty induction. No single movie can represent the incredible variety of all movies. Also, concluding that movies alone are responsible for crime in society is also a faulty induction, because this conclusion fails to consider the many factors that can lead a person to commit a crime.

This induction trap is also frequently in evidence when we try to assess risk in our personal lives. Often, the media will present a story—either as news or fiction—of an airplane mishap, a stalker crime, or something that makes us fearful. We then use this small number of portrayals to overestimate the risk to ourselves from this type of occurrence while ignoring other things (that the media do not talk about) that may pose a much higher risk to us. For example, in 1987, many news reports told about the danger of asbestos in older school buildings and the risk to children. Fear spread, as people induced a belief that all schools had problems and that their children were at risk. Almost overnight, the asbestos removal industry more than doubled its revenue. However, the actual risk of a premature death from exposure to asbestos is 1 in 100,000. Compare this to the rate of premature death due to being struck by lightning: 3 in 100,000. Also, many people believe that exposure to having X-rays made in dentists' and doctors' offices is risky. It does present a small risk, but the risk of premature death due to smoking cigarettes is 2,920 *times* greater than premature death due to exposure to diagnostic X-rays (Mathews, 1992). However, many people calmly accept the risk of smoking but feel reckless when a dentist x-rays their teeth once a year.

How can we avoid the trap of making false inductions? There are two strategies. One is to use trustworthy reference materials to find out what the general patterns really are, so we don't have to infer them ourselves, especially when our inferences would be nothing more than a wild guess. We can look up the actual rates of divorce, governmental expenditures, health risks, and so on. This requires that we become active and do some focal plane analyses to find the facts we need, rather than make faulty inferences from the skewed exemplars that show up in messages that constitute our automatic exposures.

A second strategy that can help us avoid faulty inductions is to be more tentative in our pattern inferences. We can take the perspective that we need to constantly check our inferences with more observations. When we find something that does not fit our inferred pattern, we must not discount the observation; instead, we must modify the pattern to account for the exceptions.

E. Deduction

Deduction is the skill of using a few premises to reason logically toward a conclusion. The basic procedure of deduction follows a reasoning process in the form of a syllogism, which is a set of three statements. The first statement in the set is called the major premise; it is usually a general principle or rule. The second statement is called the minor premise; it is usually an observation. The third statement is the conclusion that is derived from the first two statements.

Perhaps the most familiar example of a syllogism is the one that uses the two premises of (a) all men are mortal and (b) Socrates is a man. From this, we can conclude that Socrates is mortal. The first premise is the major one; that is, it states a general proposition. The second premise is the minor one; that is, it provides information about something specific (in this case a specific person) in a way that relates it to the major premise. Using logic, we see that the observation in the second premise fits the rule in the first premise, and we conclude that Socrates is mortal.

Deduction is the skill that the fictional detective, Sherlock Holmes, employed so successfully to make sense of clues and solve crimes. He knew a great deal about the physical world and about human behavior. He knew how to select general principles (the first statement in his syllogisms) from knowledge structures. He had keen powers of observation, so he knew what clues were the most relevant (the second statement in his syllogisms). When he observed a clue (such as a scratch on a walking cane, mud on someone's shoes, or the gardener taking walks in the middle of the night), he set up a process of reasoning in which the clue was considered in conjunction with a general principle, and he deduced a conclusion.

Deduction is the use of general principles to draw conclusions about a particular case. In a sense, deduction (which moves from general principles to particulars) is rather the opposite of induction (which moves from particulars to general principles).

We use general rules all the time. For example, if you were to walk into your house, your arms and legs would go with you. Also, you would no longer be outside. These conclusions sound silly; they *sound* silly because we are so absolutely sure they are true. But no one told you all these things; you can figure them out for yourself by deducing conclusions from general principles. By knowing some general principles about the importance of keeping your body parts together and the impossibility of being in two places at once, you could figure out the rest. As you can see, deduction is a powerful skill if used correctly and if we begin with good general principles.

Where do we learn our general principles? We either absorb them through a process of socialization or we induce them ourselves (Berger & Luckmann, 1966). Therefore, induction and deduction work together. Induction generates general principles; deduction requires the use of general principles to explain particulars. When we generate general principles, we add them to our knowledge structures. When we have gaps in our knowledge structures, we can reason from general principles to create particulars to fill in those gaps.

F. Synthesis

The skill of synthesis is used when people arrange the new element along with a selection of elements from different parts of the knowledge structure to construct a new configuration. This new configuration is not merely the addition of an element to an existing part or the adding of yet one more example to an already perceived pattern. Instead, synthesis results in the construction of a wholly new part, branch, or level in a knowledge structure. Thus, it relies on the other skills, but it is more ambitious in its goal and more creative in its execution. For example, if you take apart your car, then put it back together so it works, that is not synthesis; that is reassembly. But if you take apart three cars, then select the best parts from among the three cars, and find a way to put those selected parts together so that the new car you build works better than any of the three cars you began with, that is synthesis.

With media literacy, synthesis is the skill of reassembling all the valuable elements (identified through a process of analysis and evaluation) from a variety of messages and knowledge structures into new knowledge structures. This is done to build a new perspective, formulate a better opinion than you had before, or solve a problem. Doing synthesis well requires creativity, because the task posed for synthesis is always a partially specified problem. If it were a fully specified problem, the task would be one of assembly, not synthesis.

Like the other skills, synthesis can be conducted over a range of challenges from a quick microlevel synthesis to a large-scale creation. For example, on the micro level, when a television program breaks for a commercial, sometimes we reassemble the characters and elements in the plot line to imagine what is coming next or we imagine ourselves in the teleplay. This type of synthesis can take only a few seconds and may be more emotionally guided than intellectually complete. On a larger scale, one day we may become inspired to write an episode of our favorite show. To do this, we need a detailed knowledge structure about all the elements in the previous episodes. We need to know all the quirks about each character and possess an intimate sense of what each would do or say in any situation. Then, in writing our script, we would need to evaluate the appropriateness of dialogue, plotting points, character interactions, and so on. The final product depends on our complete command of all these elements assembled in a new, creative manner.

G. Abstraction

This is the ability to assemble a brief, clear, accurate description of something. Abstracting is what you do when you tell a friend about a book you have read or a show you have seen. This requires us first to analyze the message and identify all its component parts. Then, we must evaluate those components to select those that are most important to the message. Finally, we must assemble a short description of the message from the results of our evaluation of components.

The skill of abstracting is used when people want to relay the essence of some message to another person or to record the essence of that message in some medium so they can refer back to it later. When the message to be abstracted is complex or when the message is new and we do not have a formula to follow, the challenge of abstracting is greater.

We do this in an informal way, for example, when we tell someone what a movie was about. We try to capture the essence of the 2-hour movie in several minutes of words. We don't simply tell someone about the first several minutes of the movie. We try to tell our listener about the entire movie in several minutes.

Some of us are able to abstract better than other people. For example, let's say you ask your friend to tell you what happened on the last episode of *ER*. Your friend says, "A bunch of doctors helped some sick people." Your friend has captured the essence of the show but has not communicated anything unique about that particular episode. If, instead, your friend says, "This mugging victim covered with blood was brought in by an ambulance and the medical team went to work checking his vital signs; then Dr. Carter put a tube down his throat so he could breathe," this provides a lot more vivid detail, but it covers only a few minutes of the hour-long show. A good abstract is one that is detailed enough to convey the essence of the important events in the show but also broad enough so that all the essential happenings are covered.

The skill of abstracting relies on some of the other advanced skills discussed so far. Abstracting requires a person to break down the show into parts, evaluate the importance of different elements as to their centrality to the action, and then report those most important parts in a narrative that flows without raising any unanswered questions.

III. Summary

At an early age, people develop competencies to access and process media messages. Once learned, these competencies are used throughout life in a relatively automatic manner. These competencies are primarily recognizing referents, recognizing patterns, and associating meaning.

People who rely solely on these competencies cannot attain more than a minimal level of media literacy. Those who use the competencies as a foundation for the continual development of skills will continue to improve their media literacy. These skills are useful with partially specified problems where people need to get beyond memorized connections and construct meaning for themselves. There are seven skills: analysis, evaluation, grouping, induction, deduction, synthesis, and abstraction.

Competencies and Skills
Propositions and Research Questions

Propositions for Research

1. Competencies form the foundation of media literacy. The more competencies of referent recognition, pattern recognition, and meaning association people have, the greater their potential for a high degree of media literacy.

2. Because most of the problems encountered in processing information from media messages are not fully specified, people need to develop skills in order to actualize the potential for high media literacy.

Research Questions

1. *Conceptual*

   How do children put forth the effort needed to learn all the referents and associations? Do all children do it the same way?

   How do people make decisions about the value that accrues from media exposures and information processing?

   What combination of skills is best for which types of partially specified problems?

   Which skills can best be developed at various ages? That is, is there an age threshold for the development of each skill? Is there an optimal age for beginning to develop a skill?

2. *Measurement*

   How can we measure the degree to which a person's skills are developed?

   How can teachers evaluate the quality of divergent thinking?

3. *Practices*

   How can we get children comfortable in shifting from regarding education as the acquisition of competencies to the development of skills?

   How can we get teachers comfortable in shifting from regarding education as the acquisition of competencies to the development of skills?

   How can teachers teach divergent thinking?

PART III

Information Processing

CHAPTER 8

The Filtering Task

8

The Filtering Task

This begins a set of four chapters that focus on the tasks in the information-processing sequence. Those three tasks are: filtering, meaning matching, and meaning construction. The task of meaning matching is usually, but not always, fully specified, which means that people can rely on their competencies and automatic processing. The tasks of filtering and meaning construction are partially specified, which means that people need to use the seven skills, and the better they use these skills, the more media literate they will be.

With all three tasks, the personal locus is essential. With the task of meaning matching, the better people's knowledge structures are, the more likely they will have a wide range of competencies; and the stronger people's drives are, the more efficiently they can complete this type of task. With the tasks of filtering and meaning construction, the challenge is much higher because these are partially specified problems, so a wide range of detailed knowledge structures provide greater clarity to the task, and a stronger drive is needed to apply more mental energy to the task.

The overarching question for the topic of filtering is: How can people who live in such an information-rich environment, with so many messages aggressively competing for attention, protect themselves from the flood and at the same time avoid missing those messages they want? Answering this overarching question requires first addressing a series of component questions: (a) How is exposure different from attention? (b) Is all exposure the same? (c) What in the messages can capture and hold our attention? (d) What is it about humans that allows messages to capture our attention?

(e) Do the media condition our exposure? and (f) How can we control our exposures better? This chapter is organized to answer these questions.

I. Message Exposure and Message Attention

Recall from Chapter 3 that I make a distinction between exposure and attention. In this section, I will elaborate on that distinction.

Exposure refers to being in physical proximity to a media message such that a person is in contact with that message. Also, exposure requires that the message is within the boundaries of a person's sense organ limitations. With media messages, the two primary senses are sight and hearing. For example, if the message is visual, it must be within visual proximity to the individual, and it must be large enough and reflect or emit enough light so that the human eye can register something. A magazine cover can be a media message. If it is on a table facing up in a room someone walks through, that constitutes exposure. But if it is in the next room and the person is walled off from the potential of seeing it, that is not exposure. If the person is in the room but it is dark, that is not exposure because there is not enough light to stimulate the sense of sight. If the magazine is lying face up on the side of a hill and the person is several miles away, the person's sense of sight might permit seeing the hill but not in enough detail to see the magazine cover; thus, the image is too small for the human eye at that range, and exposure does not take place.

Attention, in contrast, is a conscious awareness of the message. Thus, attention is encompassed within the idea of exposure; that is, a person cannot attend to a message without being exposed to it. However, exposure is broader than attention, because people can be exposed to messages without attending to them. Exposure makes attention possible, so exposure refers to potentialities for attention. But for the potential to actualize, something has to happen: A person must be consciously aware of the message.

My distinction between exposure and attention is not the same distinction that Metallinos (1999) makes between perception and cognition when he says,

> Perception precedes cognition. Perception is the act or process by which the organs of reception are stimulated by physical sensations, first becoming aware of them, then categorizing and codifying them. To stimulate is to sense, to sense is to respond, and to respond is to be aware, or to be able to distinguish and codify. (p. 433)

In contrast, Metallinos says: "Cognition is the process by which the classified and intensified raw bits of information are decoded, interpreted, and turned into holistic recognizable units. Cognition is synonymous with comprehension, recognition, understanding, interpreting" (p. 433). For this theory of media literacy, the line between perception and cognition is not as important as the line between exposure and attention. During exposure, the sense organs are stimulated by physical sensations, as Metallinos points out. But the person need not be consciously aware of this stimulation during exposure; that is, a person may be in a precognitive state where automatic processes govern the decision. But a person may become aware of the stimulation (that is, the presence of a message) and therefore pass into a state of attention.

Filtering requires a decision. Filtering-in means deciding to pay attention to the message. Filtering-out means deciding not to pay attention to the message. The filtering decision can be made in either a conscious or unconscious manner. Sometimes, the decision is made in a conscious manner; that is, the person is aware of making the decision and is thus in control of the decision. But many times, the decision is governed by an automatic routine. These automatic routines make the encountering of large numbers of messages possible; it would not be possible to survive in our information-saturated culture without automatic routines that filter out messages in the environment. Thus, much of the filtering decision-making is not cognitive; if cognitive resources were required for each decision, the demands on a person's cognition would be too great.

Given the vast number of media messages in almost all environments, the overwhelming majority of those messages are not filtered in and therefore do not command attention. This does not mean that they have no effect on the individuals. For many effects to occur, exposure is sufficient; there is no need for attention. In fact, for many of those effects, exposure only is all that is required, and if a person attends to a message, the effect is prevented or is transformed into some other effect.

While the automatic governor of attention removes the need for conscious thought during the exposure situation, the governor can be created and maintained consciously or unconsciously. When it is done consciously, the person creates habits through practice, and the habits then become automatic. When done unconsciously, the media create the habits and therefore control the automatic process.

II. Exposure/Attention States

All exposure is not the same. Several models of attention have been suggested by media scholars to delineate the different types. For example,

Hawkins, Pingree, Bruce, and Tapper (1997) proposed a model of attention to media messages—specifically, television—according to how long people gaze at it. Their model includes four levels: monitoring, orienting, engaged, and staring. Monitors look for 1.5 seconds or less at a time, ranging upward to starers, who looked for at least 16 seconds at a time. Hawkins et al. found that only 11% of all looks were for as long as 16 seconds.

Another attention model was proposed by Comstock and Scharrer (2001), who argued that attention should be operationalized as three types: primary, secondary, and tertiary. Primary attention is when TV viewing is a sole and foremost activity. Secondary attention is when TV viewing is less primary than some other activity. Tertiary attention is when viewing is subordinate to other activities, such as viewing that is in the background during a conversation.

Cognitive psychologists explain that there is a range of consciousness about individual acts of cognition, a continuum from automatic processing to controlled processing (Shiffrin, 1988). The positioning of an act along this continuum is determined by the amount of cognitive resources required to execute it, which in turn is determined by the person's abilities and familiarity with a task (Pashler, 1998). Arousing content increases the resources required to process messages, thus making them less prone to automatic processing (Lang, Potter, & Bolls, 1999).

From a media-literacy point of view, it is less important to know the complex of activities people are engaged in when they are exposed to media messages than it is to know how much cognitive processing is taking place and what people's general motivation is for the exposures. The three states most important for this theory are: active searching, scanning, and screening. The primary difference among these three states is the purpose the person has for the messages, and this determines the kind of attention a person pays to those messages. Active searching requires a continuously high level of attention; scanning is conducted automatically, with a burst of attention here and there; and screening characteristically requires very little attention.

A. Active Searching

Active searching is a process of information acquisition that begins when a person is aware of a particular question. This question then motivates a search of messages until the useful message (or combination of messages) is found to answer the question. Thus, the person begins with an awareness of a goal and an awareness of some strategy to accomplish that goal. The process that a person undertakes is the applying of the strategy to reach the goal. People are fully aware of the purpose for their active searching, and they are aware of the strategy they are using to search for the answer. They continually monitor their searching activities and make adjustments to keep themselves on track toward finding an answer. The process continues in this active searching state until people reach the intended goal, which is the information they are seeking. Although people may use some automatic routines in parts of the process, the search itself requires a high degree of consciousness in the beginning (awareness of goals and strategy), the middle (the process of adjusting the strategy), and the end (determining whether the goal has been satisfied or not).

Sometimes, this state of active searching is fairly short and requires a relatively low degree of mental effort, because it can rely on habitual routines of exposure. For example, in the morning, you turn on the TV or radio to find out what the traffic is like in preparation for your drive to work. You search through the Sunday newspaper to find coupons for your favorite foods. You search through a dictionary to find the meaning of a particular word.

Other times, this state of active searching can be fairly involved and require a relatively high degree of mental effort. For example, you may be searching for some videotapes to entertain your 3-year-old daughter. You have a clear goal for what you regard as appropriate entertainment. You get on the Internet sites of companies selling videotapes and read dozens of descriptions of the tapes. But you are skeptical, because those descriptions look more like ads than genuine reviews. So you search for Internet sites of organizations that care about children, where the tapes are reviewed by child psychologists. Then, you rent a dozen tapes to check them out for yourself because the tapes recommended by psychologists look safe, but they may not interest your daughter.

The key to a successful search is to have a good strategy. For example, if you are searching for your favorite radio station you need to know whether it is a broadcast or Internet station. If it is a broadcast station, you need to know whether it is AM or FM and where on the dial it is. If it is an Internet station, you need to know how to get on the Internet and how to use a music search engine. If you are searching for the scores of your favorite sports teams who played yesterday, you need to know that scores are on a certain page in the sports section.

Searches differ in terms of the degree of mental challenge. It is relatively easy to answer the question: What is the meaning of the word *syzygy*? You open the dictionary and go to the end of the section on *s*. It is more difficult to find the answer to the question: Who was president of the United States in 1825? For this answer, you could look in an encyclopedia, but you could not look under *1825* or *President*; there are no listings for those things.

Instead, you need to figure out a superordinate concept, such as *American Presidents* or *United States* and try looking in those sections. More difficult still is finding the answer to a question such as: Why do fools fall in love? This is a partially specified problem that requires considerable creativity in putting together a strategy to arrive at a satisfying answer.

B. Scanning

Scanning, like searching, begins with an awareness of a goal. But unlike searching, scanning does not require a particular question to motivate it; instead, scanning is motivated by a general need. With scanning, a person may be in a need state for entertainment or even for comedy entertainment, but the need is not so specific as wanting to know what is going to happen to the characters on *Friends*—that would be too narrow a question for a scan; the search would have to be more focused, like a search for a particular answer.

A good example of a scan is what happens when you are driving alone in your car for a long time, and you become bored; you enter into a need state for some music to stimulate you. You turn on the radio. If you were in your home area and had a favorite radio station, you would search for its frequency so you could listen to its kind of music. But if you are away from home and unfamiliar with the radio stations and their formats in the area, you would scan, that is, switch from one frequency to another to find signals. When you find a signal, you would continue scanning until you found some music that satisfied your need at that time. If you were tired, then your need state would be for fast, loud music to keep you awake and alert. If instead you were tense from driving in heavy traffic, your need state would more likely be for softer music to soothe you and calm you down.

The process of scanning is relatively automatic; that is, it relies on well-learned routines that require little mental effort. There is no conscious strategy, so there is no continual evaluation of how well the strategy is working. The strategy is a routine that runs automatically. Returning to the example of pushing the scan button on your car radio, you rarely think about what you are doing; instead, you simply listen to what each station offers. If you can't find anything that interests you, you do not blame your strategy and try something else; instead, you blame the stations and think "The radio stations in this area are really boring!"

The attention decision also is relatively automatic and requires little mental effort. You look for a particular characteristic or two in each message and make a quick comparison of those elements with your need. If there is a match, you decide to filter in and continue to devote attention to the message. But if there is not a match, you quickly decide to filter out and move on to the next message.

C. Screening

Screening is a message-monitoring state that requires the least amount of effort, hence attention. It begins with the default of automatically ignoring messages, that is, screening them out. There is no conscious goal or strategy. The screening out continues automatically with no effort until some element in a message breaks through your default screen and captures your attention. The attention decision is triggered by the element in the message, not by the person. Thus, message designers are in control of the screening process.

The mode of screening follows from the observation by Comstock and Scharrer (2001) that there is plenty of evidence that people have low involvement with TV viewing. Comstock and Scharrer say, "Viewers most of the time are only passively involved in what they view" (p. 52). They cite studies showing that in large, representative national samples, when people are asked what they viewed the night before, few mentioned a specific program. Thus, the authors reason that many people expose themselves to television with no motive other than to monitor what is going on. To bolster this argument, they add that people typically attend to the screen only about 40% of the time, and this figure varies by type of content. If the content is formulaic, such as stereotypical characters acting out conventionalized plots, then the percentage of time spent looking at the screen is even lower.

In our culture, we spend much more time in the screening state than in the other two. Until about a century ago, there were very few media messages in the environment, so people did little screening. But today, when media messages are not just available but are aggressively competing to trigger our attention, the interaction with information has shifted from information seeking to information screening. Our capacity for information processing has not changed over the past century, so most of that screening is "screening out" or ignoring most of the messages. We are overwhelmed by the choices. To protect ourselves, we establish a default of avoiding almost all messages. Instead of encountering each message and looking for reasons to ignore it, the opposite is the case. We ignore all messages unless there is some reason to pay attention to them. This puts us in the default condition of avoidance.

This default of avoidance keeps us in a mindless condition much of the time, and thus, we allow things to happen to us outside our awareness. For example, consider going to a typical supermarket to do your grocery shopping. You probably enter the store with a list of some items (let's say

30 items) you need, and these are the items you look for, filtering out all the other 30,000 different brands of products on the store's shelves. For *each* of the 30 items you bought, you screened out 1,000 other items. When you left the store with 30 items, you had in essence rejected the purchase of 29,970 other items. You made 30,000 decisions, but because 99.9% of them were by default screening, this required little effort. Furthermore, many of your purchase decisions were made without thinking—that is, out of habit. You were programmed by advertisers, or your previous experiences with products, or by recommendations by friends. Maybe on a half a dozen selections, you comparison-shopped and read labels of competitors before making your choice. So, in essence, you experienced 30,000 decisions, and all but six were made for you before you even walked into the market. That is a great deal of efficiency. It made it possible for you to complete your shopping in maybe 15 minutes rather than 15 days, if you had to make a reasoned conscious decision about every item on the shelf. Of course, this short-term efficiency comes with a down side. You lost out on trying an incredible variety of taste treats and thus expanding your life experience into many new things. Also, you didn't carefully execute a shopping plan and therefore compromised significantly on reaching your goals. For example, perhaps you are health conscious; you most likely were not careful enough with your selections to leave with anywhere near the healthiest kinds of food. Or perhaps you think of yourself as price conscious; in typical shopping mode, you most likely did not look at the unit price on the products you selected, then compare those unit prices with those of other sizes of your brand as well as with all other competing brands.

D. The Exposure Model

This three exposure-mode model helps address one of the concerns in selective exposure literature: the degree to which people are systematic and logical in their choices. For example, Heeter and Greenberg (1985) reject the rational program selection models for TV viewing, saying that people do not assess all their options, because they are not even aware of all their options. Writing at a time when cable TV penetration had dramatically increased, Heeter and Greenberg argued that "in a television environment where only three networks are available," rational models may apply, but "in cable television environments, as the number of program options increases vastly," those models are not plausible (p. 203). People are not systematic with their television viewing, much less with all media exposure. People have developed heuristics or shortcuts that are motivated more by intuitions and motives than by logic. Once established, these decisions grow into habits.

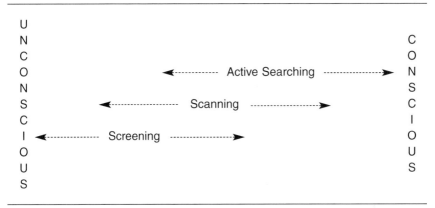

Figure 8.1   The Media Literacy Exposure-Attention Model

The Exposure Model displays all three states of exposure: screening, scanning, and active searching (see Figure 8.1). Each of these states appears on its own line, because each is qualitatively different. This is because each has a different motivation, and in each case, attention is governed by a different kind of trigger. Screening is motivated primarily by protecting the person from the flood of messages, and attention is governed by triggers in the messages themselves. Scanning is motivated by general mood states, and attention is triggered by a perceived match between a person's mood state and something in the flow of messages. Active searching is motivated by a specific need for information, and attention is governed by questions.

Each of these three exposure states is subject to a tension between a desire for unconscious processing and its advantages (primarily the efficiency of getting through the flood of messages with as little mental effort as possible) and a preference for conscious processing along with its advantages (primarily exercising a high degree of control and achieving a high degree of accuracy). This pull from both poles sets up a range within each of the exposure states. Sometimes, the unconscious pole is stronger, with efficiency as the primary criterion for the exposure situation, and other times, the conscious pole is stronger, with accuracy the dominant criterion. Notice also that screening in general is closer to the unconscious pole whereas active searching is closer to the conscious pole. There are times when scanning might require more consciousness than active searching, although the state of active searching in general will require much more mental effort than the scanning process in general; some people are highly skilled at active searching and thus can operate in a condition of automaticity, which requires relatively little effort. For example, some people have actively searched for information on the Internet so often that they have developed complex strategies that they quickly use in a repetitive fashion, almost with no thinking at all.

Recall from Chapter 3 the distinction between automaticity and mindfulness. In general, mindfulness would seem to be better from a media literacy standpoint. But automaticity is a necessary part of dealing with the media; it should not and cannot be avoided. The question should not be how to avoid all automatic routines but instead how to construct automatic routines that are most useful. A further distinction is required between low-skilled automaticity and high-skilled automaticity. Automaticity requires some skill. With some routines, a person has performed something once and, based on that very limited experience, is able to follow the same procedure again; the second time, it will require less effort and the third time less effort still. If the task is simple, it may only require a few trials before the person can address the task automatically. But here is where the distinction between efficiency and competence comes in. Automaticity allows for efficiency, but it does not guarantee competence; that is, a person may be able to perform a task over and over again with little effort, but the task usually gets done poorly. With media literacy, a premium is placed on increasing competence. So learning a task poorly and then applying that routine automatically will signal low media literacy; in contrast, learning a task to a high degree of skill, then applying the skill automatically, provides evidence of a high degree of media literacy. Therefore, media literacy is not keyed to automaticity alone. Also, media literacy is not tied to competence alone; that is, if people can process messages competently but it takes them an hour to process each message, that is not a sign of media literacy. The key is that people learn to apply strong skills well and, through practice, become able to use these strong skills efficiently.

III. The Attention Decision

The attention decision is central to the filtering task. How do cognitive psychologists conceptualize attention? Broadbent (1984) argues that attention requires a central processing unit in a person's mind and that such a unit can deal with only one thing at a time. If something else captures a person's attention, the person will not be able to pay attention to both things but must switch attention to the new thing. However, other cognitive psychologists have theorized that people can have divided attention (Spelke, Hirst, & Neisser, 1976). Divided attention is possible when people practice tasks, that is, when one or both tasks are made relatively automatic and thus each requires less than full attention.

Early models of information processing placed the locus of attention with the messages. Thus, researchers focused on the characteristics of messages to predict whether they would command people's attention or not. For example, Broadbent (1958) offered a model of attention in which he argued that humans select messages based on physical properties of the stimuli, using sensory data. This has been referred to as an early selection model because people were regarded as relying on their senses, and selection of messages is quick because it is automatic.

Cognitive psychologists have extended Broadbent's model to account for semantic content (Deutsch & Deutsch, 1963; Treisman & Geffen, 1967). This is referred to as a late selection model, because it takes longer for people to select among messages. With the late selection model, more brain activity is involved, especially in the cortex, which indicates more cognition. The late selection model requires more attention, thus reducing the capacity to process more than one message at a time. Later research (Cowan, 1995; Posner & Peterson, 1990) indicates that sensory information is processed in one part of the brain (posterior brain stem), whereas cognitive information is processed elsewhere in the anterior. This would allow for dual processing, because different parts of the brain can be used simultaneously.

Now cognitive psychologists believe that the attention decision is explained by a combination of message elements with characteristics about the person and the information task.

A. Message Elements

With regard to the attention decision, Berlyne (1960) listed the physical features of visual and auditory stimuli that can elicit attention from automatic viewing. These include intensity, contrast, change, movement, novelty, and incongruity. Subsequent research has indicated that the most important characteristic about a message is its salience (Fiske & Taylor, 1991).

Several different characteristics can make something salient. One of these is novelty. In a room full of adults, if someone brings a baby in, the baby will immediately become the center of attention. Also, if something breaks the response set, it will be regarded as more salient. If a newspaper front page is all type except for one picture, that picture breaks the set of other all print stories and will be regarded as more salient than the stories.

Like salience, vividness is also a means of getting a person's attention. Vividness is an inherent characteristic of a message. Messages are judged vivid when they are emotionally interesting, when they are concrete and imagery provoking, and when they are proximate in a sensory, temporal, or spatial way. This is one of the reasons that over time, the news media have presented stories in a more sensationalized manner (Adams, 1978; Slattery, Doremus, & Marcus, 2001; Slattery & Hakanen, 1994).

From a purely perceptual point of view, stimuli are more vivid if they are bright, complex, changing, moving, or otherwise stand out in some way from a drab background of less interesting objects (McArthur & Post, 1977). Thus, producers of films will put certain characters in a spotlight or put some costume or makeup on them to make them stand out from other characters, whom they want the audience to regard as less attractive. Detenber, Simons, and Bennett (1998) found that pictures in motion are more arousing that still pictures. Both skin conductance and self-report measures supported this finding. Also, motion pictures prompted more heart-rate deceleration, which is a reflection of a greater allocation of attention to the more arousing images. Also, Lang, Zhou, Schwartz, Bolls, and Potter (2000) reported that the rate of edits (i.e., change in images) influences arousal and memory. When the rate of edits on a television newscast increases, there are increases in physiological arousal, self-reported arousal, and memory.

These characteristics that have been found to grab attention appear to be good things at first. After all, media literacy would seem to be enhanced if people spend more time attending carefully to messages rather than either ignoring them or processing them with automatic routines. So building in these attention-gaining characteristics would seem to be a good thing for message designers. However, this is not always the case. The downside to using these attention-gaining characteristics is that doing so makes demands on a person's cognitive resources. Lang, Bolls, Potter, and Kawahara (1999) report that fast pacing and arousing content on television increase the resources needed for information processing of messages even to the point of overloading the processing system, and this results in less recognition and cued recall for specific content of messages. Also, it appears that audio overloads the system even more than the visuals. Lang, Potter, et al. (1999) report that with television viewing, the audio requires more mental effort to begin with compared to the visual information, which can more easily be processed automatically. Therefore, adding more attention-gaining elements to the audio can tax a person's cognitive resources. This again confirms that people have a limited capacity for processing messages.

Fiske and Taylor (1991) point out that salience in a message tends to polarize people's impressions; that is, if the initial impression is positive as the message holds the person's attention, the person's evaluation of the message grows more positive. "Attention can encourage stereotypic interpretations" (p. 251), they say. Also, salience requires more cognitive processing. What this means is that determining salience requires that a person look beyond the message itself and consider additional factors in the context. If the context leads the message to stand out in some way, then we can conclude that the message is salient (Fiske & Taylor, 1991).

Television is good at getting attention. Lang (2000) says, "Many of the production techniques used in television programming are designed to maximize attention. The use of production features and video content that elicit orienting and engage attention is rampant" (p. 64). The filtering decision is difficult with so much sophistication behind so many messages. Lang also argues that because of the way television succeeds in getting attention, it is poor at presenting messages that are remembered. She explains,

> Use of techniques that encourage storage of encoded information is rare. To the extent that common features of television messages do allocate resources to storage, it tends to be through the use of violent or sexual (i.e., emotional) images. People tend to use the medium to be entertained, which means controlled processing resource allocation tends to be quite low. (p. 64)

Unless messages are emotionally charged, people are not likely to encode them; thus, the messages do not get put into memory; not unless someone puts lots of cognitive resources behind doing it, and most people won't because they are not watching to learn, they are watching to be entertained. So people are programmed for the superficial experience of paying attention only.

B. Person Elements

In reaction to research that focused on message elements as determining attention, several scholars (Anderson & Lorch, 1983; Huston & Wright, 1989) put forth an active model of cognitive processing to feature characteristics about the person, specifically children in these models. These scholars argued that children are not passively waiting for formal features to capture their attention. Instead, they are actively involved cognitively in the television experience. Viewers use formal features to make their own attentional viewing choices. Thus, children learn how to sample stimuli from the formal feature cues, and they do this to satisfy their own goals (Hawkins, Yong-Ho, & Pingree, 1991; Huston & Wright, 1983; Lorch, Anderson, & Levin, 1979).

Bickman, Wright, and Huston (2001) argue for a resolution of the active and passive models. Children have different methods of seeking information, they say. At times, children know their goals and use the formal features as conscious cues to tell them whether a program will contain that information. At other times, children are on automatic pilot and use the formal features to decide whether to invest the cognitive energy to attend to the message or not.

Selective exposure is a term media scholars have used to refer to the phenomenon of how people choose to expose themselves to particular messages. This body of research and thinking is based on the idea that individuals make choices about which messages to attend to and which to ignore (for a review, see Zillmann & Bryant, 1985). This is, in essence, the filtering decision that people make during scanning. When considering all characteristics about people that could explain the filtering decision, it helps to group those characteristics into traits, drive states, motives, and prior experiences.

1. *Traits.* The primary trait related to selective exposure is the desire for information. People differ in the degree of their generalized motivations for learning and hence their overall willingness to confront new messages. People can be arrayed along a continuum according to the degree to which they embrace or avoid information (see Figure 8.2). At the high end are the active seekers, people who are generally interested in all kinds of information and the more the better. At the other end of the continuum are the chronic know-nothings, who exhibit a low interest in any new information. They generally have poor skills and knowledge structures, so the acquisition of new information carries a high cost and little return; as a result, they avoid any new information.

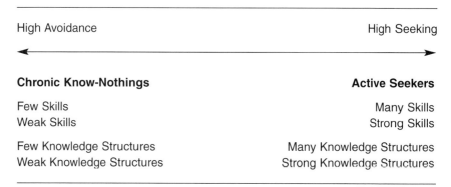

Figure 8.2   Information-Seeking Trait Dimension

2. *Drive states.* The two drive states found to be most associated with the filtering decision are uncertainty and dissonance. Because both of these

drive states are unpleasant, people seek to reduce and ultimately eliminate them.

Uncertainty arises when people are confronted with a question for which they do not know the answer or when they have a decision to make and feel that they need more information. If the question or decision is relatively unimportant, then people will have little drive to seek information. But if the question or decision is major, then the drive for information is strong, and people seek to reduce uncertainty by accessing information (Atkin, 1985).

Dissonance is also an unpleasant drive state. Dissonance occurs when a person holds two pieces of information (or is considering two positions) that are in conflict. People who experience such dissonance will seek information to reduce or ideally eliminate the dissonance. Once they have resolved the dissonance and their information sets are in balance, people will seek to avoid dissonance in the future. Thus, people who favor one side in a controversy will have a positive drive state for confirming information and a negative drive state for information that refutes their side.

In a critical review of the literature on selective exposure within cognitive dissonance theory, Cotton (1985) concludes that dissonance-motivated selective exposure is moderated by (a) level of dissonance, (b) the impact of the information choice (whether the choice is real), (c) demands for honesty and impartiality, (d) utility of the information, (e) attractiveness of the information, (f) refutability of the information, and (g) de facto selective exposure (conditions in people's environment that would make their exposure likely, regardless of their conscious choices, such as neighborhood, social class, etc.) (see Table 8.1).

Although conceptually distinct, these drive states have often been found to occur together. For example, some people may experience a high degree of uncertainty on a relatively important decision, yet still avoid the task of searching for more information they need, because they do not have confidence in their information skills or because they feel that such a search will produce the even more unpleasant drive state of frustration or even an increase in uncertainty. This will cause them to feel dissonance. On the one hand, they need more information to make a decision, but on the other hand, they need to avoid the experience of searching for that information. People will have a high drive to resolve the dissonance. Typically, people in this situation will convince themselves either (a) the decision is not that important and they will intuitively make a choice or (b) they have enough information and will use that little bit to make their decision. Either way, the decision gets made, and the state of dissonance passes.

Table 8.1   Factors Moderating Dissonance-Motivated Selective Exposure

Factor	Description
Level of dissonance	Curvilinear relationship, with moderate levels of dissonance having the highest motivation to reduce.
Impact of the information choice	Whether the choice is real
Demands for honesty and impartiality	Selective exposure is regarded as a form of dishonesty.
Usefulness or utility of the information	Whether the information is likely to serve the purpose of reducing the dissonance or not. There is no drive to seek out more information if it will serve to increase the dissonance.
Attractiveness of the information	A person will select information that is more attractive or more interesting.
Refutability of the information	If the information cannot be refuted, there is no drive to seek it.
De facto selective exposure	Conditions in people's environment that would make their exposure likely regardless of their conscious choices, such as neighborhood, social class, and so on. For example, smokers are likely to be in an environment to see more pro-smoking messages.

SOURCE: Adapted from Cotton (1985).

Sustained searching is what is referred to as vigilance in information processing (Miron, Bryant, & Zillmann, 2001). Vigilance is related to arousal and cognitive processes. As for arousal, attention decreases when levels of stimulation are excessively low. Low levels of stimulation are traced to stimulus simplicity or repetition. As for cognitive processes, Miron et al. explain that there is a sequence of decisions that "involves a progression in terms of depth and detail of cue analysis, and a continued and increasingly elaborate processing is conducive to deeper involvement with the content" (p. 156).

3. *Motives.* Motivations for media exposure can range from the very specific (wanting to listen to the latest song released by your favorite group) to the very general (such as the need for entertainment). Active searching is keyed much more to motivations for specific messages whereas screening is keyed much more to general motives.

Another way to distinguish among motives for media exposure is to group them in categories such as guidance-oriented and reinforcement-oriented motives (Atkin, 1985). Guidance-oriented motives are used for purposes of learning information whereas reinforcement-oriented motives are used by people to defend their predispositions. When people select content that is consistent with existing beliefs, attitudes, and practices, they are motivated to reinforce what they already know and believe. But other times, people want to extend their knowledge, and they want the media to guide them to new insights, facts, and opinions. Thus, people often let the media guide them into entertainment realms to pick up information they can use in their real lives. For example, McGuire (1973) says, "Entertainment content conveys a great deal of information to viewers or readers about taste in clothes and furnishing, styles of life, and appropriate interpersonal relationships," and entertainment messages are "instructive regarding how to live, how to manage, what is happening, and what it means" (p. 182).

Rubin (1977, 1981, 1983) has shown that people have two general motivations for television exposure: ritualistic and instrumental. The ritualistic mode is one where exposure is governed by habit. The medium, vehicle, time, and situation are all fixed by habit. For example, at 11 a.m. every weekday morning, Mary turns off the ringer on her telephone, turns on the TV, and watches *Guiding Light* by herself. Every Sunday afternoon during football season, Harry has his friends over, and they watch TV to follow the games; there are certain rituals they perform involving where they sit, what they talk about, how they talk, and what and when they eat and drink.

Almost all use of the media is motivated by the desire for immediate gratification (Gantz, 1981; Lometti, Reeves, & Bybee, 1977; Palmgreen & Rayburn, 1982; Rubin, 1983; Schramm, Lyle, & Parker, 1961). People select content that will satisfy those needs for immediate gratification. The pursuit of immediate gratification underlies most of the channel consumption and message selection decisions of mass media audiences, and most of this activity is inertial or indiscriminate (Atkin, 1985, p. 63).

4. *Prior experience.* Cognitive psychologists use the construct of schemas to explain a lot of what happens with human thinking. Schemas are a network of nodes linked together in memory. The nodes are images, facts, sounds, and so on. Schemas are built through experience, and they change with experience.

Priming theory posits that the most recent experiences are in the foreground in a person's memory. "Priming is specifically a name for the fact that recently and frequently activated ideas come to mind more easily than ideas that have not been activated" (Fiske & Taylor, 1991, p. 257). For example, racial categories can be primed by certain images and words, so that when people later are given a chance to think about race, those primed categories are used as expectations and constrain the way people think about race (Devine, 1989; Gaertner & McLaughlin, 1983). Celebrities are primed, and people then are more likely to pay attention to them and to associate them with certain characteristics that have been linked to them, even if those characteristics are not mentioned in the current message (Herr, 1986).

Thus, images and information about the most recent experiences are the most accessible. This means they have the greatest weight in setting goals and expectations. When a message appears in the perceptual field that links up with an idea that people have on the "top of their mind," they will likely pay attention to that message. This is referred to as accessibility. Recently and frequently activated ideas come to mind more easily than ideas that have not been activated. Related to this idea is priming. The media can prime an idea by using messages we attend to; then later, when we are in the default screening mode, the idea is still on the top of the mind, and the message in the perceptual field will have a greater likelihood of triggering awareness.

5. *Logic.* Sometimes, people handle their drives in a logical manner. For example, Atkin (1985) says that people follow "an informal cost-benefit analysis" where "content is selected when the individual anticipates that the message reward value will exceed the expenditures and liabilities associated with acquiring and processing it" (p. 64). Atkin (1985) argues that message seeking can be motivated by a deficiency; that is, people may be feeling stress and need to reduce that stress, so they seek escape. People may have other deficits (such as being bored, having nothing to do and needing to kill time, having few friends and needing companionship, feeling trapped and wanting to escape from everyday lives). The costs are efforts to obtain and decode messages. Also, Atkin says, "Message content may pose certain psychological liabilities, such as guilt feelings, fear arousal from threatening portrayals, irritation due to offensive depictions, and dissonance from discrepant messages that undermine predispositions" (p. 64). He says that attention decisions are made on an informal cost-benefit analysis using a combination of (a) the learned expectations concerning the likelihood that media offerings will provide certain outcomes and (b) the subjective evaluation of these consequences (p. 64). On the benefit side, the dominant positive motivation is enjoyment seeking, where entertainment content is chosen

for emotional arousal and cognitive stimulation, gratifications that enhance transitory satisfaction. Sometimes, decisions are made to overcome a deficit.

6. *Emotions.* Often, the attention decision is not systematic and logical. Sometimes, it is more emotional. Zillmann and Bryant (1985) argue for the importance of understanding emotions and use this point as a cornerstone of their choice model to explain how people select entertainment messages. They say that people's choice of media and content "grows from a situational context and that affective and emotional states and reactions play a key role in the formation of rather stable content preferences" (p. 157). Building on this idea, they lay out a theory of affect-dependent stimulus arrangement to explain people's media choices. They explain that individuals are motivated to terminate noxious, aversive stimulation of any kind and to reduce the intensity of such stimulation at any time. Also, individuals are motivated to perpetuate and increase the intensity of gratifying, pleasurable experiential states. Individuals then are motivated to arrange internal and external stimulus conditions so as to minimize aversion and maximize gratification (in terms of time and intensity). In this arranging and rearranging, individuals develop preferences for entertainment options; over time, these preferences are reinforced. This means that the stimulus variables that have the greatest effect on selective exposure are those that break aversion the strongest: absorption (high), behavioral affinity (low), and hedonic valence (positive).

Emotions are a large part of the selection process (Zillmann, 1982). People seek out entertainment content because of emotions and to manage their emotions. For example, people at times seek absorbing content to pull them away from a negative emotional state where they keep thinking about aversive situations; they seek relaxation and content that will not remind them of their real-life aversive situation. They want to break a mind-set where they can't stop thinking about those aversive situations. In contrast, there are other times when people want excitement, because they are bored; they want stimulation to energize themselves.

Filtering decisions can be conditioned through emotions. Zillmann and Bryant (1985) say that the process of choice begins when "an arbitrary selection is made. A particular program is encountered by chance or by mindless probing. In the latter case, basic (or primitive) attentional processes, such as the orienting reflex, may determine the initial selection" (p. 161). If the encountered message is pleasing, then the person continues the exposure; if the encountered message is displeasing, then the exposure is discontinued. This is more an emotional reaction than a cognitive one; that is, it is based on what feels good. Rejected messages stay in short-term memory and form a basis for comparing subsequent messages.

Like Zillmann and Bryant, I argue that emotions are important to the explanation of exposures and attention. The primary reason emotions are so important is because they provide the energy behind drives. Drives with no or little energy will not result in attention. It takes some mental energy to cross the threshold into attention. The more energy that is available, the more ability a person will have to use cognitive resources. The more involved the message is and the more cognitive resources that are required, the more important is the energy behind the drive, hence the emotion-eliciting properties of the message.

While most drives are states that arise in particular situations and can be satisfied rather quickly, some drives can be regarded as traits. In specific situations, a message can elicit emotions that provide the energy for a drive state. For example, a message that raises a lot of unanswered questions can produce frustration to fuel a drive state to decrease uncertainty. Another message about a controversial topic can produce anger to fuel a drive state to seek out additional information on your side of the controversy. Another message of a human interest nature can uplift a person's spirits and fuel a drive to help other people.

IV. Media Conditioning of Exposure

The mass media try to condition audiences into habitual exposure patterns. They do this by increasing the value of the messages to potential audience members. Value here is computed as the difference between audience cost (primarily in terms of effort) and payoff (primarily in terms of perceived utility of information or entertainment). The industry makes such calculations in the planning of messages, then follows through in the promotion of those messages so that potential audience members will perceive high value. The more people perceive such high value, the more people will attend to the messages, and the audience size will grow. Messages with larger audiences are more valuable to producers, because they generate higher revenues directly to them (books, magazines, newspapers, films, CDs, cable TV, and computer hardware, software, and memberships). Also, messages with a larger audience are more valuable to producers of media that benefit from revenues that come indirectly through advertisers (broadcast TV, radio, cable TV, magazines, newspapers, and computers).

One way to reduce cognitive costs to potential consumers is to use a very simple message formula. People can learn these formulas during a small number of exposures, and if the formula does not change, people can benefit from its continued use by being able to follow future exposures to messages automatically. The more the formulas are used, the more people can trust the vehicles to deliver high-value messages, and people will continue with the automatic processing. This is the process of conditioning.

This conditioning has an enormous influence on us. Because of the way media present information, we are conditioned to ask certain questions and not to ask others. We are conditioned to reside within certain need states and not others. We are conditioned to learn certain triggers and not others. This conditioning is a long-term process; it does not happen during the exposure to one message.

This conditioning is based on two factors. First, choices are constrained. Second, when we make a selection, that selected experience is reinforced.

A. Constraining Choices

The media always offer only a small fraction of possible messages. This constraint affects vehicles and information. For example, 10,000 magazine vehicles are currently published in this country, and most people have a choice of about 300 if they go into a chain bookstore and look at the wall of choices. This still looks like a plethora of choices, but many topics are not covered. Also, there is a certain "sameness" to those choices. All of these heavily promoted mainstream magazines are about the same dimensions physically. All have a cover page designed to grab attention. All have some graphics and pictures in addition to text. All have advertising messages. These similarities are not trivial, although they may at first appear to be. After all, we may ask, how else should magazines look? The very act of asking such a question indicates the conditioning has been successful. We are so used to seeing a certain model for a magazine over and over, it is difficult to imagine radical differences to the model, and if we can imagine such differences, we are likely to dismiss them by thinking something like, "Well that would never work!"

With newspapers, the model in the mid 20th century was primarily text with occasional pictures, rarely in color, and few graphics. Major stories began on page one and continued on a "jump" page. Then, Alan Neuwirth started *USA Today* in the early 1980s with a new model that was regarded as radical at the time. His model featured shorter stories with no jumps to other pages and lots of photographs, color, and graphics. His focus was on ease of reading and presentation of news that was of most interest to readers. *USA Today* offered a fresh alternative. Ironically, over time, critics of the new model gradually changed their newspapers so that the *USA Today* model is now dominant, and there are few alternatives to it.

The constraint of vehicles reflects a constraint on information. When there are no magazines on, say, the hobby of ice fishing, then that information is constrained. Even in the most mainstream of vehicles, information is still constrained. For example, major newspapers publish only a tiny fraction of the information available to them each day. A highly selective filtering process takes place at several levels. First, from among the many possible topics that could be selected for stories each day, only a small number are chosen. Second, once a topic is chosen for a news story, the information is gathered in another highly selective process. Readers do not get all the information on that topic; only certain people are used as sources of information, and other people do not get asked to contribute information. Finally, the story is told in a highly selective way.

The irony is that media companies are constantly looking for new types of vehicles and messages. If they thought a wider range of messages would work, they would offer them. However, the media are never sure if new messages will have an audience or not, and it is very risky to try something new. The costs of failure are high, especially with the media that have the largest potential audiences. With network television, the drop of a single rating point over the course of a season could cost the media company several million dollars in lost advertising revenue. So television networks do not want to wait a full season for a large audience to find each new show. If a new show does not generate a large audience almost immediately, it is canceled. So despite the desire to develop new, fresh messages, the major media are reluctant to offer the support needed to market new messages and condition new audience patterns.

B. Reinforcing Experience

A second conditioning factor is reinforcing experience with selections. Some of our selections are reinforced positively with a pleasant experience. The more reinforcement with a particular option, the more we will continue to select that option. Thus, we will consciously choose to limit our options.

The media say they are businesses that merely respond to market demand. This statement, of course, is true. But the statement is also misleading, because it makes it sound as if the media are solely responders to demand. In truth, the media also shape the demand by constraining options then reinforcing certain options over time so they condition us to an even narrower demand.

V. Locus and Filtering

Taking the major ideas reviewed above into consideration, I synthesize a model to explain what captures a person's attention in the flow of media messages. This model highlights two ideas. The first idea is that while individuals are substantially different in their traits, states, motives, and prior experiences, most of them can be typed in terms of their general approach to media messages. The second idea is that emotions are important, because they explain the degree of energy people have behind their drives.

All of us are subject to a wide variety of specific needs for media messages in our everyday lives. These needs are idiosyncratic and rapidly change. From a scientific point of view, those needs are less interesting than the general needs, that is, the large-scale needs that can explain people's approach to information in the aggregate. That is what this section focuses on.

The model described in Figure 8.3 is adapted from the locus model in Figure 5.1 to make it more specific to the filtering decision and to incorporate the ideas reviewed in this chapter. This model is useful in illustrating the differences in the way people orient to the media or their general filtering approaches. This model presents four categories of people, each category differing in terms of the person's overall approach to media messages. Thus, when a person is in a screening state of exposure, people of different types will make fundamentally different attention decisions.

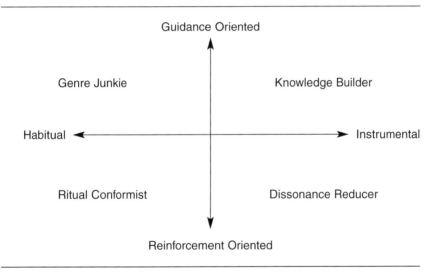

Figure 8.3   Four General Approaches to Filtering Information as Determined by a Person's Locus

The horizontal axis in Figure 8.3 represents the continuum of where the motivation comes from in the filtering decisions. At the left pole, people are motivated purely by habits; that is, they continue with the same media, the same vehicles, and the same schedules. Exposure is a ritual to them. At the right pole, people are motivated purely by specific needs for information and entertainment, and these needs can radically alter from day to day.

The vertical axis represents the continuum of purpose for the information that is filtered in. This illustrates Atkin's distinction between the guidance orientation and the reinforcement orientation. At the bottom pole, people want information that conforms to their already existing schema. At the top pole, people control the filtering consciously to achieve particular goals.

This model has four domains: genre junky, message seeker, ritual conformist, and dissonance reducer. To a certain extent, most people will find themselves described in all four domains. However, each of us has a "home" domain, one where we are much more likely to spend time.

Genre junkies are motivated by a ritualistic need to attend to large classes of messages, such as news programs, music, and so on. For example, these people will habitually read the sports pages every morning, although some messages on those pages will cause them dissonance, such as when their favorite team loses. Still, they continue to read the sports pages each morning. Their devotion is to the ritual of attending to sports more than to the need to feel good about any one message.

Ritual conformists are also motivated by rituals, but they have a narrower focus. They seek out only those messages that will support their existing beliefs. For example, if they have a strongly held political position, they will devotedly read those magazines, watch those commentators on television, following those call-in radio programs, and read those books that support their positions. They continually seek confirming evidence of their positions. They are not motivated solely by reducing dissonance, because they rarely feel dissonance; that is, they rarely encounter messages counter to their beliefs. However, their drive remains high, because they feel that they can never get enough exposure to messages that support their beliefs.

Knowledge builders are motivated by specific needs for particular information as those needs arise. Once that need is satisfied, that particular drive is gone; that is, they are not motivated to go back to those messages again and again, so their exposure is not ritualistic or habitual. They are not afraid of finding messages that disagree with their previously held knowledge sets or opinions. In fact, they like to find disconfirming messages; these messages engage them in the pleasurable challenge of reconciling and synthesizing new information.

Finally, dissonance reducers are motivated by specific needs, but only for messages that will reduce a negative drive, such as temporary uncertainty or dissonance. Unlike ritual conformists, dissonance reducers are not motivated to return habitually to shows and magazines that support their positions. Once their dissonance is reduced, there is no drive for further attention.

Automaticity and awareness are possible in all four groups. The ritualistically motivated people are not always driven by habit in the sense that they make mindless automatic decisions. They are often aware of their attention decisions. Also, the instrumentally driven groups are not always aware of their decisions; that is, their decisions can be made automatically.

VI. Knowledge Structures and Filtering

Let's return to the two questions that were posed earlier in this chapter when we dealt with the problem of being overwhelmed with information. These questions are: (a) How can we sort through all this information in terms of importance? and (b) How can we make decisions about how much to retain?

The answer to both of these questions is: Use good knowledge structures. Good knowledge structures help people orient to what is most important when they make their filtering decisions. Knowledge structures are maps. They illustrate which are the main branches of knowledge, which are smaller branches, and which are twigs.

When people encounter media messages, they can compare the information in those messages to the information they have in their existing knowledge structures. If they already have that information, they do not need to relearn it. If they do not have that new information but it is relevant to a central branch of knowledge in their structures, then it becomes important that they learn it. If the new information is relevant only at the "twig" level, then they must decide whether they want (and have time) to grow that part of their knowledge structure. If so, then they will need to learn it. But that type of learning will be more efficient, because they already have the context for that bit of information, so they know where and how that new information fits in the overall picture. If, instead, they do not have time to learn this new "twig"-level information, they know that they still have a firm foundation of learning and that ignoring this new information is not going to harm their knowledge structure much. If they do not have a knowledge structure for some new information, then they have no basis for judging whether this new information is of central importance or whether it is relatively trivial. Making judgments of this nature is the mark of an educated person. It is not how much information people have memorized that makes them educated. Being educated means that people have the "maps to the world," and they can use these maps to keep themselves oriented to what is most important, to make good judgments about new information, and to know where to go to get additional accurate information. If they keep their focus on building these maps—knowledge structures—they will be able to get above the tidal wave of information that is threatening to drown all of us in facts and images. Knowledge resides in the structure, not with bits of information alone.

The stronger knowledge structures people have, the more literate they are. To be media literate, we need to have an in-depth understanding of the media across a broad range of topics, such as production techniques, narrative structures, character patterns, and thematic indicators; knowledge about industry practices, motivations, and perceptions of audiences; knowledge about the full range of media effects; and a self-monitoring awareness about the variety of ways the human mind can process information from the media.

VII. Summary

We are constantly exposed to messages from the media; we cannot avoid exposure, but we can control our attention by altering our exposure states from the automatic ones of screening and scanning to searching. The attention decision can be triggered by characteristics of the message or states/traits of the individual.

It is to the media companies' advantage to condition audiences to habitual exposure. Thus, the media can create a predictable and smooth revenue flow. They accomplish this conditioning by presenting audiences with messages of high value, that is, messages that require little from audience members while giving them a lot in return for that small effort. Once audience members experience this high value, they come back for more of the same message, which is again provided by the media. In this way, people can depend on a good exposure experience and not have to undertake the risks of a search in which they will have to expend much more energy and may not find messages they like.

When people undertake filtering tasks, they can keep their costs low if they have a strong locus and elaborate knowledge structures. If the locus has sufficient drive energy, people will not find it too burdensome to look for alternative messages. Also, with highly developed knowledge structures, it will be easier for people to know where to look for those additional messages and know where to catalog the new information they find.

Filtering
Propositions and Research Questions

Filtering Propositions

1. People will typically stay in a state of automaticity where exposure is automatic unless:
   (a) They are in an active searching mode directed by a specific need for some kind of message or information, or
   (b) They are in a scanning mode directed by a general need until something in a message indicates that the message could satisfy that general need, or
   (c) They are in a screening mode and something in the flow of messages triggers their attention.

2. In active searching mode, analysis and evaluation are the most valuable skills. Strengthening those skills will reduce the costs of active searching.

3. The mass media condition people to stay in the scanning and screening modes by constraining choices to a relatively few simple choices of messages, then reinforcing the selections that people make.

4. A person's locus shapes his or her filtering decisions. There are four general types of people as indicated by their locus:
   (a) Genre junkies are motivated by a ritualistic need to attend to large classes of messages as indicated by a genre.
   (b) Ritual conformists seek out only those messages that will support their existing beliefs.
   (c) Knowledge builders are motivated by specific needs for particular information as those needs arise.
   (d) Dissonance reducers are motivated by specific needs, but only for messages that will reduce a negative drive, such as temporary uncertainty or dissonance.

Filtering Questions

1. How can the searching mode be made more valuable to people; that is, how can the costs of searching be reduced while the payoffs are increased?

2. Are there certain need states that make searching easier?

3. What is the full set of message characteristics that can trigger attention?

4. What is the relative power of different message characteristics to trigger attention? Is trigger power relatively constant across time? That is, are there certain message characteristics that have always appealed to humans and always will? Or does trigger power change when people get habituated to certain characteristics and those characteristics lose their novelty or salience? Is trigger power relatively constant across people?

5. How can people be trained to recognize a wider range of characteristics in messages as potential triggers?

6. Are there triggers that are purposely misleading in media messages? If so:
   (a) How can people be trained to tell the difference between genuine triggers and misleading triggers?
   (b) Are there natural abilities within certain people to enable them to perceive the difference quickly and easily between misleading triggers and genuine ones?

CHAPTER 9

The Meaning-Matching Task

9

The Meaning-Matching Task

The task of meaning matching is primarily one of decoding referents in media messages. These referents can be a word, an image, a sound, or any unit of a message that can be perceived. Once people recognize a referent, they must attach meaning to it; this is done through accessing their memory to find a link between the referent and its associated meaning. These meaning associations are typically learned from sources outside the person. For example, early in elementary school, a teacher pointed out a word on a page, such as *dog*, which is a referent, and he or she told us what that word meant, thus fixing its meaning in our memory. Associations between referents and meanings can usually be learned in one exposure, then once learned, they can be repeatedly accessed automatically with little effort.

The task of meaning matching—much more than either the tasks of filtering or meaning construction—relies on competencies rather than skills. In the previous chapter, it was shown that the filtering task relies primarily on skills, especially analysis and evaluation. The product of the filtering task is then input into the meaning-matching task, where competencies are used to locate convergent meaning in a person's memory. These elements of meaning are then moved forward into the meaning-construction task, where they are rearranged by using the skills of grouping, induction, deduction, abstracting, and synthesis.

Because meaning matching relies on competencies that are learned at a relatively early age, most people are fairly competent at this type of task. Once people have acquired the competencies of the task, meaning matching is usually accomplished with great efficiency, because people can perform it automatically.

The origin of *meaning* is different depending on whether the task is meaning matching or meaning construction. With meaning matching, meaning is assumed to reside outside the person in an authority, such as a teacher, an expert, a dictionary, a textbook, or the like. Society has sanctioned a certain meaning for each word, and these meanings become the convention. Institutions have the responsibility for passing these meanings down to each generation. The shared meanings make communication possible; unless people share meanings, one person cannot communicate an idea to another person, because there are no shared meanings for referents that can serve as the bridge between the two minds. In contrast, meaning construction is an individual process where people transform messages they take in and create meaning for themselves.

The meaning-making task has two fundamental steps. First, a person must recognize the referents in a message; second, the person must connect the referent with some meaning that is stored in memory. Recall from Chapter 7 that I am using the term *referent* as others might use the term *symbol*: to refer to units in messages that signal meaning. Referents are any unit of signaled meaning in a message. For example, if I present the word *dog*, that should signal the same class of animals to all readers. If I present a picture of a four-legged creature about knee high, wagging its tail, and being held on a leash, that picture is also a referent for the same meaning. Or if I play a tape of a bark, then that, too, would be a referent for the same meaning. Referents can be a word, a picture, a graphic, a drawing, a movement, a sound, a touch—anything that signals an association with a denoted meaning.

This chapter focuses attention on the meaning-matching task by dealing with five issues. First, we examine how people acquire the associations between referents and denoted meaning. Second, we look at the meaning-matching process people follow when they recognize a referent in a message. Third, we examine several different types of meaning matching. Fourth, we examine closely several specific challenges in the meaning-matching task. And fifth, we focus on the task of meaning matching and its implications for media literacy.

I. Acquiring Meaning-Matching Knowledge

By the time most people reach adulthood, they are able to speak, read, and write a language. How do we acquire these competencies?

A. Absorbing Associations and Memorizing

The early part of life for all humans is occupied with the task of learning to recognize referents and understanding what they mean. These referents are, essentially, sensory stimuli. Infants look at their hands and study the shape through the movement of color patterns on their retinas. They have to learn that the color and shape they see are a sensory representation of a part of their bodies. Infants also learn to recognize the pitch and tone of their parents' voices. They need to recognize that sometimes the voice is happy and sometimes it is anxious. Toddlers need to learn what is safe to touch and what is hot or sharp. They must recognize thousands of sensory stimuli as distinct referents and then learn their definitions, that is, their meanings as prescribed by authorities.

People learn these definitions by absorbing the associations. For example, a young child who touches a hot stove will quickly absorb the association of the stove with pain. Children learn to associate certain body movements with certain goals. Children absorb the association of certain expressions on the faces of their parents with certain feelings. Early childhood is consumed with the task of learning to recognize certain things as referents and absorb the association of those referents with their denoted meanings. Thus, the emphasis is not on constructing a personal and unique meaning but rather on absorbing the association that is naturally presented in the environment, that is, the presented meaning.

Children enter another layer of referent recognition when they enroll in school. The primary goal early in school is to help children learn how to look at lots of squiggly lines on paper and break them down into individual referents. Then, children learn to recognize words and numbers. With some referents, there is a natural connection with a meaning (between fire and pain on touching, for example). However, with many media referents (such as words, headlines, graphics, etc.), there is no natural connection between the referent and a meaning so children cannot absorb these connections on their own. Someone must teach these connections, and children must memorize those connections. This memorization has a convergent goal of getting everyone to accept the same definitions, so the referents trigger the same meaning in everyone, thus making communication possible. The task for the person is to find those meanings and acquire them. Thus, parents and the educational institution are the primary authorities for sharing this information with the next generation. The media also have attained status as a major source of this type of information.

It is easy to tell whether students have learned to recognize referents by asking them to point to particular words, numbers, colors, characters, objects, and so on. It is also relatively easy to check whether students have learned the prescribed meanings by asking them what those referents mean, that is, to define words or draw pictures for those words. The important competencies at this age are recognizing referents and memorizing the denoted meanings for those referents.

In the upper grades of elementary school (middle school) and even throughout high school, the development of competencies is still important. Teachers instruct students how to recognize a wider range of referents and to memorize the authority meaning associated with them. Examples include pictures of historical figures; additional mathematical terms in geometry, calculus, and so on; figures of speech; chemical symbols, and so on. All of this memorization of words, ideas, people, dates, and happenings serves to create in each student a body of shared meanings that makes possible efficient communication on a wider range of topics. If people are missing this type of information in certain areas, they cannot make sense of messages in those areas. For example, people who are raised in a family of English-only speakers will learn to hear the different words and sentences when they are spoken. They will easily make matches of sounds to meanings. But if they find themselves in a household of Spanish-only speakers, the language will sound like noise to them; that is, they will not be able to break the sounds into words or sentences, except perhaps if the speakers pause between each word. However, listeners who hear discrete sounds will still not be able to match the discrete sounds to the denoted meanings.

Another example is reading the written word. People who have not learned to recognize written referents and memorize the convergent definitions of each referent will not be able to read print. They will be regarded as illiterate. Of course, the idea of literacy in this sense is limited to reading the written word. There are many other kinds of illiteracy. For example, some people are computer illiterate. This means that they do not recognize referents (such as icons, hot buttons, drop-down screens, and so on) on a computer screen, or if they do recognize some, they do not know what the referents mean. The term *illiteracy* usually refers to an inability in some meaning-matching task, and this inability can be traced to a person not being able to recognize referents or to attach commonly agreed-upon meaning to those referents.

Some scholars talk about *cultural illiteracy*, by which they mean either (a) that people cannot recognize enough of the common referents of their culture or (b) that people cannot associate those referents with the authority meanings. When there is not much shared meaning across people in a culture, the society is fragmented; that is, people do not share enough common meaning to converse with each other efficiently. As a result, a person referring to events would have to stop continually and explain to listeners what those events mean.

As a person learns the definitions for referents and practices recognizing referents and accessing definitions, the process of meaning matching becomes more and more automatic. Eventually, certain referents become very familiar, and the appearance of one of those referents immediately evokes a definition with almost no mental effort. As this becomes more automatic, our speed at processing referents increases as does our confidence in our ability to access the memorized meaning accurately. There is little chance we will get lost in this process, and there is little demand for creative activity or any kind of thought process that is not automatic.

B. Elements in Memory

Once learned, the referents and associated definitions are stored in a person's memory. There is a great deal of research and theorizing about memory, and there are many distinctions about types of elements in memory, such as episodic versus semantic memory (Barsalou, 1992); autobiographical memory, which is memory for representations of personal events (Shum & Rips, 1999); declarative versus procedural knowledge; explicit versus implicit memory (Schacter, 1987); propositional, temporal, analog, and affect (Fiske & Taylor, 1991); and words and images (Paivio, 1986). All of these distinctions are important to cognitive psychology in general, but when we narrow the focus down to media literacy, the most important distinction is between factual information and social information. Factual information typically comes from formal learning. Thus, it is more carefully (rationally and consciously) processed than social information. Factual information is like semantic information whereas social information is more like episodic memory, except that social information includes that which is learned either in real life or through exposure to the media. Either way, social information is autobiographical in the sense that it happened to the person, either in social interactions with real people or in parasocial interactions with characters in the media.

The distinction between declarative and procedural knowledge is important from an educational point of view, for example, to those who are planning to teach someone how to type or solve a math problem. But with media literacy, this is not as important a distinction. Social knowledge can be both (and usually is both) declarative and procedural. When you watch characters be "cool" in a movie, you learn the facts of what they wore and how they acted, but more important, you also acquire the feeling that you could dress and act that way and thus be cool. In essence, it is the procedural possibility that makes the declarative knowledge important to you.

C. Organization of Memory

How are the bits in memory organized? Fiske and Taylor (1991) say that the basic model of memory used by cognitive psychologists is the associative network. Tulving (1983) theorizes that elements in a person's memory can be independent, minimally connected units. For this form of organization, the schema is a useful explanation. Schema are networks of nodes and pointers. The nodes are referents and definitions, and the pointers are the links between the nodes. Some links are short; that is, the nodes are close to one another and thereby conceptually linked tightly. For example, an image of a cat and the word *cat* are adjacent nodes with a short and well-developed link. Other nodes are farther apart, especially when the person has not had much experience in associating the two. Some nodes are linked to only one other node, such as something that is simple and new to you. For example, you are introduced to the host of a party. You have a node with the person's image and another node with his or her name. Later, when you see that person to say goodbye, it is easy to link up the face with the name. In contrast, some nodes have links to a great number of other nodes. For example, if someone mentions the name of someone you know well (your mother, father, sibling, or best friend), you are likely to work out from that name node to many, many others, each with an image, a story, adjectives, emotions, and so on.

With these associative networks, when people encounter a referent in their environment, they quickly access that referent in memory and move out the link to the associated definition. If they want more information on the referent, they move out through other links to the next set of most closely associated nodes. Thus, this model of thinking is called the *spreading activation model*. Because ideas are linked in networks, when people access one idea, they are able to make associations to other closely linked ideas.

Cognitive psychologists have speculated that there are more sophisticated organizational patterns beyond a simple associative network, such as hierarchy (Collins & Quillian, 1969; Kolodner, 1984) or thematically and chronologically structured histories or streams (Barsalou, 1988; Conway, 1996). For example, Rips, Shoben, and Smith (1973) set up a test of the Collins and Quillian claim by reasoning that *pig* is a mammal and that mammals are animals, so therefore the link between *pig* and *animal* is longer (and has to go through an intermediate node of mammal), so that if people were told to think about pig, it would take longer for them to verify that a pig is an animal than that a pig is a mammal. But they found the opposite, and they concluded that the node of *animal* is closer to *pig* than the node of *mammal* is to *pig*.

The simplest form of organization is the associative network. Because these are the easiest to construct and maintain, cognitive psychologists believe the schema organization is prevalent. Other forms of organization are more like knowledge structures.

II. Process of Meaning Matching

Matching the meaning of any message from the media requires a process. Sometimes, the process is short, such as matching one easy–to-recognize referent to one simple meaning. Sometimes, the process is long and involved, such as working with many referents of different kinds, such as auditory, visual, word, pictures, social situations, and so on.

A. Steps in the Process

The meaning-matching process has two phases. In the first phase, people encounter a message and must recognize the referents within it. In the second phase, people match the referents with the meanings they have stored in their memories. This second task is essentially one of recalling definitions as triggered by referents. Meaning matching is a relatively easy task when definitions for referents have already been acquired and when they are easily accessible.

Almost everyone learns how to conduct meaning-matching activities well and usually at a relatively early age. Even young children know that the box with a glass front is a television set. They know that the dark plastic thing that is about as big as their forearm is a remote control device and that it has buttons that can turn the TV on and off.

1. *Recognizing referents.* All media users must first go through a process of extracting elements from the chaos of raw stimuli that composes any message. Without this step in the process, no meaning can be perceived. This process is primarily perceptual, because it requires a person to scan the perceptual field, usually visually or aurally or both. This process is also cognitive, because the person needs to know what referents are.

Sometimes, this process is almost purely perceptual, such as making sense of the perceptual elements on a television screen. The television screen is really individual dots arranged in a grid of 525 lines, each containing several hundred glowing dots. The hue of those dots is limited to three primary colors, but when you move back a few feet from the screen you can see the blending of those three primary hues into an entire rainbow of colors. Also, you no longer see the dots or even lines; instead, you see images. While the dots on the screen do not move, it appears that the images of people and objects are moving on the screen. How is this possible? Your mind blends the individual primary colors into combinations. The blinking off and on of different colored dots leads your mind to perceive that there are objects on the screen and that they are moving. We learn to recognize that the individual pixels are not useful referents; instead, we look for more macro units of referents, such as blocks of color that represent people and objects.

In a movie theater, the screen is blank half the time, but these blanks are so brief that the human eye cannot perceive them. If the film projection speed were slowed down to less than 12 frames per second, people could see a flicker. This flicker is the perception of interruptions or blanks between the individual frames appearing. When frames are projected at the rate of 24 per second, as they are in movie theaters, the blanks appear too briefly to be perceived by humans. Furthermore, the still picture of each individual frame is not be perceived as a still picture, because it is replaced too quickly by another still frame. The human mind cannot process each still frame, so it "perceives," instead, motion or the differences across the individual frames. The human mind does not recognize individual frames or the blanks in between as referents; instead, it looks for more macro units of referents.

Some referents are words, so we need to know what a word is compared to a letter, a sentence, a line of type, and so on. Some referents are elements in pictures, so we need to be able to recognize form, dimension, and perspective. Some referents are audio, so we need to be able to recognize voice, music, and sound effects. Some referents are movements on a screen; we need to be able to recognize a cut, dissolve, pan, zoom in, and so on.

With newspapers, young children will look at the front page and "see" the same thing as an adult, but they will not be able to extract many elements. They will recognize that certain things are pictures, but they will not be able to extract any of the words or graphics, that is, they will not be able to distinguish the boundaries of the referents there. With radio, children will "hear" the sounds but not be able to recognize the boundaries between the songs, jingles, stingers, happy chat, serious news, and ads.

Children begin orienting to the TV screen as early as 6 months of age (Hollenbeck & Slaby, 1979). They are able to start recognizing referents and learning the meaning of those referents. Children as young as 12 to 24 months demonstrate learning that can last up to 24 hours after exposure (Meltzoff, 1988). Attention to the TV screen increases as children age until about age 10 (Anderson, Lorch, Field, Collins, & Nathan, 1986). During this time, children are learning more referents and larger form referents. At age 10, they are well into the concrete operational stage (Piaget & Inhelder, 1969), so they have the cognitive capacity to handle referents of different sizes. Also, their experience has reached a point where they can process those messages in a relatively automatic manner.

Referent recognition is a fairly sophisticated task. People are able to "detect and process edges and other discontinuities in display, [and] they infer detailed world structures by extrapolating from partial views" (Pomerantz & Lockhead, 1991, p. 11). However, once we are able to automate this task, it appears very simple to us.

At what level is the referent? Some referents are micro (such as a letter or a word) whereas others are much more macro (such as a novel or an entire body of an author's work). For example, when you analyze a novel, you have lots of options for what a referent is. At the macro level is the entire story. Within this macro unit of entire story, there are subunits: chapters, paragraphs, sentences, and words. Some units are larger than the message, such as the author (and his or her body of work), the vehicle setting (with medium and surrounded by which vehicles in that medium), and the culture (history). The more levels people recognize, the more options for analysis and the more media literate they are.

Some scholars make a distinction between syntactic and semantic elements of television. For example, Bickham et al. (2001) talk about a difference between syntactic and semantic parts of a message, where syntactic markers are the formal features of a message and semantic parts deal with its content. As examples of syntax, they cite the lap dissolve between scenes, whereas scary music communicates the meaning of the movie. But I believe this is a confusing distinction and one that really provides no explanation of either the content or its effect on viewers. Instead, it is better to think of all things in the show as referents, each with a syntactic property that serves as a signal and a semantic property that is an associated definition.

Sometimes, people recognize and process referents at a level that is too micro. In this situation, they need to look for patterns across those micro referents, and the pattern becomes a more macro referent. Media messages include all sizes of referents, and therefore there are many choices of macro referents. Deciding what is the referent is a task governed by a person's purpose for the exposure. For example, for someone looking up a word in a dictionary to determine its spelling, the letters are the referents, and the arrangement of those letters into a word is the pattern. For someone interested in grammar, the referents are the words and clauses in sentences, and the macro referent is the sentence or paragraph.

The larger the assortment of referents, the more interpretation is required. For example, with smaller assortments (such as letters into words and words into sentences), most people use widely accepted formal rules without thinking. Readers carefully follow the construction rules of grammar and sentence syntax with little interpretation. But as referent sets become much larger and complex (such as plot development and narrative conventions), people must exercise much more interpretation; they move from the task of meaning matching, which is largely accomplished with competencies, into meaning construction, which requires skills (see the next chapter).

We also must recognize patterns in the visual media. Messaris (1994) argues that children first need to learn to interpret still images because of their two dimensionality, lack of color, and reduced detail. Then, the issue of literacy moves to the more complex task of interpreting the interplay of pictures, speech, music, graphics, and special effects, a task required by viewing film and television. At each of these levels, we must know how to spot patterns among the referents. Production techniques can help us identify these patterns, but we must learn how production techniques cluster into patterns. For example, there are formulas for the way a camera frames an object so as to reveal its image as a coherent object, action, or space through the successive presentation of partial views. We must learn how production techniques tell us what a character is feeling and thinking through the juxtaposition of facial close-ups and contextual cues.

2. *Associating referents with meaning.* After we have isolated a referent, we must interpret it, that is, match the referent with a meaning that has been previously learned. For example, we memorize the definitions of words and the conventions of grammar and expression to be able to read. From the experience of listening to radio, we know that certain sounds signal the lead-in to news, certain voices convey humor or seriousness, and certain sounds convey danger or silliness. With television and film, we learn the meaning of a flashback, an extreme close-up on a character's face, character stereotypes, and what to expect in the unfolding sequence of a detective show. We have learned to connect certain referents with certain meanings.

How is matching accomplished? Once people recognize a referent in a message, they automatically access the relevant node in the relevant schema. This referent node is connected to a definition node and perhaps several other characteristics relevant to the referent, each with its own node. When the definition is closely linked to the referent, the path that connects the nodes is short and usually well traveled. The more a person makes an association (between referent node and definition node), the more traveled is the path that connects them.

Retrieval from memory begins with a referent that cues a path to a memory bit. We check the stored information and make an assessment of how closely the stored information matches the cue (probabilistic assessment). If there is a high probability of match, then we think we have the memory. If the match is low probability, then we cycle through other paths to retrieval, sometimes having other cues triggered.

As an example, let's say people open the newspaper and read a sentence: "The President met with his Cabinet today." The individual words *the, met, with,* and *his* have easy associations with one meaning. *President* requires a bit of context; the capitalization and the story itself would give readers enough to make the connection as the President of the United States and evoke that person's name and image. The word *today* requires a bit of context; readers need to look at the date on the paper to find out if it is today's newspaper, in which case today means today, but if this were yesterday's newspaper, the word *today* in text would mean yesterday. Finally the word *Cabinet* requires a knowledge of how the executive branch of government is structured and that the word does not refer to a piece of furniture but instead to a set of close advisers. The reader is required to bring some context to the situation, but those demands are so small and the task of bring context is likely to be accomplished by all readers the same way, so this task remains within the domain of meaning matching, because it requires very little interpretation or construction.

B. Automaticity

With many meaning-matching tasks, the link between a referent and its prescribed definition is usually short and strong; thus, the association can easily be made. Also, with most referents, the links are singular; that is, there is one and only one link to a definition, which keeps things simple. When the links are singular, short, and strong, the associations are made consistently, quickly, and habitually. The meaning-matching task is typically automatic.

Once the person has familiarity with the referent and its common definition, the meaning matching can be done with almost no effort or thought. The tasks of referent recognition and meaning matching are relatively automatic and, therefore, can be done in a parallel manner. This means that a person can do several automatic tasks at once. There is no bottleneck of information processing, such as the one Broadbent proposed. Broadbent's (1958) bottleneck model says that a person's mental apparatus includes a central processing system that receives inputs from sensory channels and compares them with items stored in the memory system to determine their meaning. Overload of the central processor is prevented by means of a selective filter interposed between the central processor and the outside world, which sifts incoming stimuli by letting through those that have certain properties and excluding others. For example, at a party where there is music and loud talking, people will filter out everything but the sounds of the person to whom they are talking. If someone tries to monitor two conversations at the same time, a bottleneck occurs because the mind cannot shift back and forth between the two simultaneous conversations. But if a person is watching a familiar TV show and making small talk with a roommate, both can be accomplished at the same time through parallel processing, because both processes are automatic. When a person is engaged in a process that is not automatic, the processing is serial; that is, it requires the person's full attention, and other tasks get bottlenecked waiting for mental resources to become available.

III. Types of Meaning Matching

There are four types of meaning matching according to how it is used to solve problems: authority-generated meaning matching, automatic meaning matching, context-reliant meaning matching, and deductive meaning matching.

A. Authority-Generated Meaning Matching

The first time people encounter new referents, an authority (such as a parent or a teacher) needs to point out the referents and provide the definitions for them. For example, a young child who is learning to read will frequently encounter a new word. The child must point to the word and ask an authority what that word means. When we get older and we encounter a new word, we look it up in a dictionary. In both these examples, we do not construct meaning for ourselves. Instead, we want to know the conventional meaning, so we ask an authority. For all the words and other referents we recognize and "know" the meaning of, there was an initial exposure when we could not do this. We needed to access an authority, then absorb that prescribed meaning.

Often, people can learn this information on first hearing, but sometimes, the meaning must be repeated. Until it is learned to a degree that the person (a) recognizes the referent, and (b) matches the definition to it, the person must rely on an authority to generate the meaning. Once we have absorbed the meaning, we move on to one of the other forms of meaning matching when we encounter that referent.

B. Automatic Meaning Matching

Once we have learned to recognize a referent and absorb its meaning, then that association stays with us in memory. Next time we see that referent, we quickly make the association with its meaning. The process is automatic.

This is the most common form of meaning matching. If it were not, then the meaning-matching task would continually require a degree of effort that would make its use prohibitive to the degree it is used. For example, after people learn to read a written language, the meaning-matching task of reading is largely automatic and returns to the authority-generated realm only when they encounter a word or referent that they do not recognize and must ask someone or something (such as a dictionary) for help.

C. Context-Reliant Meaning Matching

There are times when we will easily recognize a referent and look for an association with a definition, but then find that the association is not singular; that is, several definitions are associated with that particular referent. In this case, the process of meaning matching requires a bit of conscious reflection. In this conscious reflection, the person needs to make a decision about which association to sanction, that is, which is the proper definition for the referent *in this situation*. To make this decision, the person needs to consider the context of the referent.

Context-reliant meaning matching is more involved than automatic meaning matching. The person needs to concentrate not just on the focal referent but also on contiguous referents to make some sense of the context. With automatic meaning matching, the task is always fully specified. However, in some situations, you can recognize the referents, but there may be several different definitions for those referents. Thus, the task is only partially specified. Nevertheless, people can still solve the task on their own by looking at context.

With context-reliant meaning matching, people look at the referents contiguous to the focal referent as context, and the context can be used to select the most appropriate definition for the referent in question. For example, the word *bad* is likely to have more than one meaning. *Bad* can mean "not good" but it can also mean "very good." Which meaning do we match? It depends on the context of the sentence in which it is used.

Context is also important to consider with sets of referents. For example, the idea conveyed by a sentence often involves more than the simple sum of the meaning of each word. The arrangement of words and the grammar as well as punctuation are important. For example, if two characters are kissing, and one says, "Don't! Stop!" that conveys a very different meaning than if the character says, "Don't stop." The way the sentences are arranged into paragraphs and stories conveys more meaning than the simple sum of the ideas conveyed in each sentence. If you read about a wife telling her husband, "You are so funny," the meaning can change given the overall story. If the husband just insulted his wife, her comment would likely be sarcastic. But if the husband just told a joke and everyone was laughing very hard, the wife's comment would likely be a compliment. Determining the meaning of words, sentences, and stories is a complex process that is often dependent on contextual cues.

In all of these examples, the sense of the messages cannot be fully derived by making associations with only the focal referent, because there are several potential meanings for the focal referent. To make sense of the focal referent, we must also consider the contiguous referents and factor the context into the selection of a definition. Although the task is more complex, it is still a fully specified task; that is, people have enough information in the focal referent and the surrounding referents to derive one and only one meaning from it. Also, while this requires more effort than a simple matching of meaning, it can still be accomplished in a relatively automatic fashion.

In accessing the context, there are times when people need to do more than consider the focal referent in the context of contiguous referents. Sometimes, people must try to infer patterns from the referents provided. The inference then becomes a meta-context. One way of doing this is to think about the sender of the message and see the message from that person's point of view. This is called local rationality. Every message sender has multiple goals, and many are in conflict with one another. Human problem solvers

> possess finite capabilities. They cannot anticipate and consider all the possible alternatives and information that may be relevant in complex problems. This means that the rationality of finite resource problem solvers is local in the sense that it is exercised relative to the complexity of the environment in which they function. (Woods & Cook, 1999, p. 149)

The person sending the message is working from a particular perspective that supports the message. Understanding that person gives the receiver the ability to get inside the rational system that is the world of the sender. Thus, knowledge structures are even more useful than associative networks. Knowledge structures include much more information that can help the receiver understand the world of the sender; this cannot be achieved with simple associative networks.

With context-reliant meaning matching, people often take a shortcut and simply choose the first association they find without bothering to check to see if other definitions are associated with the referent. When there are several definitions, one of those associations will usually occur to the person first.

D. Deductive Meaning Matching

At times, the task of meaning matching relies on the skill of deduction. With deduction, people observe a specific occurrence and access a general principle to explain it. The general principle is the conventional definition rule. People perceive a set of referents that becomes a larger set referent, then they look for a principle that could explain that larger set referent. This is more complex than looking for a simple referent and making a simple match. For example, when people are watching a new family situation comedy, they might access a principle that family sitcoms feature a father who is a buffoon, a mother who is the strong rational family member, and kids who are quirky. This is the family sitcom formula; people who know this formula (general principle) are in a good position to quickly and efficiently construct the meaning of the show they are watching. But if they do not know this formula, then they need to construct the general principle; thus they need to use induction to infer one.

IV. Challenges in Meaning Matching

People can make many mistakes in the meaning-matching task. One set of mistakes can be traced to people relying on faulty authorities for definitions. Another set of mistakes concerns faulty schema, and a third set of mistakes is due to people encountering partially specified problems and treating them as if they were fully specified.

A. Faulty Authorities

Sometimes, people use faulty authorities. This often happens with media messages. People listen to pundits who are presented as authorities on talk shows, but often, those pundits are hired not because they are authorities but because they are controversial or because they look good on screen.

Also, sometimes, people will ask another person for the designated meaning, thinking that the person they select is an authority when in fact he or she is not. If the selected person does not know the authority meaning but does not admit this ignorance, instead preferring to make up a meaning and pass it along, that meaning could be faulty. When people then memorize the faulty meaning, they think they are memorizing the conventional and shared definition when that is not the case. Later on, people may be surprised to learn about other preferred meanings, and when this happens, they are likely to think the other people are wrong. Thus, faulty definitions can get reified as authority definitions.

Sometimes, we ourselves are false authorities; that is, someone asks us for some information. We think we know the accurate answer but we don't; often, we provide an answer as if we did know the accurate one. This happens with questionnaires that ask our opinion on something, and we offer our expert opinion even though we did not have an opinion until we were asked for one.

This type of problem is even more serious when we are not sure what the question is really asking. An example of this is when someone asks you, "How many hours of TV do you watch a week?" Before you can reply, you have to make sense of the question. You need to use linguistic skills to break the stream of sounds uttered by the other person down into words. This requires a good deal of phonological knowledge. You also need to know the meanings of the words, using everyday meanings for hours, TV, week, and especially watch. You need to know how the words are structured by grammar (that is, which are verbs, nouns, subjects, objects, etc.) and how to use this information to assess the meaning of the sentence. So you need to match many individual referents that are of different kinds and at different levels of generality.

This procedure is used to find the literal meaning of the question, but you are not done yet. You also need to know enough about the context of the measurement to make sense of the questioner's intention, because this will further determine the meaning of the question and hence influence how you should respond. Let's say the person is a teacher in a media class who wants you to fill out a questionnaire. In that case, the teacher may be making a distinction between different types of TV—broadcast TV, cable, or perhaps tapes played on your VCR. Which should be included? You would need to look at the questions carefully or remember what the teacher said as far as the class's definition of TV. Or perhaps the questioner is a parent who sent a child to his or her room with instructions not to watch any TV. Or perhaps the questioner is your friend, who hates TV and is trying to be ironic.

Or perhaps the question is in a diary from the A. C. Nielsen Company, which compiles the official ratings of television programs based on diary responses. In this situation, you must think about what does it mean to watch television? What if you are in the room in front of the set, but you are reading a magazine, and the sound is turned down? What if you are in the next room, but you are carefully listening to the sound of the program until you can return to the room where the TV is on? What if your TV is broken, and you sit in front of it for an hour each day staring at it in disbelief?

Context matters. If the situation directs you clearly to take certain contextual features into consideration, then the problem is fully specified, and you can automatically match meaning and arrive at a meaning that anyone else would. However, often, the situation is ambiguous, so the task is partially specified; different people will interpret contextual cues differently and thus come up with different meanings for the same referent. This moves us out of meaning matching and into meaning construction.

B. Faulty Schema

Some associative networks are faulty. When this occurs, one of two problems with the schema usually results. One problem is that people have misperceived a message and encoded it incorrectly into their schema. Cognitive psychologists for a long time now have known that memory functions nothing like a camera or tape recorder. "Mental representations are constructed by the perceiver rather than being direct copies of available stimulus information" (Smith, 1999, p. 252).

A second problem is that the associative structure is missing nodes or links; for example, certain elements of the event are closely connected and therefore easily accessed, while other elements are missing or are unconnected to the nodes first accessed (Conway, 1996). When this happens people may know that some information about the event is missing and may continue to try to search for connections to that information; but when that accurate information is not present, people may follow connections to elements from other events, thus believing them to be connected to the event in question. "The information you retain and recall about an incident is merely one of many possible representations of that event. . . because the selectivity of perception and memory makes it impossible to remember all that occurs in even fairly simple everyday events like washing the dishes" (Shum & Rips, 1999, p. 98).

C. Partially Specified Problems

There are times when the meaning-matching task appears simple on the surface, but this appearance may be deceptive because the underlying task is really only partially specified; that is, people do not have enough information to match the meaning on their own, even by looking at the context. If the problem is truly partially specified, then it is likely to fall within the realm of meaning construction (see next chapter) rather than meaning matching.

V. Meaning Matching and Media Literacy

A. Personal Locus

The meaning-matching task is almost always performed in a state of automaticity. This provides great efficiency in processing messages. When people are in an automatic state of information processing, they quickly match meaning by using the most accessible schema and allowing the associations in that schema to show them the meaning. For example, when people see some blood or gore in a television program or a film, they quickly access their violence schema. Thus, the orienting node for the violence schema is graphic-ness, that is, how much blood and gore are shown (Potter et al., 2003). If viewers perceive a lot of blood and gore, they will accept the meaning that the show is violent even if there is only one act of aggression. Conversely, if people do not perceive any blood or gore, they will conclude the show is not violent even if there are dozens of gunshots, punches, and stabbings. Thus, judgments of whether a show is violent or not may have very little to do with number of violent acts or the ways in which those acts are portrayed, except for graphic-ness. The schema for violence in the general public is a relatively simple one, relying almost exclusively on graphicness. People continually apply this automatically to match meaning. As you can see from this example, there are times when meaning matching results in faulty meanings. People need to expend more mental energy, and this requires a stronger personal locus.

While the meaning-matching task is relatively automatic, there are times when people do need to expend some mental energy. For example, when people identify a referent in a message, they must find an orienting node in their schema that is relevant to that referent. If a person cannot find a relevant schema or a relevant orienting node, then mental effort is needed. Also, if a person finds an orienting node that is not singular—that is, the node is linked to more than one definitional node—then the person must make a choice. Of course, there are shortcuts for this choice if one of the links is primed, but when this is not the case, the person must expend more mental effort by considering context or using deduction. If a person's locus is weak, the energy will not be there; instead, that person will stay in the automatic state, ignoring all demands to make nondefault choices. Efficiency is maintained but at a high cost of accuracy and control.

A strong personal locus is less critical to the meaning-matching task than it is to the other information-processing tasks, because so much of this task can be accomplished well automatically. However, some cognitive demands still arise in this task, and a strong locus is necessary to provide the energy and awareness needed to face these challenges well.

B. Knowledge Structures

Knowledge structures are less critical to the performance of this information-processing task than the other two—filtering or meaning construction. The meaning-matching task relies primarily on the relatively simple associative networks of schema. However, sometimes, people have to decide which of multiple links to an orienting node to select; in such times, they need more context to their decision, and thus a well-developed knowledge structure would be better to draw from than a simple schema.

VI. Summary

Meaning matching is an essential step in processing information. When people encounter messages, they must recognize the referents in those messages and access the conventional definitions of those referents. These definitions are learned from authorities early in life, then stored in memory. When referents occur, these trigger an association with the remembered definition. Meaning matching relies on competencies that are learned early in life then practiced automatically from that point forward.

There are several types of meaning matching; they differ in terms of how challenging they are and how much people can rely on automatic processing. None of these four types of meaning matching is as challenging as meaning construction tasks, which are the subject of the next chapter.

Meaning-Matching
Propositions and Research Questions

Propositions for Research

1. People will remain in a state of automaticity with meaning-matching tasks as long as they can easily associate referents with denoted meaning. If they cannot, they will either go to an authority to learn the denoted meaning of the referent, or they will give up the task.

2. People will remain in a state of automaticity with meaning-matching tasks as long as the orienting node is linked to one and only one definitional node.
   (a) If the orienting node is linked to more than one node, but the information in each node is complementary with the information in all other nodes linked to the orienting node, people will stay in the state of automaticity and choose one node for meaning.
   (b) If the orienting node is linked to more than one node, and the strength of the connection to one node is much stronger than the strength of connection to any of the other nodes, people will stay in the state of automaticity and choose the strongest linked node for meaning.

3. When the links are singular, short, and strong, the associations are made consistently, quickly, and habitually. The meaning-matching task is typically automatic.

4. When people are in a state of automaticity, they can engage in parallel processing and do several things at once. This provides great efficiency in message processing.

Research Questions

1. *Conceptual*
   How do children put forth the effort needed to learn all the referents and associations?

   Do all children learn to match meaning the same way?

   How do people make decisions about the value that accrues from media exposures and information processing?

   In what sense are the following competencies dichotomous and in what sense are they continuous?
   • Recognizing patterns
   • Context reliance meaning matching
   • Use of deduction in meaning matching

   How do people choose the level for a referent and what triggers the need to look for patterns across referents to arrive at a more macro referent?

2. *Measurement*

How can we map a person's schema?

How can we validly identify nodes?

How can we validly identify the length and strength of linkages?

Is response time a sufficient measure of length of linkages?

3. *Treatments*

When people encounter a new referent, what treatments stimulate the need for searching authorities for the meaning of that referent?

How can costs be minimized and rewards maximized in those treatments?

Can treatments be used to condition a strong drive trait for meaning matching?

Questions for Practices

1. Basic: What is the most efficient way to teach meaning matching?

2. Advanced: How can people be encouraged to expend the mental energy needed to snap out of automaticity when need be?

CHAPTER 10

The Meaning-Construction Task

I. Types of Meaning-Construction Challenges
   A. Under-Information Challenges
   B. Over-Information Challenges
   C. Barren Information Challenges

II. Accessing More Information
   A. Outside Sources
   B. Inside Sources
      1. False memories
      2. Confusing media world knowledge with real-world knowledge
      3. Inert knowledge

III. The Reasoning Process in Meaning Construction
   A. Heuristics
   B. Assuming Shared Meaning

IV. The Media Literacy Perspective
   A. Context and Knowledge Structures
   B. Skills
   C. Personal Locus

V. Summary

10

The Meaning-Construction Task

There is a difference between matching meaning and constructing meaning. Recall from the previous chapter that matching meaning is primarily decoding, that is, using schemas to access the association between a referent and a definition. To be prepared for meaning matching, people acquire information from authorities outside themselves. This information can be learned in one exposure and, once learned, can be repeatedly accessed automatically with little effort.

In contrast, the meaning-construction task is much less automatic. It requires an awareness of process as well as goals for the processing. It also requires a higher degree of mental energy to work with skills rather than relying on simple competencies. These skills are necessary, because, with meaning construction, people are confronting partially specified tasks and must create their own interpretations from messages. Thus, constructing meaning is more of a challenge, because less is given to the person by the message, and more is required from the person by the task.

This chapter first deals with the types of challenges posed by the meaning-construction task. Then, it examines the issue of accessing the additional information that is needed with all partially specified problems. Next, it examines the reasoning process. Finally, we look at how meaning construction fits into the media literacy perspective, particularly with knowledge structures, skills, and personal locus. The next chapter completes the treatment of the meaning-construction task by illuminating its traps.

I. Types of Meaning-Construction Challenges

The general challenge of meaning construction is to solve partially specified problems. This means that the problem is missing something that prevents the person from being fully guided. This missing piece must be "filled in" by the person in order to complete the task of constructing meaning. This filling in cannot be done with competencies; it requires skills. Also, the filling in needs more than simple schema, because a person's schema is missing nodes and links needed to fully specify the problem. The meaning-construction task needs well-developed knowledge structures.

Let's take a closer look at the nature of partially specified problems. Below, we will examine three types: under-information problems, over-information problems, and barren information problems.

A. Under-Information Challenges

These are problems that are presented to us with information missing, so they appear to be partially specified problems. The challenge for solving this type of problem is to access more information, either from personal knowledge structures or from additional sources of information.

This "filling in of information" serves to render the problem fully specified. However, completing the information set does not also transform the task into one of meaning matching, because it lacks the convergent solution. People are likely to bring different sets of information to the problem, and each information set bends the construction process in a different direction. Because people's knowledge differs substantially across individuals, the inputs into the process of solving partially specified problems can substantially differ (Smith, 1999). Thus, people arrive at different meanings rather than converging together on the authority meaning. Each person places a high value on his or her constructed meaning, so we cannot say that one solution is the correct one and the others are faulty.

For example, let's say you listen to a political pundit talk about how bad a particular piece of legislation is. The pundit is very entertaining as she gives reason after reason for trashing the proposed legislation. She has convinced you that this is an important issue, and you should have an opinion on it. But should you have a negative opinion about the legislation? It can't be all bad; why would elected officials have introduced the legislation if it is as worthless as the pundit makes it out to be? This is a partially specified problem. You want to construct your own meaning on this issue. You search through your existing knowledge structures to think about your opinions on similar issues, but this issue is different, so the problem remains partially specified. You decide to actively search out more information on the issue from a variety of sources. But what sources do you use? You do a focal plane analysis of *TV Guide* looking for public affairs shows that might deal with the issue. You go to the local magazine rack and look for publications on the issue. As you exposure yourself to the information, you evaluate it. You take the information elements you evaluate as good and see if there is a pattern, then generalize that pattern into a conclusion that becomes your opinion on the issue.

In the search for information and the processing of it, you have considerable freedom, because you are not guided by a set of rules that render the problem fully specified. That freedom offers you many options, all within your control to accept. At the easy end of that option array is accepting the opinion of the pundit and making it your own. This requires little effort and no skill. At the other end of that option array is the challenge of carefully constructing your own opinion after searching widely for all available information on the topic, then carefully evaluating each bit of information, looking for patterns, and finally synthesizing your own personal opinion that acknowledges the strengths from all sides of the controversy.

B. Over-Information Challenges

Sometimes, problems are presented to us with too much information. The amount of information may be overwhelming, presenting us with a figure-ground problem; we get lost in all the trees and cannot find the forest. In this case, we must sort through the information and discard that which is irrelevant. We must also make the more difficult discriminations about which information is background to the more relevant foreground information. When the problem does not provide guidance to make these sorting decisions, then the problem is missing something, and the problem is partially specified. We are confronted with examples of this type of problem every time we turn on the television. There are so many viewing options. Even if we decide we want to watch a movie, there may be half a dozen movies on at any given time.

Sometimes, we are presented with a problem that offers multiple options and multiple criteria to select options. If we use Criterion A, we will clearly select Option X; but if we use Criterion B, we will selection Option Y. Which criterion do we use? The problem has not specified a criterion, so all criteria are relevant, and the problem is therefore overspecified. Our first task in solving such a problem is to simplify by rejecting all but one of the possible criteria. For example, let's say we begin watching a movie, and we are confronted with the problem of deciding whether it is good enough to continue watching or we should switch to another movie. What do we look for in the movie to solve the problem of deciding if the movie is worth watching or not? There are many criteria. Do we focus on the actors, the setting, or the plot; the overall look of the movie; or the genre? When we can select a clear criterion, we use that criterion as a filter and reduce the information set down to a manageable size.

C. Barren Information Challenges

Recall from above that there are under-information problems, and the task is first to get more information. But there are times when there is no way to access additional information that will fill in all the gaps to solve the problem in a systematic manner. These are barren information problems.

The challenge for solving a barren information problem is to engage in a reasoning process that allows one to bridge the gaps in information rather than to be stopped by those gaps. This can be done with hypotheticals, where people can ask "What if?" questions and speculate what would happen if X were the case. In this way, people are plugging X into the gap as a bridge, and this allows them to move on down the path to decisions about the overall meaning of a message. Of course, it is important that people not lose sight of the nature of X: that it is speculation and not accurate information. Instead, people should keep in mind that the bridge allows them to continue down a path to a solution that is only tentative.

To illustrate the barren information type of problem, let's return to our TV viewing example. Let's say you have switched through all 500 of the channels on your cable service, and you cannot find anything that fits your need for entertainment. You look through the *TV Guide* and cannot find anything listed there that would fit your need. There seems to be no information available to help you solve your problem. Most people would throw up their hands at this point and think "There is nothing on TV that is any good!" then proceed to watch a randomly selected show, thinking it is terrible. A way out of this problem is to speculate with hypotheticals. People could think about what would be the ideal show for them to watch now. What kind of a genre? Who would be the actors? What kinds of settings and scenes would the movie contain? In answering these questions, they are likely to envision a movie that does not exist. Then, they could go to the video store and ask the clerks if they have such a movie. The clerks, if they are good, will likely suggest some movies similar to the customer's vision.

II. Accessing More Information

With all three types of partially specified problems presented above, there is a need to check for more information. People cannot tell if a problem is an under-information type of problem or a barren information type of problem until they try to find more information. Also, when people work on problems that are initially presented to them as being over-information, and they pare away irrelevant information, they often end up finding that some crucial information may be missing, so they, too, need to search out more information. There are two places to look for more information to elaborate the problem at hand: outside sources and inside one's self.

A. Outside Sources

Additional information to solve partially specified problems can be gathered from sources outside the person. With outside sources, there are some obvious things to be concerned with, and these are—in order of how difficult they are to ascertain—credibility of the information source, the accuracy of the information, and the completeness of the range of sources.

The credibility of the information source is the easiest to ascertain. One needs to consider if the source, whether it is a vehicle or a person, is a reasonable conduit for the information. Therefore, a scientist who has made a discovery is likely to be a good source of information about that discovery. However, some people who are close to the generation of information should not necessarily be regarded as credible. For example, if a political candidate makes a blunder, that candidate's press secretary is close to the candidate—and, hence, the generation of the blunder—but the press secretary is not likely to be a credible source of information about why the candidate blundered; the press secretary's agenda is to spin the blunder to make it look planned and actually a brilliant move. So for a source to be credible, the source needs not only to know the accurate truth but also to be trustworthy enough to transmit the truth.

The accuracy of the information is also an important consideration. To test this, people need to check the information against more than one source. If all sources provide the same information, then, many people think the information must be accurate. However, accuracy is not determined by elections. People should give credibility to consensus information only when the various sources of that same information are each expert and trustworthy.

The completeness of the range of sources is the most difficult to test, because it requires a constant search for more *types* of sources. By types, I mean sources that are likely to present a different perspective on an issue and, hence, different information to support their perspectives. The mass media tend to simplify issues by reducing them to two sides. For example, in political races, the mass media typically limit their coverage to one candidate from the Republican Party and one candidate from the Democratic Party.

B. Inside Sources

When looking inside oneself, it is better to rely on well-organized knowledge structures than on informally derived schemas containing unconfirmed intuitive impressions cobbled together with heuristics. Good knowledge structures help people see the context of the problem more fully, and this helps in (a) focusing on the central essence of the problem and not getting lost in the details, (b) providing more information to fill in the gaps, and (c) selecting criteria to make good choices to proceed down a path to a useful solution.

Good knowledge structures also help people keep track of the information they have. Typically people are not very good at being aware of what they know. Meta-memory judgments are judgments about information that exists in one's memory. These judgments have generally been found to be accurate in the sense that people know whether they have some information on a topic or not, but much of the information they have is inaccurate (Payne, Klin, Lampinen, Neuschatz, & Lindsay, 1999). I will discuss three types of inaccurate or inaccessible information below.

1. *False memories.* Individuals are vulnerable to illusions of remembering. False memories may arise from external suggestive influences or when people mistake their internal thoughts (associations, fantasies, and dreams) for what actually happened. People are often confident in false memories and sometimes claim to remember details of the episode in which the event supposedly occurred. One explanation for false memories is that, sometimes, people will store information from different kinds of experiences together. Then, when they go to access some of those memories, other closely stored memories are also recalled as being part of the same event (Smith, 1999). Also, "potential sources of inaccuracy in memory reports include not only the respondent's locating and using the wrong representation in memory, but also defects in the perceiver's interpretive and constructive processes" (Smith, 1999, p. 252).

2. *Confusing media-world knowledge with real-world knowledge.*
Sometimes, the information we bring to bear on a problem may be an accurate memory, but that it is from the wrong "world of experience," thus making its applicability to this problem questionable. For example, we may get disoriented and use a media narrative schema that we have developed through media exposures when we should be using an event schema, which we have developed through exposures in our everyday social world. If we go to a party and ignore all of our previous experience at real-world parties and instead expect to participate in a party that would take place in a Hollywood movie, this can get us into trouble or embarrass us, or at minimum makes us feel enormously disappointed when the party turns out not to be as glamorous or intense as we expected.

One of the problems with schemas and their organic growth of linkages is that media schema can easily get linked with real-world schema. When we initially make an association between images and meanings, it is easy to remember whether the image was from a media message or a real-world encounter (for examples of these schemas, see Table 10.1). But over time, the linkages can get rearranged, and we can confuse media and real-world images; thus, we might see a real-world image and trace its meaning back into a media meaning. This is another reason why knowledge structures are better than schema: The higher degree of construction that goes into fashioning knowledge structures makes it less likely that the two worlds will become confused later.

For many reasons, it is tempting to use media-world information for real-world problems. One reason is that the media provide a wider range of messages than does a person's real social life. People need a wider range of schema to deal with the types of people they see in the media but do not encounter in their interpersonal interactions—for example, national political figures, major entertainers, professional athletes, psychopathic killers, the very rich, and so on. People also need a wider range of event schema to understand what it means to play a sport professionally, to be a person living in Iraq, to be a knight looking for the Holy Grail in medieval times, or to be an astronaut on a futuristic voyage to another galaxy.

Another reason is that the media have a sense of authority about them. Thus, when we read something, we feel it has been written by an expert so we should believe the claims in the message. Because cameras have recorded images of actual events and these are presented as news, we are likely to believe those images. Also, the repetitiveness of the messages contributes to its expert effect.

The more consciously we pay attention to our world, the more elements we notice and the more we add to our existing schema. We are constantly

Table 10.1   Types of Schema

Schema Label	Description
Real World Schema:	
Person schema	You have a schema for every person you know. Each of these schema include the physical characteristics and personality traits of that person. For acquaintances, the schema are very sketchy, but for your closest and longest friends, the schema are highly elaborate.
Self schema	These are all the images you have of yourself. Most people have developed a more elaborate schema about themselves than any other single thing.
Role schema	These are your expectations for how people should behave in certain situations. You have a role schema for behaving as a student in the classroom, one for behavior at a family reunion, one for a job interview, one for a party with friends your age, etc. Each of these roles is very different, because each has a different goal and requires a different set of attitudes and behaviors.
Event schema	These are expectations you have that unfold over time, and as such they can be regarded as scripts. In the long term, you have a script that tells you what you should be doing in the next few years and what you should be doing in 10 or 20 years with your imagined career and family. In the short term, you have scripts that guide what you should say in conversations; that is, if a person is funny, you respond one way, but if the person is a bore you respond another way.
Media Schema:	
Character schema	The media deal in stock characters (that is stereotypes) that we can easily recognize. Our character schema are what make it possible for us to have such a sense of recognition.
Narrative schema	These are the formulas of storytelling used by the media. They contain elements that cue us as to whether the media message is a fictional story about crime, a news story about crime, a comedy, and so on.

Setting schema	Settings influence our expectations. If an armed robbery takes place in a liquor store in a poor urban neighborhood, the meaning of that crime can be different than if it takes place in the bedroom of an upper middle class family home in a small rural community.
Thematic schema	These schema help us recognize the moral of a story. For example, if a bad character is punished for his behavior, the theme is usually that crime doesn't pay or honesty is the best policy. But if a good character is continually punished, the theme can be something quite different, such as the world is unfair or good guys finish last.
Rhetorical schema	This is the viewer's inference about the purpose of the storyteller. Is the primary contribution of the story to provide information or to entertain? Is the story trying to teach us a moral lesson or provide us with a fantasy escape? Is the story meant to be humorous, and if so how: slapstick? satire? irony?

developing our schema, adding to them and subtracting elements that we find not useful or that belong in other schema.

When it comes to people interpreting media portrayals, it is useful to think of two levels of intention. One level is inside the portrayal itself; that is, the more viewers understand the motives and personalities of all the characters, the more they can assess the meaning of interactions within the plot. But there is also a second level, and this is involves the creators of the portrayals, that is, the writers, directors, actors, and so on. This is clearly illustrated with the characteristic of humor. In the *Three Stooges*, Mo is an angry man with low tolerance for the mistakes of his partners. He is seriously upset when Larry or Curley makes a mistake, and he retaliates with the intention to punish them with physical harm. There is nothing humorous on this level. However, viewers know that these portrayals are meant to be a comedy; that is, the writers are constructing situations to make the viewers laugh. People are aware of the creator's intention when it comes to humor; but unless they realize this, they can miss the intention of other creators and thereby not "get" the humor. Thus, the difference between watching media portrayals and social interactions in real life is that there is another level of concern. That is, there are two levels of motives.

3. *Inert knowledge.* When people are presented with a problem on a topic, they naturally go to the most relevant knowledge structure and seek out information to provide more context for their meaning construction. But often, there will not be enough—or any—information that will help with the current problem. In this case, people need to seek out the information in other knowledge structures. This is relatively easy if the knowledge structures are linked, but often they are not. It is difficult to find relevant information catalogued in a nonlinked knowledge structure. In such a case, the knowledge is regarded as being inert (Woods & Cook, 1999). This means that people may possess some knowledge and be able to use it in one situation or with one type of problem, but they cannot access it to solve another type of problem; thus, this knowledge is inert.

To avoid the situation of inert knowledge, people need a high degree of coupling. Coupling is the degree to which the components in a system are linked up. The more the components are linked, the more the effect of a problem in one component can cascade and influence other components (Woods & Cook, 1999). However, when every node is linked with every other node, the structure is not efficient. The large number of links makes the network very complex. Also, the activation of any one node will necessarily spread out to all nodes, and this provides too much information. A better way to organize nodes is through nesting, where like ideas are nested together and fully linked within a nest. Then, the nests are linked together. This is rather like an outline. This form of linking offers efficient access to all nodes in a branching pattern and thus eliminates the possibility of accessing all nodes through spreading activation whenever one node is accessed.

III. The Reasoning Process in Meaning Construction

Solving a partially specified problem requires a realization that a purely logical process is not possible. That is, the gaps in information required to be purely systematic prevent a step-by-step logical reasoning process. This is not to say that there is no chance to be logical at all. Instead, it requires that people understand the various challenges in the meaning-construction task: Some tools that are most useful for working on certain parts of the problem are logical, and some tools required for working on other parts are not. To illustrate, let's consider how people use rules to categorize objects. Hampton (1982) conducted a study in which he asked his participants: Are typewriters office furniture? Participants struggled with the logical inconsistency that typewriters belonged in an *office* in many ways but that typewriters were not *furniture* in many other ways. People who use logic exclusively will not be able to provide a satisfying answer to this question.

Cognitive psychologists have long recognized that the human mind is not a machinelike calculating device; instead, it can take shortcuts, reason intuitively, and be subject to emotion. If the mind could not do this, we could not solve partially specified problems. This idea of nonrationality shows up quite prominently in cognitive psychology. For example, Hammond (1966a) says all judgments fall along a continuum ranging from analytic at one end to intuitive at the other, with quasi-rational in between. Barsalou (1992) says, "Many psychologists have concluded that human knowledge does not follow logical form closely. This is not to say that human knowledge is illogical, but only that other factors play more significant roles. In other words, human knowledge is generally nonlogical" (p. 150). Simon (1957) argued that humans are neither rational or irrational; instead, humans show a bounded rationality; that is, some reasoning processes are relatively rational but not completely systematic. Simon created the idea of *satisficing*, which is a strategy that does not require us to consider all possible options and then carefully compute the relative merits of each as a means of maximizing our gains and minimizing our losses. Instead, we consider options one by one until we find one that satisfies our minimum level of acceptability, then go with that option. The advantage of this strategy is that it minimizes the number of options we must consider before making a decision.

Not all people approach problem solving and thinking the same way. Cognitive psychologists have come up with many different explanations for how people make decisions in their everyday lives. In synthesizing those explanations, Fiske and Taylor (1991) list four views of human thinkers. First, *consistency seekers* are people motivated to seek consistency across attitudes as well as consistency between behaviors and attitudes. This is the view espoused by Leon Festinger. Second, *naive scientists* are motivated to act systematically to gather data and logically make decisions. Attribution theorists, such as Fritz Heider, see people this way. Third, *cognitive misers* view people as limited in their capacity to process information, so they take shortcuts when they can. Fourth, *motivated tacticians* are regarded as fully engaged thinkers who have multiple cognitive strategies available and choose among them based on goals, motives, and needs. Sometimes, people are motivated by accuracy and sometimes by efficiency.

There is wisdom in all four kinds of explanations. Any given person probably exhibits characteristics of all four. However, most people are more like one of the types in their basic approach to thinking, that is, the one they use most often. When the demands of a given situation require a change in method, they can switch to another type. For example, someone might be a naive scientist and try to gather good information and think out each decision carefully but, if he or she is overwhelmed with information, might switch to a cognitive miser style and make decisions quickly to get through all the choices that need to be made in a given morning.

A. Heuristics

Heuristics was originally conceptualized to mean techniques that people use in everyday problem solving as shortcuts to a formal logic process. When people are motivated more by efficiency than by accuracy, they want to arrive at a solution to a problem as quickly as possible, so they take shortcuts, that is, use heuristics. Tversky (1972) introduced the idea of heuristics as rules of thumb or mental shortcuts that people use to reduce the amount of effort they need to expend in solving problems rationally. Heuristics are judgmental shortcuts that people use in times of uncertainty. Rather than gather more information systematically and reason carefully, they are more motivated by efficiency, so they want to take shortcuts to arrive at conclusions quickly and thus reduce their uncertainty. Fiske and Taylor (1991, p. 381) explain that heuristics are helpful especially when people seek efficiency, that is, a means to arrive at a reasonable solution as quickly as possible. To do this, people employ heuristics because of time constraints, complexity, volume of information, or uncertainty about the information.

But heuristics are more than shortcuts. It is too limiting to think of heuristics only as techniques for people in a hurry. It is better to think of them more broadly as alternatives to a formal logical process of problem solving. When a formal logic process is available, then heuristics are, of course, shortcuts. But sometimes, a formal process is not available; in this case, heuristics are the only alternative. This is the case with most partially specified problems. Remember the problem $24 = X + Y$; solve for X and Y? No formal process is available to take you to one and only one accurate answer. So you use a heuristic to bridge the gaps in information. In this case, we speculate that X is 1 for instance. This then allows us to solve for Y with certainty.

Often, heuristics are the only tools available to solve partially specified problems. When confronted with a partially specified problem, people are constrained in their options. One option is to ignore the problem. The other option is to make a valiant effort to construct a solution, using the partial set of information you have, knowing full well that there is a good chance your solution may not be a good one. Those who choose to undertake the challenge of solving a partially specified problem can either make a wild guess or try to do a bit better and use a heuristic.

The risk in using heuristics comes not from using them as tools to solve problems per se; rather, the risk comes from using them as shortcuts when a better process of reasoning is available to the problem solver. Thus, if the heuristic is the only tool available, its use is good in the sense that it can reduce uncertainty; but if more powerful or systematic tools are available, then its use is usually a poor choice, because the person could reduce uncertainty to a higher degree and much more accurately by using other tools. Thus, it is a mistake to oversimplify, because that will result in distortions or misconceptions (Woods & Cook, 1999).

In summary, there are two reasons for using heuristics. They are helpful when we are confronted with a partially specified problem and cannot get enough information (either from outside authorities or our own knowledge structures) to make it fully specified. Therefore, to bridge the gaps in the problem, we need to use a heuristic.

The other reason we use heuristics is to save time and energy. We humans have a choice of how much mental energy to put into problems. We have the capacity to be systematic, precise, and accurate, but we can also be non-logical, subjective, and intuitive. The meaning-construction process is not objective, nor is it uniform across individuals. It is subjective and as such, different people construct different meanings for the same event or message. This is because people make different selections of parts of a message, different inferences from the elements, and different interpretations about what they perceive. For example, a man figures he needs a new car and can afford to spend about $25,000, so he opens the newspaper to look for car ads. The quickest shortcut would be to look only at prices and stop when he finds a car that costs about $25,000. This would take only a few minutes, and the problem would be solved. But there are many alternatives to this simple strategy, and all of them would likely result in a better decision. The man could even use a formal logic strategy if he first determines what his criteria are (in addition to price) and weights the relative importance of each criterion. By doing this, he is filling in the gaps of a partially specified problem and making it fully specified. Then, he would systematically gather information about each car for sale rating each car on each of his criteria, weighting the ratings by how important each criterion is, then computing a score for each possible purchase. The car with the highest score then becomes his choice.

Thus, there are two kinds of heuristics: shortcuts and bridges. Shortcuts are used when there are alternatives, but the person wants to avoid those alternatives. When people are guided by a need for efficiency, they take a shortcut to get to a solution as quickly as possible and thereby avoid a more formal decision path. Think of a decision path as the sequence of squares around the outside of a board game, like Monopoly. Proceeding square by square around the edge of the board takes longer than cutting across a corner and missing some of the squares. But going square by square gives you experiences that you will need to arrive at your destination; that is, you pick up things along the way.

A bridge heuristic is used when the problem solving path has a gap; that is, there are elements missing that are not part of the problem, making the problem partially specified. If you stop at the gap, you cannot proceed all the way to the end of the task, so you must use some kind of a heuristic to bridge over the gap.

B. Assuming Shared Meaning

In all communication situations, people have a concern about shared meaning. Often, people will hold what is called *common ground* (Clark & Marshall, 1981); that is, they share the same knowledge. In these situations, communication can take place well. But when the sender and receiver do not share common ground, they need to uncover the problem in their conversation and clarify meanings, thus restoring the value of the communication. This is especially challenging with mediated communication. Senders know general things about their audiences (such as their demographics) in order to create their target audiences, but senders are largely ignorant about substantive characteristics. Also, there is no chance for feedback. This lack of true interaction raises three levels of problems: (a) receivers know they do not understand the sender's meaning but cannot ask about it, so they are frustrated; (b) receivers think they may not be understanding the message as intended by the sender but cannot confirm this suspicion; or (c) receivers believe they understand the sender but do not, so false impressions arise and are reinforced. The last problem is the most serious, because receivers do not know they are misunderstanding, so they cannot discount the message. The media are particularly good at creating this third problem, because they make people believe that there is common ground by presenting images, characters, events, and so on that look familiar and are easily understandable to receivers. But often, these things require a higher degree of complexity to communicate well. Because the media often do not deal with complexity, they mislead audiences.

IV. The Media Literacy Perspective

A. Context and Knowledge Structures

With meaning construction, people confront partially specified problems, so they need to consider context in helping them fill in the gaps. They need to move beyond the task of understanding the literal meaning of a message and also deal with the issue of *why* the information was communicated. To reach this level of understanding, people must consider the message sender's intention, their own objectives for the message, and characteristics of the message itself. The sender may be using irony or satire, may be transparently trying to lie (Joe Izusu commercial), or may be trying to hide something (as a suspect in a murder story).

There are different kinds of meaning, and people need to consider context to be able to sort through the different kinds. Wyer and Gruenfeld (1995) make a distinction between literal meaning and what they call pragmatic meaning. Literal meaning is that which is on the surface and normative, that is, what is expected when the sender's and receiver's intentions are obvious. Pragmatic meaning is what is received, and it may not be what the sender intended. Wyer and Gruenfeld conclude that the "interpretation of informa-tion that is received in a social context, and therefore its impact on judg-ments and decisions, is likely to be guided as much by perceptions of its pragmatic implications (i.e., why the information was conveyed) as by its semantic meaning" (p. 86). The cognitive effort people spend in meaning construction is affected by their drives and goals.

The media, however, do not always provide enough context, even with relatively simple factual material. For example, Marton and Stephens (2001) conducted a content analysis of stories published in the *New York Times* that reported the use of polling data and found that the stories rarely con-tained enough information to help readers make a judgment about the qual-ity of the polls. The American Association for Public Opinion Research has guidelines that newspapers should follow when reporting polls. They rec-ommend including information on 12 topics, such as who sponsored the poll, exact wording of questions, population under study, sampling tech-niques used, sample size, and rates of nonresponse. The authors analyzed 500 articles reporting surveys from 1989 to 1997 and found that half the articles did not meet as many as 6 of the 12 standards.

B. Skills

The two major skills used in the process of meaning construction are deduction and induction. With induction, people look for patterns across messages, then infer a general pattern. With deduction, people observe one specific occurrence and access a general principle to explain it. For example, recall from the previous chapter that when people are watching a new family situation comedy, they can access a principle that family sitcoms feature a father who is a buffoon, a mother who is the strong rational family member, and kids who are quirky. This is the family sitcom formula; people who know this formula (general principle) are in a good position to quickly and efficiently construct the meaning of the show they are watching. But if they do not know this formula (or do not have a general principle to use in order to deduce meaning), then they need to construct the general principle; thus they need to use induction to infer one.

The deductive process is relatively simple when people can access a general principle from their knowledge structures. They then reason from the general principle and the observation about the new message to make meaning of a current message. Cutting (1991) says, "There are deductions, which are sure, and inductions, which are not. Each is made up of premises and a conclusion. Deductions are well understood in logic; inductions are hardly understood at all" (p. 42). Thus, it is very challenging to use induction. The central problem is how people know if they are really able to equate a characteristic in Message X with a characteristic in Message Y and say that the two characteristics are the same and therefore can be regarded as being part of the same pattern. Perhaps X and Y are really different, and you are really comparing apples and oranges. Also, how do people know when they have enough examples to allow them to induce a pattern with confidence? Are two examples enough to constitute the basis for inferring that a pattern exists among all possible examples?

We make inferences all the time. It is believed (in connectionist models of human thinking) that a person uses a number of related experiences to construct a general representation automatically; it is not a conscious decision to do so or not to do so. As people acquire more examples that are related in some way, they are automatically connected to one another, and the connections gain more weight with the more examples; also, these examples become a set that is then linked to a general representation for the set (category name or concept). The more examples included in the set, the stronger the link to the representation that focuses on the characteristics that linked all those examples together. For example, when you see a bird fly, then another bird fly, you link the two together in a set of examples that are represented by the characteristic of flying. As more examples are found, they are put in the same category, and the connection to the "flying" representation for the category is strengthened.

People are generally more confident of their ability to use deduction than induction. This is due to what is called *hindsight bias* (Fischhoff, 1982). If you give people the outcome of something and ask them how it was possible that the thing occurred, they can reason backward from the conclusion and feel that their explanation is a good one. But if you tell people about some events and ask them to predict how the course of events will turn out (inducing a pattern), they are less sure of their conclusion.

C. Personal Locus

Meaning construction is a challenging task. To do it well, people need a strong personal locus. In fact, the personal locus makes more of a difference to the quality of this task than to either of the other two information-processing tasks. There is a wide range of quality in meaning construction. People will move toward the higher quality end of the continuum to the extent that they have a high drive state to energize them to consider all the traps and work to avoid them (see the next chapter) and to keep their awareness high as they go about all the steps and use the skills necessary to construct meaning well. Typically, they will need to access additional information to more fully specify problems, and to do this well, they need to avoid taking heuristic shortcuts as much as possible.

V. Summary

Meaning construction requires people to solve partially specified problems. Too little information leaves gaps in the meaning-construction process. Too much information can confuse people about what is most relevant to the task. Barren information is also a challenge, because it requires people to find a way to bridge gaps in the process when no information is possible.

Additional information can come from either outside the person or inside the person from already existing knowledge structures. Guidelines were presented for both sources. The reasoning process was examined, and the chapter concluded with the meaning-construction task being examined within the media literacy perspective.

Meaning Construction
Propositions and Research Questions

Propositions for Research

1. People will be more likely to construct meaning when their personal locus is strong, as characterized by one or both of the following conditions:
   (a) They have a strong drive for control.
   (b) They prefer mindfulness over automaticity during exposures.

2. People will be more likely to construct meaning (rather than accept the meaning in the messages) when the information-processing flow presents one of the following characteristics:
   (a) People are faced with a strong skepticism about the meaning in a message.
   (b) People are faced with an information task that has strong negative consequences if they act on faulty meaning.

Research Questions

1. *Conceptual*

   To what extent do people recognize the difference between meaning-matching and meaning-construction tasks?

   To what extent do people recognize the difference between fully specified and partially specified problems?

   To what extent do people recognize the difference between bridge heuristics and shortcut heuristics?

   Given a meaning-construction task, to what extent do all people go about constructing their meaning the same way?

2. *Measurement*

   How can we map a person's knowledge structures?

   How can we validly identify the information?

   How can we validly identify the structure of that information?

   Is response time a sufficient measure of length of linkages?

3. *Treatments*

   How can researchers articulate their research treatments well when media literacy treatments can never be fully structured by the researcher? Media literacy treatments are always complexes that are composed of what participants bring to the study as well as what the researcher designs. Key to the treatment complex is an understanding of participant skill profiles as well as their relevant knowledge structures.

Questions for Practices

1. What is the most efficient way to teach the meaning-matching task?

2. How can people be encouraged to expend the mental energy needed to snap out of automaticity when need be? What characteristics make meaning construction most attractive so that people will be more drawn to this task and more willing to expend the additional mental energy above what is required in automaticity?

3. How can we:
   (a) help people strengthen all higher order skills, especially induction and synthesis?
   (b) help people build a wider range of knowledge structures so they have context on a wide range of topics?
   (c) help people elaborate knowledge structures so they have deep context on a given topic?
   (d) help people better understand their locus so they can more clearly envision their goal for meaning construction?

CHAPTER 11

Traps in Meaning Construction

11

Traps in Meaning Construction

M eaning construction is a challenging task. One reason for the challenge is that it presents partially specified problems. Another reason is that the process includes many traps that can divert people's thinking and lead them to construct faulty meaning. At times, the traps can even prevent people from constructing any meaning at all.

Generally speaking, these traps can all be traced to a lack of resources by the person constructing the meaning. According to the applied cognitive psychology research, the chance for human error increases when the demands of a task are out of balance with the resources available to the person who must complete the task (Woods & Cook, 1999). When people do not have enough time, energy, information, or skills to construct meaning well, they will make mistakes; that is, they will arrive at interpretations that are faulty in some way. When people are lacking resources, they are likely to use a heuristic, and heuristics always present a danger of making errors.

Recall that there are two types of heuristics: shortcuts and bridges. Shortcuts are used when there are alternative methods, but the person wants to avoid those alternatives. A bridge heuristic is used when the problem-solving path has a gap; that is, there are elements missing from the problem, thus the problem is partially specified. Both can result in a faulty decision-making process.

This chapter displays how heuristics can lead to errors in interpretations. The presentation of these errors is organized by skills. First, we look at traps in the skills of analysis, grouping, and evaluation. I categorize these in this chapter as preparatory skills, because they produce a product that is fed into the more complex processes requiring the skills of induction and deduction. Induction is often referred to as the bottom-up process of reasoning; it begins with particulars and reasons to general principles. Deduction is often referred to as the top-down process of reasoning; it begins with general principles and then reasons to explanations for the particulars. The skills of induction and deduction are so central to meaning construction that each gets its own extended section in this chapter.

I. Traps With Preparatory Skills

When people are confronted with a meaning-construction task, they typically must do some analysis of the message, evaluate the elements they identify in the message, and then take the elements that are favorably evaluated and group them. In performing these tasks, people need to be aware of traps so they can prepare for them and thus reduce the chance of getting caught in one of the traps that would prevent them from constructing good (accurate and useful) meaning.

A. Analysis

Analysis is the skill of breaking things down into component parts. Not all parts of a message are equally important to the construction of meaning, but before a person can evaluate the usefulness of each element, those elements must first be identified. There are three traps with analysis: framing, selecting a unit of analysis, and sizing the unit.

1. *Framing.* Think of framing as a picture frame that limits a person's view of a total phenomenon and focuses attention on that which fits in the frame. Framing can take place in three ways. First, media make necessary selections because they cannot present everything, and those selections limit the audience's perspective on the total phenomenon. Second, message constructors purposely limit the presentation to manipulate receivers. Third, our mind-set creates a frame and determines our selections.

Framing limits the meaning-construction process by constraining the product of an analysis. When the media leave some element out of their messages, we cannot find that element no matter how well we analyze the message. So when the media limit the number of components they cover regarding a given issue, our analysis will result in a limited number of components and miss the other components that the media do not provide. An example of this is the news. News scholars have long studied the way news stories are framed and how that leads to the construction of different interpretations (Biocca, 1991; Entman, 1993; Gamson, 1992; Pan & Kosicki, 1993; Price, Tewksbury, & Powers, 1996). This is a large literature, but to illustrate, Price et al. (1996) said that all news events can be organized into three frames: conflict, consequences, and human interest. The conflict frame shows certain people or groups competing against other people or groups. The consequences frame focuses on the outcomes of some event or policy. If the news media frame a race for a political office as a conflict, then readers will have an easy time finding information about who is the front runner and who is the challenger. But readers will have hard time finding much information on issues.

News is not an accurate reflection of what happened during the day. Instead, it highlights the unusual, so that deviance becomes the frame for breaking news; that is, if something is out of the ordinary, it fits the frame and is likely to get presented by the news vehicles. For example, Pritchard and Hughes (1997) demonstrated that journalists do not report all crime; journalists are much more likely to report crime that rarely occurs compared to the everyday type of crime. The authors found four kinds of deviance as explaining most the decisions journalists make. They found that status and cultural deviance are the most important predictors of newsworthiness, for example, when people involved in crimes are high status (well known, rich, etc.). Cultural deviance is when an act is thought to be unhealthy, unclean, or perverted; when a crime deviates from the culture's norms about being healthy, clean, or normal, it has a greater chance of being covered.

There is not the obvious bias in news that many critics may argue. For example, D'Alessio and Allen (2000) conducted a meta-analysis of 59 quantitative studies of partisan media bias in presidential election campaigns and found no reason to conclude that there was gatekeeping bias (preference for printing stories about one candidate or party over the others), coverage bias (relative amounts of coverage each party receives), or statement bias (favorability of coverage toward one party over the others).

The media are clear in framing political news, especially strategy framing and issue framing (Rhee, 1997). The frames serve to narrow the range of interpretations of the message. The framing can be signaled through headlines in print media (Bleske, 1995; Geer & Kahn, 1993), audiovisual components in television (Crigler, Just, & Neuman, 1994; Graber, 1990), metaphors (Fowler, 1991; Johnson & Taylor, 1981), and referents (Bennett & Lawrence, 1995).

A second way that the media frame issues is when they construct their messages to serve their own goals, even when those messages have a good chance of misleading us. Ads do this all the time. Framing has also been important in understanding how people comprehend advertisements, especially political ads (Iyenger, 1991; Schenck-Hamlin, Procter, & Rumsey, 2000). For example, Thaler (1980) illustrates this in a study in which participants were asked to imagine themselves driving down a road, needing gas, and seeing two signs. The sign for Gas Station A says that gas is $1 a gallon but that there is a discount of 5 cents for paying cash. The sign for Station B says that gas is 95 cents but that there is a surcharge of 5 extra cents per gallon for customers who use their credit cards. In essence, both stations are charging the same, but Station A makes people believe they can save money while Station B frames its charges as a penalty for customers who use a credit card. Most people were found to prefer Station A, because it makes people believe they are saving money when in fact they are not. Advertisers know about framing. If they can make people believe they are getting the same product from them at a cheaper price than they are getting from their competitors, then people will buy from them. However, rarely do we test those claims for ourselves; it is easier to take them at face value.

A third way framing shows up is when our mind-set creates a frame and determines our selections. Even when the media put a complete set of elements into a message, framing can still limit the analysis; in this case, the framing is traceable to the person, not the message. Often, people have a mind-set that guides them to look for certain elements and ignore other elements. This mind-set is a frame that influences the analysis. People's mind-sets can lead them to ignore information that does not conform to their expectations. When the discrepant information is observed, it is discarded or discounted (Woods & Cook, 1999). For example, Zillmann, Taylor, and Lewis (1998) found that dispositions were an important predictor of the emotional reactions people have to news reports. They found that when people held a favorable disposition toward someone, they experienced heightened enjoyment when the news reported good fortune, and they suppressed such reactions to bad-fortune reports. In contrast, when people held unfavorable dispositions, enjoyment was heightened when they heard bad-fortune reports and suppressed when they heard good-fortune reports. The individual's frame significantly influences interpretations of the message.

The wrong mind-set can cause failures in problem solving. Neisser (1976) says there is a perceptual cycle that relies on two processes. We begin with a mind-set that guides us to focus our attention on certain events, objects, and tasks. But then when unique events in the environment occur, they shift the focus or mind-set and trigger new lines of thought.

The media can create a mind-set through priming. Priming "refers to the effects of the content of the media on people's later behavior or judgments related to the content" (Roskos-Ewoldsen, Roskos-Ewoldsen, & Carpenter, 2002, p. 97). Priming has been found to be an important influence with a wide range of messages, including those that involve violence (Anderson, 1997; Josephson, 1987), political opinions (Iyenger, Peters, & Kinder, 1982; Krosnick & Kinder, 1990), and stereotypes (Hansen & Hansen, 1988; Power, Murphy, & Coover, 1996).

2. *Selecting units.* Messages offer meaning cues at different levels of analysis. When the meaning cues differ across levels of analysis, it is important to choose the best level of analysis for the purpose of the meaning construction. Choosing the wrong level of analysis will result in a faulty meaning construction, even if the skill of analysis itself was applied in a high-quality manner. For example, a television narrative looks very different if you conduct the analysis at a scene-by-scene level than it does if you take a more macro level of the entire episode of a program. My colleague Stacy Smith and I found this to be the case when we compared meaning cues for violence using the National Television Violence Study database (Potter & Smith, 1999). If the analysis is done at the scene level, the bad guys get away with most of the violence; that is, they repeatedly avoid punishment and are frequently rewarded for their violent acts. But if the analysis is conducted at the level of the overall narrative in the show, the bad guys are almost always caught and punished. Thus, the meaning of violence in terms of reward and punishment is radically different by level of analysis. At this point, people may be tempted to ask which level of analysis is more correct. That is the wrong question, because the accuracy of the analysis is high at both levels. The question instead should be which level of analysis provides the more useful set of evidence for constructing the meaning of violence on television.

3. *Sizing.* Related to the concern about level of analysis is the size of the unit. If the size of the unit is too large, it may be impossible to perceive uniqueness across the elements. If the size of the unit is too small, there will be too much detail for other skills (such as grouping and induction) to handle. For example, if you were analyzing the population of all 280 million people in this country, you could use states as units, one unit for each of the 50 states. But this unit is too large, because there is so much variation among the people in any given state that it is impossible to perceive a uniqueness shared by all the people in a state that would distinguish them from all the people in another state. What do all the people in Alabama share (other than address) that makes them different from all of the people in Tennessee?

If the unit is too small, this is also a problem. If you were going to use the individual person as the unit in the analysis of the U.S. population, you would end up with 280 million units, each having to be described in sufficient detail so that each person is different from all the rest. Thus, you end up with so much detail that you cannot use the results of the analysis in a grouping or induction.

Another trap with sizing is something called conjunction error. When we describe a person with adjectives, the addition of each adjective increases the uniqueness of the person, but it also reduces the size of the group of possible people who share all the characteristics specified in the adjective list. This, of course, sounds logical, but often, people get confused thinking that the more adjectives you use to describe something, the larger the group to which the adjective set refers. For example, Tversky and Kahneman (1983) asked college students what percentage of men in a survey had one or more heart attacks. The estimates averaged 18%. Then, they asked the same people what percentage of men in the survey were both over 55 years of age and have had one or more heart attacks. The estimates to this question averaged 30% to the second question. The pair of estimates is faulty because logically, the second estimate would have to be lower than the first estimate. The first estimate had one condition to limit the sample whereas the second estimate had not only the first condition but an additional condition to limit the sample. Therefore, the second estimate must be lower, but as you can see people often get confused and make the conjunction error.

B. Evaluation

Evaluation is the comparing of some message to a standard. If the message meets the standard, then it is accepted; if not, it is rejected. People who do this systematically compare every message to the standard. When we have many options, we do not try to make all the possible comparisons and then weight the importance of each evaluation on all the criteria before making a decision. Instead, we take a shortcut.

Arguably the most prevalent shortcut when we have many options is what Tversky (1972) called the "elimination by aspects" strategy. In elimination by aspects, we focus on one criterion, then eliminate all the options that do not meet that one selected criterion. If that does not reduce the options down to one, then we select another single criterion and eliminate all options that do not meet that second criterion. We keep going until we get to one option. This shortcut is more efficient than a complete evaluation process. However, if we choose an unimportant criterion to begin the process, we may end up eliminating the best options early and end up with less desirable ones from which to choose.

C. Grouping

People who conduct an analysis with units of too small a size will end up with a large number of units, each of which is unique. This creates an impossible condition for grouping; that is, the distinctiveness across units is so high that there is no commonality, thus making grouping impossible. For example, if you say you saw a movie about an 8-year-old boy named Evan who immigrated to this country, walked with a limp, and had a scar on his right arm, you would lead your listeners to picture Evan vividly in terms of the detail you provided, but your listeners would not be able to place Evan in a group because he is too unique. Then, if you asked your listeners to provide more detail about Evan, they could not because they would have no group information from which to draw. In contrast, if you said you saw a movie about a fraternity boy and left it at that, your listeners would be able to pull up their "frat boy" schema, which is likely to include all kinds of detail about clothing, attitudes, voice patterns, and behaviors.

II. Traps With Induction

The human mind is continually looking for patterns to reduce the chaos into predictable patterns and to explain how the world works. The skill of induction helps us do this. We look for patterns across elements, then try to generalize that pattern. When we do this well, we are applying the scientific method and thereby generating useful knowledge. However, a wide variety of traps prevent people from doing this well.

A. Inferring a Pattern

Five of the many traps with inferring a pattern are presented in this section.

1. *Attribution.* People look for connections all the time—connections between cause and effect, connections between a person's beliefs and behaviors, and connections among events. Frequently, people will observe an outward manifestation of something and try to infer an inner cause. This is what social psychologists refer to as attribution.

Some attributions are to internal states and others are to external conditions. Internal causality means that the person did the deed because of who he or she is. External causality means the person did the deed because of situational pressures. Fiske and Taylor (1991) reviewed the large literature on attribution and identified six types of attribution errors (see Table 11.1).

Table 11.1   Six Types of Attribution Errors

Error	Description
Fundamental attribution error	Attributing people's behavior to their dispositional qualities rather than to situational factors
Actor-observer effect	The tendency to explain others' behavior as due to dispositional factors and one's own behavior as due to situational or unstable factors
False consensus effect	People self-generate a consensus, then use this to justify their decisions; people overestimate how typical their own behavior is
Self-serving attributional biases	The tendency for people to take credit for successes and deny personal responsibility for failure
Self-centered bias	Taking more than one's share of responsibility for a jointly produced outcome, regardless if the outcome was successful or not
Attributions of responsibility or blame	Blame the media for violence in society

SOURCE: Adapted from Fiske and Taylor (1991, pp. 66–86).

These errors are not the same for everyone. For one thing, people differ by locus of control; that is, people with an internal locus of control are more likely to attribute actions to personal responsibility, whereas people with an external locus are more likely to blame fate or situations for actions. Also, people have different attributional styles, which is the tendency to make particular kinds of causal inferences rather than others across different situations and across time.

2. *Illusory correlation*. Often, people look across many elements and infer a pattern of correlation in which some elements are believed to be related to other elements or to cause a change in other elements. People will find correlations where they expect to find them, even when those correlations do not really exist. Illusory correlation is overestimating the degree of a relationship. Two such traps (ecological fallacy and the butterfly effect) are especially troublesome to inferring patterns.

3. *Ecological fallacy.* The ecological fallacy is the inferring of a causal relationship between two things merely because they occur together. An example of this is the inference that immigrants commit more crimes than other people in this country. In the 1950s, it was found that crime rates were the highest in neighborhoods where immigrants were most numerous. Some people used this "co-occurrence" to argue that immigrants were a cause of crime. But a careful analysis of this situation revealed that immigrants were forced to live in neighborhoods where crime rates were high, because they could not afford more expensive housing in safer neighborhoods. Immigrants themselves committed very few of the crimes (Strauss, 1996).

4. *Butterfly effect.* The butterfly effect is named after the belief that if a butterfly flaps its wings today in the Amazon basin, it will trigger a chain of events that will eventually lead to rain in your hometown next week. The problem with this "connection" is that there are too many simultaneous effects occurring, any one of which could account for the rain. You would need to analyze each link in the long causal chain from the Amazon to your house to see if there were any faulty links that would invalidate the jumping from a particular cause to a far-removed effect.

5. *Dilution effect.* After we finish an analysis and have a set of elements, we need to conduct an evaluation to sift through those elements and remove the irrelevant ones before we try to infer a pattern. If we do not remove the irrelevant elements, they will dilute the set of information. Thus, the relevant information can get lost in the set, and the pattern we infer is based more on irrelevant elements.

6. *Continuity bias.* Sometimes, when people infer a pattern, they ignore examples that do not fit this pattern. In their quest for efficiency, they cut corners by not considering the elements that do not fit the pattern. They say they are looking at the big picture and don't want to let a few exceptions spoil the pattern, so they ignore the exceptions to preserve the continuity of the overall pattern. This is continuity bias.

When we see an exception to a pattern, this creates dissonance. To reduce the dissonance, people need to rework the pattern and come up with a new one to account for the elements that did not fit the old one. This requires additional work and usually results in a more complex pattern. If the task is not of high importance to people, they will likely not want to expend the effort to work out a more complex pattern; instead, they will simply ignore the discrepancies to the simple pattern and focus only on the continuities, that is, the elements that do fit the pattern.

The media frequently depend on our continuity bias. For example, filmmakers will not present all the detail about what happens to each character; they leave out scenes knowing that audiences will fill in the gaps and create a continuity of the story for themselves. Messaris (1994) points out that filmmakers frequently juxtapose images to play on viewers' quest for continuity so that viewers put the images together in a pattern of time and place.

The continuity bias is so strong that when filmmakers make mistakes with continuity, these frequently go unnoticed by viewers. For example, Levin and Simons (2000) found that people do not notice continuity problems (shots within a scene not matching on perceptual details) in movies. They presented their participants with a film in which Bob and Mary were talking. The camera alternated a two-shot of both people with close-ups of each person individually. In some shots, Bob was wearing a blue sweater, and in other shots, Bob was wearing a green sweater. They found that few participants noticed the change in color of Bob's sweater. Levin and Simons concluded that there was "a striking tendency for people to perceive events as continuous and consistent despite large perceptual inconsistencies that occur right before their eyes" (p. 362). The continuity bias prevented people from seeing a difference in sweater color, because attention was likely on the flow of the conversation. Overlooking small errors like these is not a serious impediment to constructing good meaning. However, the continuity bias can lead to confusions where a movie subtly slips in flashbacks or flashforwards, and the viewers do not interpret them as such.

7. *Simulation heuristic*. This is the constructing of hypothetical scenarios to try to estimate how something will come out. For example, when news stories are left unresolved, people are motivated to achieve closure (Allport & Postman, 1947; Graber, 1988; Gunter, 1987). To do this, people are likely to infer retrospectively a plausible resolution to the issue or event, using their cognitive schema. These inferences are typically conclusions that the event will turn out OK or that there will be positive outcomes. This has been referred to as a positivity bias (Metzger, 2000; Petty & Cacioppo, 1981).

B. Generalizing

Once people infer a pattern across elements, they generalize to a larger class of elements. This part of the induction process also has its traps. First, people tend to use too small of a sample. In the extreme case, people observe a single behavior of one person and generalize to the behavior of all people. Second, people are likely to use a nonrepresentative sample. Even when this type of sample has many cases, its size does not overcome its faulty nature.

Third, some generalizations are what is called motivated. This means that people's emotions or values get in the way of making good generalizations. Instead, they will generalize a pattern to create evidence to support an argument they are making.

III. Traps With Deduction

Deductive problems with meaning construction usually stem from the selection of a faulty general principle. A second type of deductive problem is using the wrong principle when we have accurate ones available to us. In this section, I will present 10 traps that plague deductive reasoning.

A. Representative Heuristic

Throughout our lives we generalize patterns through induction. The act of generalizing is making a claim that the pattern we observe is typical and that it can be applied to a large number of—perhaps all—people. Our beliefs about what is typical then become our general principles. We use these general principles about how the world works to explain individual occurrences. For example, one of the general principles many people have in the area of health is that men are more likely than women to suffer a heart attack and, furthermore, that once a man reaches middle age, his risk of a heart attack is higher than when he is younger. Let's say we watch a movie where Harry, a middle aged man, starts complaining of acute chest pains. We are likely to conclude that Harry is having a heart attack. Later in the movie, we see Crystal, a young woman, complaining of chest pains. We would use the same principle to conclude that she is not having a heart attack. We see the same behavior on the screen but construct a very different meaning for Harry's behavior than for Crystal's behavior. We use our general principles about typical behaviors and typical characters all the time as we process media messages. The representative heuristic is a useful tool, because it allows us to bridge lots of gaps in stories and quickly construct meaning about who various characters are and to build our expectations about how those characters should behave.

We often use the representative heuristic as a bridge heuristic; that is, it helps us bridge a gap in information. We may be wrong in our inferred bridging, but when it is our only alternative, we use it to reduce uncertainty. To illustrate this, Kahneman and Tversky (1973) posed the following problem. A high school offers two programs. In Program A, boys are in the majority at 65%, while in Program B, boys are in the minority at 45%.

There is an equal number of classes in each program. Now, if you enter a classroom at random and observe that 55% of the students are boys, what is your best guess as to which program this class is part of? If this is the only information we are given, we are likely to say that the class belongs to Program A, because there are more boys in the class; that is, this one class is more representative of Program A. There is a good chance that we are wrong, but there is a better chance that we are correct. Thus, this representative heuristic gives us a way to reduce uncertainty a bit, and that is a helpful bridge heuristic.

The media tend to work against the usefulness of the representative heuristic because of their fixation on presenting the untypical, the deviant, and the bizarre. This is clearly the case with fiction, where storytellers create unusual characters and untypical situations. If we construct our general principles from this social information, those principles might have usefulness in helping us understand media stories, but they will have little value in real-world applications. The same can be said for information presented in news programs. For example, the evening news on TV or the daily newspaper are much less interested in presenting an accurate picture of the events of the day than they are interested in presenting the most unusual events and people, so as to capture and hold your attention.

The media intuitively know about this representative heuristic, so they present anecdotes of what is untypical. When we see these, we are surprised and say "How about that? Who would have guessed?" That gets our attention. For example, we all know we should eat healthy and exercise to live a long life, but the press will sometimes show us a contrary view: Rudy ate a pound of greasy bacon every day, smoked two packs of cigarettes, and drank a quart of whisky, and still lived to be 99 years old. The news media tell us the exceptions to representativeness. But over time, after we are exposed to a steady diet of exceptions, we generalize new patterns from those exceptions and arrive at a distorted idea of what is representative. Then, when we use the representative heuristic, we deduce wrong conclusions.

B. Misunderstanding Probabilities

Associated with the problem of using the representative heuristic in a faulty manner is the problem that people have with understanding probabilities. For example, many people do not understand that the probability of each coin toss is independent of the pattern of coin tosses. With a fair coin, people understand that there is a 50% chance of a heads coming up, and a 50% chance of a tail coming up. That is a general principle most people accept. Let's say you flipped a coin six times and got the following pattern:

H, H, T, H, T, T. If you asked people what the result of the seventh toss would be, most people will say there is a 50% chance for a head and a 50% for a tail. However, if you show a person another pattern (H, H, H, H, H, H) and ask what the next result will be, most people will say there is a high probability of a tail, reasoning that the existing pattern cannot go on forever; there must be a tail to get the results back to an overall 50-50 pattern. But this is an error, because the next coin toss is independent from all the others and has its own 50-50 probability. The coin has no memory and no motivation to put things back in order, but our minds do. This is called the gambler's fallacy, and it is an example of using the representative heuristic in a faulty manner.

Another facet of this problem has to do with computing joint probabilities. Bayes developed a system of statistical reasoning to enable people to reason from a starting point to predict the probability of a particular event occurring. This form of reasoning requires people to construct a decision tree-type diagram to illustrate each decision point and the options available, then to estimate the probability of each option at each decision point. To work this system of combinations of probabilities in a chain, people need to be able to recognize all the decision points along a particular path and multiply together all the associated probabilities. For example, if I turn my TV on now, what is the probability of seeing a new episode of a show I like? First, I know that about one third of all programming time is non-program content (commercial messages, teasers for shows, promos, PSAs, etc.), so I have a two-thirds chance of seeing a program. Then, I know that of all programs I am likely to see, I like only 20%. Third, I estimate that about 40% of all programs are reruns. So what I must do is multiply 67% (program probability) by 20% (probability of liking show) by 60% (non-reruns) to arrive at the combination probability. Thus, the chance of turning on the TV and seeing a new episode of a show I like is about 8%. People rarely use this procedure for two reasons. First, it is difficult to estimate the series of individual probabilities, and often, we have no idea what these should be. Second, we need to compute the product, and this is difficult to do in one's head quickly. If the decision is important, however, this is a useful tool.

C. Misunderstanding Percentages

Many people have difficulty understanding the meaning of percentages. A percentage, of course, is an expression of the relationship between two numbers. The problem of misunderstanding is in evidence when people add two percentages (or average two percentages) and ignore differences in the bases. Here is an extreme example. A baseball player in August thinks that he can dramatically raise his batting average by having a good week. Let's say his batting average is .200, and he thinks that if he can bat .500 this coming week, he will raise his overall batting average to .350—that's a simple calculation of the average of .200 and .500. But if the .200 average is based on 300 at bats and the next week he gets only 12 at bats, then the .200 average should be weighted 25 times as much as his hoped for .500 in the coming week. So batting a phenomenal .500 the next week would indeed raise his overall batting average, but only to .212.

Ignoring base numbers is perhaps the greatest trap in dealing with percentages. For example, let's say I describe a person as dishonest, power hungry, and a presidential candidate. Then, I ask people if they think this person is a congressperson or an insurance salesperson. Most would say the person is a congressperson because of the characteristics. However, this is faulty because they would be ignoring the base numbers. There are fewer than 500 congresspeople while there are millions of insurance salespeople. Let's say that 90% of congresspeople have those bad characteristics; this computes to 450 people. Now, let's say that only 1% of a million insurance salespeople have those characteristics; this computes to 10,000 people. When we consider the base number, it becomes very clear that the answer cannot possibly be the congressperson.

We have likely seen at least one news story that reports about how the divorce rate has grown in this country. Often, these stories will say the divorce rate is now 50%, but what does this really mean? Let's analyze it. This figure is a percentage, and like all percentages, it is computed from two numbers. What are those numbers? If we compare the number of marriages with the number of divorces in any given year, we get a ratio of 2 to 1. In other words, there were twice as many marriages last year as there were divorces, or expressed another way, the number of divorces last year was 50% of the number of marriages. However, this makes it sound as if half the married people get divorced each year; this interpretation is wrong. If we change the base number of the comparison, we get a very different number. Let's compare the number of divorces last year with the number of total existing marriages at the beginning of that year. When we make this comparison, we get a figure of about 1%. This means that last year, 1% of all existing marriages ended in divorce by the end of that year. Which is the correct divorce rate: 50% or 1%? They both are. The difference is attributable to a difference in the base of comparison, where both bases of comparison are legitimate. Because the bases are different, they are answering different questions. If the question is what percentage of existing marriages will end in divorce this year, the answer is 1%. But if the question is what is the percentage of the number of divorces this year to the number of marriages this year, the answer is 50%. If we don't analyze a claim that the divorce rate is 50%, we can be misled to believe that half of all marriages will end in divorce this year.

Percentages can be misleading, but if people understand that they are really simple comparisons and always ask the source what is being compared, then the deceptive trap can be avoided. The same principle applies to all numbers reported in the media. Numbers should not be avoided, because they could be deceptive; such avoidance is itself a trap. We must avoid the trap of becoming so skeptical of statistics that we don't believe any of them. Not all statistics are equally credible—or faulty.

D. Halo Effect

Another problem is the halo effect, where we believe someone's explanation merely because we believe he or she is an expert or because we trust him or her. But even experts are sometimes wrong because of faulty reasoning. We must analyze their claims to see if this is one of the times they are right.

Just because people are regarded as experts does not mean that they are right all the time. For example, economists continually are developing sophisticated mathematical models to predict facets of the stock market or the economy. Meteorologists use supercomputers to predict weather trends, yet are often wrong. At any given time, there are many different predictive outcomes, and almost all of them will be wrong. If you accept one of these unquestioningly, you will probably select a wrong one. To protect yourself, carefully look across all the predictions at a given time to see what the majority say. Or look at the history of a particular model to see what its track record is. Some models are better at predicting the performance of certain stocks; however, be careful to understand that better is not the same as perfect. My predictive model may be better than any of the others because I am right 35% of the time, while everyone else is right only 20% of the time. If you invest with me, it will be better than using other models, but you will still lose money most of the time.

E. Availability Heuristic

The availability heuristic is the tendency of people to evaluate the frequency or likelihood of an event on the basis of how quickly instances or associations come to mind. Because those instances are more salient in their mind, the events are assumed to be more frequent or prevalent in the real world. For example, Tversky and Kahneman (1983) asked undergraduate students whether there are more words in the English language that begin with the letter L or whether there are more words with L as the third letter. Most students said there are more words that begin with the letter L. This is an illustration of the availability heuristic: It shows that it is easier to think about the first letters in words than to spend the mental energy to think about third letters in words.

We make decisions based on the information that is most available to us, and this can get us into trouble. For example, if you ask two partners in a marriage individually to list who does which household chores and what proportion each contributes, you are likely to get both saying they do 80% (Ross & Sicoly, 1979). Of course, it is not possible that both could contribute such a strong majority of the work; however, this is how it appears to the respective partners because the information on their own work is more available to them than the work of the other.

The availability heuristic is especially important to the topic of media literacy. People get a great deal of social information from the media, and for some people, they get much more social information from the media than from real life. When these people interact with others in real life, the principles that are most available to them are the generalizations from media portrayals. Therefore, these people will constantly be accessing the wrong principles and will continually be constructing faulty meanings for what is happening in their lives.

F. Self-Enhancement Bias

People tend to rate themselves above average; that is, most people think they are slightly healthier, happier, smarter, and so on than the average person. This lays the foundation for a third-person bias and a first-person bias.

1. *Third-person bias.* This is the tendency for people to think that other people are at greater risk than they themselves are. For example, with media effects, people will attribute greater harmful media effects on others while believing that they are relatively risk-free (Eveland & McLeod, 1999). Peiser and Peter (2000) found that people tend to perceive others as more inclined toward undesirable viewing behaviors, especially if those others are perceived to be less well educated. This effect is also likely to be attributable to other factors, such as self-perceived knowledge or expertise (Salwen & Dupagne, 2001).

2. *First-person bias.* There are times, albeit more rare, when people think they are at greater risk than other people. Some people have a high drive to believe the media content. When this happens, they can overestimate the influence of the content on themselves. However, if a person has a desire to not believe, then there is a third-person effect; that is the effect is not strong on the person but stronger on other people (Eveland & McLeod, 1999).

The third-person effect is situationally specific, argues Perloff (1999). When messages say something socially desirable about people or their group, there is likely to be a first-person effect, that is, people overestimate that desirable thing in their group. But when the messages say something undesirable about their group, they underestimate that thing about their group.

An explanation for this self-enhancement bias comes from social identity theory, which says that people gain self-esteem from their social group memberships to the extent that they can positively contrast their in-group with various out-groups. So they like exposing themselves to media messages with attractive characters who are like them, and this increases the value of their group. Harwood (1997) found that people prefer viewing stories with characters their own age. Viewing this content serves to help people identify more strongly with certain social groups, and this enhances their self-image.

G. Projection Bias

Frequently, people will project their own opinions onto other people, thus believing that all people think like they do. For example, Gunther and Chia (2001) studied news coverage of an issue, then looked at public opinion on that issue. They found that public opinion was largely wrong about the facts of the issue and that the distortions were influenced by personal opinions.

This projection bias is related to something called pluralistic ignorance. If people don't have an opinion about something, they often guess what the majority of people think. Often, these guesses are wrong. But when people do not know their guess is wrong and believe they are right about public opinion, then they create a situation of pluralistic ignorance (O'Gorman, 1986; Shamir & Shamir, 1997).

People infer public opinion by relying on their own subjective assessments of media content. People do not always take the facts into consideration; instead, they are likely to look at how a news story is told; that is, stories with a positive slant will influence people to believe that public opinion is positive on an issue, even if the story presents facts to the contrary (Gunther & Christen, 1999).

H. Appropriateness Heuristic

People make judgments about the behaviors and reactions of others in terms of how appropriate those behaviors and reactions are. Bucy and Newhagen (1999) use this appropriateness heuristic as an explanation about how people can accurately assess the performance of their leaders, even when they do not have much political knowledge; that is, people can read the nonverbal behaviors and make a judgment.

I. Base Rate Versus Exemplars

In most media messages, information can be categorized as being either base rate or an exemplar. Base rate includes facts and figures; they can be specific, such as actual percentages, or general, using terms such as *many, some,* or *lots* (Brosius & Bathelt, 1994). In contrast, an exemplar is episodic information that describes "causes, importance, and consequences of the problem under consideration from the unique perspective of an individual" (Brosius & Bathelt, 1994, p. 48). These are stories, examples, and testimonials.

Research has shown that people typically use exemplar information to create attitudes (Perry & Gonzenbach, 1997). Also, when a message contains many exemplars, people will generalize from them to make base rate inferences, and these often are inaccurate.

People often like to infer patterns from exemplars rather than accept base rate data; this has been found to be the case frequently with news stories. In constructing meaning from news stories, people seem to be most influenced by vivid examples and their own personal risk related to those events. For example, a series of news stories about one gruesome crime can influence people to believe that crime is a problem and one that is increasing in their locale, even when crime is going down and even when such figures are also reported. Thus, vivid examples can be more influential than base rate data (Baesler & Burgoon, 1994; Berger, 2000; Brosius & Bathelt, 1994; Gibson & Zillmann, 1994). Berger speculates that a vivid example of a crime can create an emotional response that prevents the person from using base rate data when they are presented.

J. Overconfidence

Overconfidence is another trap. When people are asked to provide answers to questions, then estimate how confident they are that their answer is correct, they tend to overestimate their level of confidence. Thus, they are compensating for the possibility for being wrong by telling themselves they are right (Fischhoff, 1988).

VI. Summary

Meaning construction is a challenging task; to do it well requires considerable use of skills. Many times, people employ shortcuts in lieu of the active application of these skills. When this happens, people are in danger of making faulty constructions of meaning. Often, the faulty nature of these constructions is not that serious. However, sometimes, the faulty constructions have serious consequences. To increase their media literacy, people need to understand when faulty constructions have serious consequences, then take steps to engage their locus more fully and exercise a stronger drive for more careful construction of meaning so as to avoid the traps.

This chapter detailed many of the traps that prevent people from making useful and accurate meaning constructions. These traps were presented in relation to the skills that people employ in the various stages of meaning construction. The two skills that are associated with the greatest number of traps are the skills of induction and deduction.

Traps in Meaning-Construction Propositions and Research Questions

Propositions for Research

1. Meaning construction is plagued with traps because:
   (a) people are faced with partially specified problems and must make a choice about whether to devote resources to doing the task well or taking shortcuts to complete the tasks quickly.
   (b) there is a very limited amount of resources to devote to these tasks.

2. People who have more highly developed skills and more elaborate knowledge structures have more resources to bring to meaning-construction tasks and are therefore more likely to avoid traps.

3. Traps are keyed to skills.
   (a) The better people are at the skills of analysis, evaluation, and grouping, the more they will be able to avoid traps in preparing information for meaning construction.
   (b) The better people are at the skill of induction, the more they will be able to generate useful and accurate general principles.
   (c) The better people are at the skill of deduction, the more people will be able to select relevant and accurate general principles and to apply them in the deductive process to construct meaning.

Research Questions

1. *Conceptual*
   Are the traps situation-specific, or are they generic to all types of meaning-construction tasks?

   If some traps are found to be generic, which of those:

   are most prevalent?

   are most serious to preventing the construction from being good (accurate and useful)?

   are associated with meaning that has the strongest consequences to a person's life?

   To what extent is faulty construction a matter of lack of knowledge versus lack of drive?

2. *Measurement*
   Can we measure people's encountering traps directly or must we infer this from the observable characteristics in people's reported constructions?

3. *Treatments*
   Which treatments can trigger in people an awareness of traps and their own faulty reasoning?

   Which treatments can trigger in people a drive to avoid traps and to construct higher quality meaning?

PART IV

Practices

CHAPTER 12

Practices

I. The Interpersonal Context
   A. Interpersonal Mediation
      1. Restrictive mediation
      2. Co-Viewing
      3. Active mediation
   B. Use of Program Ratings
   C. What Works?
      1. Restrictive mediation
      2. Co-viewing
      3. Active mediation
   D. Family Communication Styles
   E. Critique of Interpersonal Influence and Recommendations

II. The Institutional Context
   A. Current Curricula
   B. Barriers
   C. Curriculum Design Issues
   D. Teaching Issues
   E. Assessment Issues
   F. Critique of Curriculum Concerns and Recommendations

III. Summary

12

Practices

U p to this point in the book, practices have been in the background, although practices have been an underlying theme throughout the book. While I have focused attention on the importance of media literacy, how it should be defined, and how people process information, the implicit message has been that people can use this perspective to increase their own media literacy.

In this chapter, I bring practices into the foreground as we look at what people (especially parents) can *do* in interpersonal settings to help others (especially their own children) increase media literacy. Then, we look at what the institution of education has done or what people think it should do to help students with their media literacy. The underlying theme of this chapter is that interpersonal practices as well as institutional practices can benefit from a cognitive theory of media literacy.

The primary value of this chapter, I hope, will be to underline the importance of a theory of media literacy. That is, this chapter will demonstrate that the topic is an important one for many reasons and to many people. Any theory of media literacy is ultimately one of informing practices. As a result, it is important to get a sense of what practices have a history, which have been found to be effective, and what barriers are preventing other practices from evolving.

This chapter will demonstrate that we are at the beginning of the challenging task of helping others gain more control over meaning in our media message-saturated culture. This is not to say that no work has been done in this area; to the contrary, many people have worked hard for years to test different techniques, develop courses, and design curricula. However, this work has been largely exploratory and fragmented. Even so, this effort has served to begin building a good base of knowledge about some techniques that seem to work and a few that do not. This chapter will attempt to provide a snapshot of where we are in these efforts.

I. The Interpersonal Context

What can individuals do to help other individuals become more media literate? This is the question underlying this section of the chapter. The research I review in this section has four characteristics. First, it is focused exclusively on children as targets of the techniques. Second, it emphasizes parents (or sometimes siblings, peers, or caregivers) as the agents employing techniques to help children. Third, the research deals almost exclusively with one medium: television. Fourth, the purpose of employing the techniques is to help the targets avoid what the parents feel are negative effects.

A. Interpersonal Mediation

Mediation is an umbrella term that encompasses the techniques parents use to help their children with the media, particularly television. This is a concern because children are watching a great deal of TV, and they are likely watching alone because many have their own TV sets. Jordan (2001) reports the result of a nationwide random sample that found 87% of American households with children have at least two working TV sets in the household. Children are reportedly spending about 2.5 hours per day watching television and almost another hour a day in front of a screen playing video games or on the computer. This is far more time than they spend on homework, about 1.1 hours per day. This degree of exposure has many parents concerned, and they want to do something to protect their children from potentially harmful effects.

Researchers have surveyed parents and found many mediation techniques in use. There are so many techniques and names for techniques that several scholars have observed that the literature on this topic is amorphous, with a wide variety of treatments and measures. This makes the literature difficult to synthesize into a neat set of findings (Austin, Bolls, Fujioka, & Engelbertson, 1999; Nathanson, 2001a). In reviewing 30 years of mediation research in a chapter for the *Communication Yearbook*, Nathanson (2001a) argued,

> Research in this area has not proceeded from a common understanding. This problem is most evident in the lack of a consensus regarding what the term

mediation means. The mediation construct itself has not been adequately defined, leaving us with only a vague idea of what specific behaviors it encompasses. (p. 116)

Therefore, a premium is placed on organizing this thinking. One effort to provide such organization was conducted by Valkenburg, Krcmar, Peeters, and Marseille (1999) in their analysis of random survey data of Dutch parents and their usage of television with their children. They factor-analyzed their data and arrived at the conclusion that there were three techniques, which they labeled as instructive mediation, restrictive mediation, and social co-viewing. With instructive mediation, parents explain or discuss certain aspects of programs. In restrictive mediation, parents set rules for viewing or prohibit children from viewing certain programs. In social co-viewing, parents and children simply watch television together.

Nathanson (2001a) attempted an explication of mediation of children's television viewing and posited that it is composed of three components: active mediation, restrictive mediation, and co-viewing. Active mediation consists of conversations that parents or other adults have with children about television. This talk need not be evaluative. Restrictive mediation involves setting rules about how much, when, and which types of television can be viewed. Co-viewing involves parents and children watching TV together; no conversation is required, and guidance is unfocused. Because this three technique scheme is useful as an organizing device, I will use it to structure the following review of what parents use to help children.

1. *Restrictive mediation.* Several research studies have examined restrictive mediation, in which parents set rules about television usage (Bybee, Robinson, & Turow, 1982; Roberts, Foehr, Rideout, & Brodie, 1999; van der Voort, Nikken, & van Lil, 1992; Weaver & Barbour, 1992). It appears that many households do not have any rules for TV viewing in general. For example, about half (49%) of all children in one study said they have no rules for TV viewing in their households, and 42% of children said that TV is on most of the time in their house (Rideout et al., 1999). However, Jordan (2001) reports that about 61% of parents said they have rules for TV viewing.

What are the rules? Of those families who said they have rules, 92% said they prohibit certain programs, 76% said they require their children to finish homework or chores before viewing, and 69% said they limit the number of hours their children are allowed to watch (Stanger, 1997).

Who uses the rules? The parents who have rules for TV use tend to be mothers who are educated and highly concerned about the negative effects of television (Brown, Childers, Bauman, & Koch, 1990; Bybee et al., 1982; Valkenburg et al., 1999; van der Voort et al., 1992). The children who receive restrictive mediation tend to be younger, but there are no gender differences (Abelman, 1999; Brown et al., 1990). Among children 8 years and older, 61% in one study said they have no rules (Roberts et al., 1999).

Parents who have rules appear to be motivated not by a general concern about exposure but more by a fear that certain content will trigger negative effects. For example, Valkenburg et al. (1999) found in a Dutch survey that parents who have viewing rules are motivated by the concern that their children will watch something that will either scare them or teach them to behave aggressively. This concern was also found by Krcmar and Cantor (1996), who reported that 90% of parents in an American sample said they limit their children's viewing of violent content. Also, Jordan (2001) reports that more parents were concerned about what their children watch on TV (70%) than they are about the amount of TV they watch (19%).

2. *Co-viewing.* The research is inconclusive about how often co-viewing occurs. For example, Valkenburg et al. (1999) found co-viewing more common than active mediation. Jordan (2001) reports that 93% of parents said they watch TV with their children at least once in a while. Also, Sang, Schmitz, and Tasche (1992) found that while co-viewing decreases with age, even with adolescents at 14 years of age, about half were still co-viewing with at least one parent.

Other researchers have found co-viewing to occur rarely (Dorr, Kovaric, & Doubleday, 1989; Lawrence & Wozniak, 1989; Lin & Atkin, 1989). For example, Lawrence and Wozniak found that most viewing was solitary and that when children did view with a family member, it was usually a sibling. Dorr et al. said that co-viewing is more common with older children, who were likely to watch shows the adults also like. But among children 7 years of age and older, 95% in one study never watch TV with their parents, and even among children ages 2 to 7, 81% never watch with their parents (Rideout et al., 1999).

Co-viewing is more likely to occur with mothers (Bybee et al., 1982; McDonald, 1986; van der Voort et al., 1992) and parents who have a more positive orientation toward television (Austin & Pinkleton, 1997; Dorr et al., 1989; Nathanson, 2001a).

3. *Active mediation.* Active mediation is not one technique but an umbrella term for many techniques, usually verbal, that parents use when viewing with their children. As Messaris and Kerr (1984) explain, parents who use active mediation will typically discuss the reality status of programs, make

critical comments about behaviors their children witness of characters on television, and provide supplemental information about topics introduced by the television messages. In a survey of caregivers, Nathanson, Eveland, Park, and Paul (2002) defined active mediation as talking to the children and asking them questions about the content. Austin et al. (1999) found four types of mediation approaches that parents used when viewing with the children. These are: nonmediators (parents who talk about television with their children infrequently), optimists (those whose discussion primarily reinforces television content), cynics (those whose discussion primarily counters television content), and selectives (those who use both positive and negative discussion strategies). Austin et al. also illuminated a difference between positive mediation, which is pointing out the good things in a television message and encouraging children to emulate those good things, and negative mediation, which is pointing out the bad behaviors of characters and being critical of what is portrayed.

Active mediation is rare. Several studies have found that there was generally no dialogue when a parent and child were viewing together (Austin, 1993a; Himmelweit, Oppenheim, & Vince, 1958). A Gallup poll indicates that when parents and a child were viewing television and same offensive material came on the screen, parents were seven times more likely to ignore it by quickly changing the channel than to discuss the offending content with their child (Austin, 1993a). There is evidence that the active mediation comes at the request of children (Reid & Frazer, 1980; Stoneman & Brody, 1982); that is, sometimes, children ask their parents questions while viewing.

Patterns indicate that most of the active mediation is done by mothers and that it is not related to the child's age or gender (Austin et al., 1999; Austin, Knaus, & Meneguelli, 1998; Bybee et al., 1982; van der Voort et al., 1992). Active mediation has also been found among caregivers at day care centers. Nathanson et al. (2002) conducted a survey of 265 nonparent caregivers of second through eighth graders. They found the caregivers provided more active mediation and censorship for violence than for sex on television. They found that when caregivers thought they had effective strategies of active mediation, they were more likely to use mediation when there were high-threat situations. But when the caregivers did not feel they could mediate effectively, they were more likely to use restrictive mediation.

B. Use of Program Ratings

Some tools are available to parents to help monitor their children's exposure. One of these tools is the ratings of films provided by the Motion Picture Association of American for the past three decades. However, in repeated studies, about one third or fewer parents were found to use the MPAA age-based ratings system (Abelman, 1999; Bash, 1997; Mifflin, 1997).

In the mid 1990s, Congress mandated program ratings for television programs so that this information could be fed into a V-chip, which was required on all television sets sold in this country after 1999. However, parents were slow to learn about the ratings. Six months after the introduction of the ratings, Greenberg, Rampoldi-Hnilo and Hofschire (2000) conducted a survey of fourth, eighth, and tenth graders and found that these children and adolescents seldom used the ratings. The survey was repeated a year later, and the findings were the same; about 30% of mothers were not aware of the ratings at all, and those who were aware of the ratings gave them below-average grades for clarity (Rampoldi-Hnilo & Greenberg, 2000). Similar results were found in a pair of Kaiser-funded studies. In one Kaiser study, 82% said they were aware of the ratings, but among those who were aware, only half said they used the ratings (Foehr, Rideout, & Miller, 2000). These figures remained largely unchanged a year later when the survey was repeated (Kaiser Family Foundation, 1999). It appears that parents who are most in need of the ratings are least likely to use them; the ratings are used most by parents who already carefully monitor their children's viewing (Abelman, 2000; Greenberg & Rampoldi-Hnilo, 2001). The development of the TV ratings has done little to stimulate other parents to become more involved in the monitoring of their children's viewing.

In a nationwide random sample, 72% said they are aware of the TV ratings systems and that their children are also aware of the ratings system. However, only 39% said they used the ratings on a regular basis (Jordan, 2001). Also, in a Kaiser Family Foundation report (1998), only 7% of parents could correctly interpret the symbol (FV) for violence in children's programming.

The television ratings system has been widely criticized as not being accurate or useful. For example, there is evidence that the V-chip is not as helpful as hoped (Kunkel et al., 2002). They found that while the age-based ratings (TV-G, TV-PG, TV-14, and TV-MA) were reasonably accurate, the content descriptors (V, S, D, and L) were not being used on the vast majority of programs that contained violence, sexual behavior or dialogue, and adult language. Furthermore, there is evidence that only a small minority of parents are even aware of the meanings of the labels (Kaiser Family Foundation, 1999; Schmitt, 2000). For a more detailed discussion of this topic, see Potter (2003).

C. What Works?

Many interventions have been tried. In reviewing this literature, Nathanson (2001a) shows the complexity inherent in mediation. Some techniques work while others do not; some work with certain kinds of parents or certain kinds of children; and the effects are varied, ranging from cognitions (learning about television messages), attitudes (developing skepticism about ads and news), perceptions (of television reality), and behaviors (including aggression, viewing habits, and response to advertising). For example, Nathanson (2001b) found that parental attitudes were a strong predictor of what techniques a parent used and the effect those techniques would have on their children. Parents with negative attitudes concerning violence on television used active and restrictive mediation whereas parents with positive attitudes used co-viewing. From the child's perspective, restrictive mediation signaled parental disapproval of the content, and co-viewing signaled approval of the content; interestingly, children interpreted active mediation as parental approval of the content (Nathanson, 2001b).

1. *Restrictive mediation.* There is a difference of opinion about the effectiveness of restrictive mediation. Desmond, Singer, Singer, Calam, and Colimore (1985) argue that it has been found to be a useful technique. In contrast, Nathanson (2002) found that restrictive mediation was related to less positive attitudes toward parents, more positive attitudes toward the content, and more viewing of the content with friends. This appears to be opposite of what parents intend as an outcome of using this strategy. Nathanson says, "Unfortunately, parents' good intentions in using restrictive mediation may actually contribute to the harmful outcomes parents wished to prevent in the first place" (p. 221).

2. *Co-viewing.* Like restrictive mediation, co-viewing has had mixed results in the research literature. Co-viewing has also been found to be associated with negative outcomes such as coming to believe that television characters are like real-world people (Messaris & Kerr, 1984) and learning aggression from violent television (Nathanson, 1999). Also, Nathanson (2002) found that co-viewing was related to more positive attitudes toward viewing of television violence and sex. These were interpreted as unintended effects. Nathanson concludes that "parents' consistent pattern of co-viewing objectionable television with their adolescents encourages the youngsters to develop similar media habits" (p. 223).

Co-viewing has been shown to have positive outcomes, such as increasing the learning of educational content (Salomon, 1977). Children who co-view with their parents say they enjoy the programs more (Nathanson, 2001b). However, even when positive effects are found, they are usually fairly weak. For example, Austin and Pinkleton (2001) found that while co-viewing had a positive effect on political socialization, other factors, such as skepticism and negative mediation, had more impact.

Peers are also influential during the adolescent years. Nathanson (2001c) found that peer mediation is more influential than parental mediation during adolescence. Specifically, she found that peer mediation promotes more of an orientation toward antisocial behavior, which then leads to aggression. Thus, the positive influence of parental mediation serves to reduce aggressive behavior, but the negative influence of peer mediation serves to increase it.

3. *Active mediation.* Active mediation techniques have been found useful to help children reduce unwanted effects from viewing television (Austin, 1993b; Nathanson & Cantor, 2000; Nathanson & Yang, 2003). Active mediation seems to work better than more punitive techniques. Parents who try to reason with their children while disciplining them are more effective in reducing the harmful effects of exposure to violence than those parents who use physical punishment (Desmond et al., 1985; Singer, Singer, & Rapaczynski, 1984).

Children who experience active mediation in general are less vulnerable to negative effects of all kinds: cognitive, attitudinal, emotional, and behavioral. As for cognitive effects, active mediation has been successful in teaching children to be more skeptical toward television news (Austin, 1993) and in creating better understanding of television plots (Desmond et al., 1985). With children, parental involvement in media exposure serves to influence learning. Children increase their understanding and recall of both central and incidental program content when adults provide comments to guide their children's attention and understanding during viewing. However, most parents do not usually provide critical insights during TV viewing with their children (McLeod, Fitzpatrick, Glynn, & Fallis, 1982; Roberts, 1973).

As for attitudes, active mediation has been found to reduce perceptions of reality of television messages (Messaris & Kerr, 1984), even with television news (Austin, 1993a), and reduce negative cultivation effects (Rothschild & Morgan, 1987). Nathanson and Botta (2003), reporting results of a survey of adolescents and their parents, found that when parents commented on body images of characters on television, adolescents were more likely to process the images and experience negative emotions. These negative emotions had an impact on behaviors in the form of unhealthy eating or eating disorders.

Active mediation has been helpful in shaping emotional responses to media. Cantor and Wilson (1984) found that negative emotional responses to frightening films could be allayed with active mediation at least with older children (more than 9 years old). Cantor (2001) provides some good advice for parents of children who are experiencing negative emotional effects from the media, especially horror content. Also, Hoffner (1997) talks about the effectiveness of prior knowledge of a happy outcome in reducing fear for some children.

As for behavior, active mediation has been found to lower levels of aggression (Corder-Bolz, 1980; Grusec, 1973; Hicks, 1968; Nathanson, 1999; Nathanson & Cantor, 2000; Singer et al., 1984) and reduce the influence of advertising (Reid, 1979).

Nathanson (2001c) found that peer mediation was more effective than parental mediation. She found that peer mediation led to more positive orientations toward antisocial television, which in turn led to greater aggression. Of course, the intention of parental mediation is to inhibit negative media effects, but peer mediation facilitates harmful outcomes.

The success of mediation techniques is also tied to the type of person who is the target. For example, Nathanson and Yang (2003) demonstrate that certain techniques work well with younger children (5 to 8 years old). These techniques were to emphasize the factually inaccurate nature of a show or to emphasize how socially unrealistic the portrayals were. But these techniques were not found to work well with older children (9 to 12 years old). The authors speculated that perhaps the older children already understood those lessons and did not want to hear a lecture, feeling that such advice was pedantic or condescending. Also, some techniques work better with one gender. For example, Nathanson and Cantor (2000) tested a mediation technique of getting children to become involved with victims of violence in cartoons rather than the aggressors. This worked with boys but not girls; that is, it was successful in preventing boys from increasing their aggressive behavior subsequent to viewing the violence in the cartoon.

Mediation works better when parents are more active during television viewing (Austin, 1993a). Parents need to ask questions continually and engage their children in discussions about the meaning of actions. Parents need to explain the meaning of words, pictures, narratives, etc. Cantor (2001) provides an analysis of particular cognitive and noncognitive strategies that can be used when dealing with children's fright reactions to horror shows in the media. She says that in general, preschool children benefit more from noncognitive than cognitive strategies. Among elementary school children, both types of strategies work well, but children prefer the cognitive strategies. Cognitive strategies rely on a person verbally casting the threat in a different light. "When dealing with fantasy depictions, the most typical cognitive strategy seems to be to provide an explanation focusing on the unreality of the situation" (p. 215). In contrast, noncognitive strategies "do

240 Practices

not involve the processing of verbal information and appear to be relatively automatic" (p. 214). One noncognitive technique is visual desensitization, which showing a person repeated images that are sequenced to build from nonthreatening to very threatening so the person is gradually desensitized. Also, Desmond (1997a) provides some detailed suggestions about how parents can do things in their homes to increase the media literacy of their children, particularly to help them with their perceptions of reality, and to increase their knowledge about production techniques and the commercial nature of the media.

Role modeling has been found to be a successful technique. Often, children will select their own role models, but parents in active mediation can influence the models children choose and sensitize them to certain characteristics of those characters that make them good role models. Children are likely to model their behavior after attractive characters they see in the media. This modeling can be shaped by interpersonal strategies, especially from parents who are themselves good role models (Austin & Meili, 1995; Hogan, 2001; Slater & Rouner, 2002). For example, Austin and Meili (1995) found that children use their emotion and logic to develop expectations about alcohol use in the real world when they see alcohol used by characters on television. When children rely on both real life and televised sources of information, children are more likely to develop skepticism about television portrayals of alcohol use when they rely on parents as primary sources of information and behavioral modeling.

Slater and Rouner (2002) observe that social cognitive theory has been a useful explanation for the effectiveness of educational messages in entertainment programs because of role modeling. However, they argue that the elaboration likelihood model is an additional explanation, especially for those people who do not have role models on shows; these people are likely to have low involvement, and this makes them even more susceptible to the influence of such messages. Thus, if these people were highly involved and were likely to argue against the messages, their low involvement defuses the counterarguments.

D. Family Communication Styles

Research on family communication patterns is often evoked by mediation researchers as a context for the explaining why certain types of families use particular mediation techniques. The earliest conceptualization on family communication styles and how they relate to media use can arguably be traced to the 1970s, when several media scholars used family communication patterns as a possible explanation for how the media are used in a household and how those varying uses could account for differences in effects (Chaffee & McLeod, 1972; Chaffee, McLeod, & Atkin, 1971). These scholars speculated that there were four types of families in terms of how they regard other family members and how they communicate. The consensual family encourages a high degree of communication that is cooperative, not conflictual; communication is open and continues until all family members can agree. In contrast, laissez faire families allow members to disagree but do not encourage communication about those disagreements. People get to be who they are as long as they allow others to be who they are. The pluralistic family is one in which conflict is high and people openly debate their positions. The protective family is characterized by strong authority figures who preserve harmony and family unity, but discussion is not tolerated. Rules govern behaviors to preserve the common good of the family, and those rules are strictly enforced.

Family communication style has been used as an explanation for mediation techniques. For example, Krcmar (1996) found that protective families were more likely to have rules for media use and to enforce them more strongly. In a later study, Krcmar (1998) showed children clips of violence while varying the perpetrator's motives and punishment of the violent act. She also measured the child's family communication patterns and found that children who were from households with higher levels of communication were more likely to see motivated violence as more justified. Children who were from families where control was important were likely to see punishment for violence as less justified. In addition, children who were more control oriented and who had perceived the violent clip as justified chose aggressive story endings significantly more frequently than other children.

F. Critique of Interpersonal Influence and Recommendations

Given the few scholars who have worked on this topic of mediation, it is a positive sign that the literature is as strong as it is. Still there are many gaps. I will address five concerns with the existing literature and provide direction for where future research can make the strongest contributions.

First, as useful as Nathanson's three types of mediation scheme is, this needs further development. There are so many techniques that we need more of a taxonomy to display the variety of those techniques in an organized fashion. This taxonomy would be useful to researchers who want to design treatments to test the relative effectiveness of several techniques in one study. Also, it would be of use to practitioners who want to know their full set of options when they design instructional modules. A large part of this effort will be in developing definitions for the different techniques. For example, today, it is unclear where the lines are drawn between restrictive mediation, co-viewing, and active mediation. What is a rule? Is it a prohibition, or can it be a requirement? Does it count if it is not enforced? What counts as enforcement? Without a clear definition of a rule, it is impossible to compare findings across studies on restrictive mediation. Another key term is co-viewing. Does it mean parent and child in the same room while the TV is on? Can the parent be talking to the child? If so, how much talking does there need to be for something to change from co-viewing to active mediation? Or does the difference lie in what is said rather than in how much?

With active mediation, so many possible techniques can be used. We need a taxonomy of different techniques to classify them and give each a definition that can be shared by researchers. Then, research needs to be conducted to determine which techniques work under which conditions and with what types of children. Next, we need to know which techniques work best so that we can devote our limited resources to the techniques that have the greatest chance of succeeding. Finally, we need to consider how to sequence techniques into an overall strategy that builds systematically and efficiently toward a higher degree of media literacy.

Second, we need to expand our samples, especially in regard to age. Today, the literature is composed of studies in which the targets are almost always children. Parents (or sometimes siblings, peers, or caregivers) are usually the agents employing techniques to help children. We need to pay more attention to adolescents. Also, adults are totally ignored as targets of mediation. As controversial as this might sound, I argue that there is great value in designing studies where the children are the agents of the mediation and the parents are their targets. When taking a multidimensional perspective on media literacy, we must consider that many children are more media literate in certain ways than are their parents. If research can identify where these areas are, then the developing of media literacy in families can be more of a cooperative and mutually beneficial enterprise.

Third, we need to test techniques beyond the medium of television. The current research deals almost exclusively with television. While television is important, we know that children spend a great deal of time with other media, especially computers, and when they grow into adolescence, they will spend a great deal of time with radio and recordings.

Fourth, we need to shift away from collecting data in self-report questionnaires and do more observation in natural settings. Much of the current literature is based on self-report data. There is reason to be skeptical of data like these, which are so sensitive to many uncontrolled threats to validity. This lack of validity seems to be in evidence when we examine the discrepancy between what parents say and what their children say in surveys that ask questions of both groups (Austin, 1993b; Carlson, 1990; Greenberg, Ericson, & Blahos, 1972; Lyle & Hoffman, 1972; Tolan, Gorman-Smith, Huesmann, & Zelli, 1997). Typically, parents report more rules, more family interaction, and less TV viewing. For example, in a survey of parents and their first-grade children, 40% of mothers said they have rules limiting their children's viewing, but only 19% of their children said they had such rules (Lyle & Hoffman, 1972). There are several reasons why the discrepancy might exist. One reason is desirability; few parents like to admit they do not care what their children watch on TV. Another reason for the discrepancy might be the difference in defining rules between parents and children. For example, Holz (1998) conducted focus group discussions with children and found that many children say there are rules that the parents lay down but that those rules are inconsistently enforced so they don't count as rules.

We need to conduct the observations in a longitudinal manner. We need to be more careful to distinguish between unusual behaviors triggered by the demand conditions of research and the habitual patterns. Also, when people are subjected to interventions and exhibit some change, we need to monitor those people over time to determine if the change is a lasting one or if those people return to their old habits shortly after the intervention.

Fifth and finally, we need to think more about how we can design techniques to move beyond increasing awareness and also strengthen the locus. We need to figure out how to motivate people to increase their drive states and to condition them so that the positive drive states become drive traits. This requires much more consideration of the emotional elements in the endeavor. Cognitions are important and should not be overlooked, but there is more to developing media literacy, especially if it is to be lasting. Most important, we must realize that any techniques we try (or that parents try with their children) are merely "priming the pump" activities. That is, we cannot be there every step along the way with other people on their journey to greater media literacy. The most we can do is to show people the path and motivate them to take the steps themselves. Showing them the path is the cognitive part. Motivating them is the emotional part.

II. The Institutional Context

This section shifts our attention to a more macro level. First, I will briefly show the fragmentary nature of media literacy curricula in this country, then examine the barriers that prevent a more unified approach to media education. Next, we'll address three issues of curriculum design, teaching, and assessment. This section then concludes with a critique of curriculum concerns and recommendations.

A. Current Curricula

Critics have observed that the United States lags behind many other countries in developing media literacy courses and curricula in public schools (Brown, 1991, 1998, 2001; Considine, 1997; Davies, 1997; Kubey, 1997; Piette & Giroux, 1997; Sizer, 1995). The long list of countries that are far ahead of the United States with media literacy curricula include Australia, Canada, Great Britain, South Africa, Scandinavia, Russia, and Israel, as well as many other countries in Europe, South America, and Asia (Brown, 1991; Piette & Giroux, 1997). For example, Australia has had mandated media education from kindergarten to 12th grade since the mid 1990s. This curriculum stresses aesthetics and semiotics, with a liberal humanist approach to the popular arts (Brown, 1998). Also:

> In the U.K. and some Latin American counties, empowerment of media consumers is paramount often focusing on industry control through corporate and governmental hegemony. Media education there stresses "representational" and oppositional ideologies, power, and politics and ways to participate in mainstream media or construct alternative media outlets. (Brown, 1998, p. 45)

Critics point out that the relative lack of attention to media education in the United States is a serious problem, because the United States is the most media-saturated country in the world. More time and money is spent on media consumption in the United States than in any other country in the world, yet our educational system virtually ignores media education (Sizer, 1995). This is not to say that there are no media literacy efforts in America's schools; however, their existence is rare and largely unsupported by the institution of education. For example, Brown (2001) attributes the teaching of media literacy in this country to "isolated teachers [who] introduced mass media topics into their classrooms, usually within the context of traditional content such as English or history social studies" (p. 683). He continues, "Schedules already crowded with curricular mandates had no time for yet another addition, so whatever media study could be introduced was typically integrated into already existing courses" (p. 683).

Some states have been discussing media literacy and trying to get initiatives going. Kubey (1998) notes "significant statewide initiatives" in New Mexico and North Carolina, with "noteworthy developments" in Wisconsin and Minnesota. A few years ago Hobbs (1998) reported that media literacy concepts are included in the curriculum frameworks in more than 15 states, and "ongoing efforts are in place in many U.S. school districts. Interest in media education is even growing among mainstream education organizations and health professionals, including the National Association of Secondary School Principals and the American Academy of Pediatrics" (p. 24). Initiatives are growing, but we need to monitor whether this talk about the importance of media literacy and its inclusion in mission statements translates into meaningful implementation.

B. Barriers

Why is there so little sustained effort to develop and implement media literacy curricula in the United States when there are many good efforts in other countries? There appear to be many obstacles for further development of media literacy (see Brown, 2001; Considine, 1997; Davies, 1997; and Kubey, 1997; for a more complete treatment of these).

Arguably the most critical obstacle is the lack of centralized decision making concerning education in the United States. Brown (1998) points out that curriculum decisions are spread out over 15,000 school districts, each with its own school board and administrators. Kubey (1998) elaborates on this argument by pointing out that the United States is a huge country with a highly diversified population and no central governmental policy on media literacy to pull things together. Also, only 4% of U.S. educational expenditures come from the federal government (Kubey, 1998). Thus, in this country, the power to make curriculum decisions lies at the state and especially local levels. Each of these decision-making bodies has its mix of personalities, needs, and political agendas.

Lack of attention to the special circumstances in each school's culture was to blame in large part for the failure of media literacy efforts that were tried in the 1970s (Anderson, 1983). Hobbs (1998) points out that "media literacy initiatives have been most successful in school communities where teachers, parents, and students have a shared, common vision about their love-hate relationship with media culture" (p. 23). Brown (1998) says, "If media literacy studies are to survive and grow, administrators in school systems and at individual schools must endorse and support them. [Media studies] should not be left wholly dependent on the initiative and energy of isolated teachers" (p. 52). Brown calls for a more holistic and continuing approach.

To succeed, a curricular program of media literacy must be developed through collaboration among teachers, administrators, specialists, and parents, who together must build it into the systematic education process. Media study should not be a mere appendage of a random elective course, nor should media technology be used merely as a tool or aid to teach other subjects. That means developing studies geared to the participants' successive levels of cognitive development based on educational and behavioral research findings. It also means continuing and integrating studies into successive grade levels through the school years. (p. 52).

But all this comes with a high cost. Other curricula must be replaced with the media literacy one. Teaching media literacy also requires a sustained commitment that includes substantial training of teachers. Hobbs (1998) says,

> The most successful efforts to include media literacy in schools have taken 2 or more years of staff development to build a clearly defined understanding of the concept as it relates to classroom practice among a substantial number of teachers and school leaders within a school district. (p. 23–24)

Then once trained, the teachers need to be supported continually by the institution rather than left on their own. Hobbs (1998) explains that a study of teacher performance in Great Britain yielded depressing results. Among the teachers who completed training in media literacy education, about 40% ended up doing nothing, 25% did something moderately well, 10% did something creatively exceptional, and the remaining 25% did something embarrassing, dangerous, or just a waste of time.

Unless resources are provided, there are significant barriers to implementation. For example, one recent study reports that while most high school teachers believe the study of media is important, 40% do not teach it at all because of constraints on time and curriculum space (cited in Brown, 2001). The same pattern was found in Maryland, where language arts teachers regarded media literacy as important to teach, but the lack of training, materials, and time prevented many from teaching it (Koziol, 1989). Brown (2001) observed that few teachers receive training to deal with the challenge of teaching media literacy, either in their college degree programs or in workshops for teacher certification. However, most teachers feel that they are qualified to teach media literacy, even though only about one third have any training.

Curriculum designers often look to media literacy scholars for guidance. However, scholars disagree about what media literacy is and what its goals should be (see Chapter 2). Two of the more pressing definitional issues when it comes to curriculum design are tone and texts. As for tone, Brown (1991) complains that "many media workshops and curricula are protectionist and defensive. They seek to inoculate consumers against blandishments of images and messages of media entertainment, news, and advertising" (p. 45). As for texts, Hobbs (1998) observes that while media texts have always been essential in education, rarely are those texts "considered beyond their function as conveyers of information" (p. 25). They need to be the objects of inquiry (Kress, 1992). People need to analyze the corporations who produce and disseminate those texts and understand their motives. Also, the texts themselves need to be analyzed for what they leave out, how they are structured, and the basis for their claims, both from an aesthetic and moral perspective.

This diversity of opinion gets magnified as we move out to consumer activists, teachers, and school administrators, who have a range of opinions concerning what a media literacy curriculum should be composed of, what should be taught, how it should be taught, and how its effect should be assessed. The good thing about this diversity is that it provides a wide range of ideas for instruction and a variety of curriculum models to the many different school systems in this country. If most of the school systems were entrepreneurial and willing to search out the techniques that would fit the special culture in their district, then this variety would pay big dividends. But most school districts are conservative about change. Teachers and administrators already feel they are asked to cover too many topics, so they cannot add another one without a strong reason.

The diversity of ideas among scholars appears more as an academic debate than as a convincing argument to shift resources. If scholars are to present a convincing argument, they need a perspective that integrates the best thinking into a clear set of principles that can guide their decision making on three key issues: curriculum design, teaching, and assessment.

C. Curriculum Design Issues

Three main questions are associated with curriculum. All three apply to both K through 12 and higher education. The first is what is the purpose of the curriculum? The second is how should media literacy fit into the curriculum (Bazalgette, 1989; Hart, 1997; Quin & McMahon, 1997)? The third is what are the key elements/principles of media literacy that should be taught?

In building a curriculum, there is a tension between the often competing goals of training students for specific tasks that could help them get a job and educating students in a liberal manner to be prepared for our complex society (Buckingham, 1998a, 1998b; Kubey, 1998). In the United States, many media education programs in higher education define their missions in terms of preparing students to become practitioners in the media industry (Christ & Hynes, 1997; Rowland, 1999). This narrow focus is challenged by the work being done in media literacy. Because media literacy debates are normally about K though 12 education, training students for employment is rarely a key element in the discussion. As for media educators in higher education, the key concern is what would happen to their programs if they did not teach production and writing skills for employment. What would these programs have to offer if their purpose was instead to educate students to become media literate citizens and consumers (Blanchard & Christ, 1993; McLaren et al., 1995; Sholle & Denski, 1994)? The point is that because media have become intertwined with people's professional, civic, and personal lives, a media literacy orientation suggests that the primary purpose of media education should be to educate students broadly.

This does not mean, however, that all media literacy advocates reject input from people working in the media industries. In the United States, many media programs in higher education pride themselves on developing links with practitioners (Limberg, 1994; Metsger, 1996). Some people involved in the K through 12 media literacy movement suggest that practitioners, working closely with media educators, have much to offer media education (Bazalgette, 1997; Masterman, 1997). In Great Britain, academics and practitioners were able to agree that media education should foster "the development of a critical spirit" while encouraging "collaboration with professional people and agencies in both fields" (Commission 1, 1992, pp. 222–223).

If the aim of media education is to teach students to become practitioners, then the question that needs to be asked is: which practitioner role should be selected in which industry? Do media educators in higher education really want local news broadcasters coming in and telling their students how to perpetuate the status quo in local newscasts? Or, would it be better to get someone from the telephone industry to explain how fiber optics will transform people's ability to send and receive media information? Or should someone explain the regulatory environment that has allowed certain companies to flourish and others to wither? Do we want speakers supporting the current system or challenging the status quo?

Exposing students to industry practices and practitioners raises the issue of whether or not to train students in the current techniques of media production. This is one of the current debates in the K through 12 media literacy movement (Hobbs, 1998). On the one hand, this exposure could lead to a greater understanding among students about how messages are constructed. Messaris (1998) argues that asking students to produce media messages is a good technique to sensitize them to how they treat visual images as natural analogies to underlying meanings in those messages. This greater understanding could increase their skepticism. Zettl (1998) argues that production is an important way of knowing the world and provides a model that helps frame production questions.

However, Lewis and Jhally (1998) believe the teaching of production could be detrimental to heightening student awareness. They argue:

> [Many assume that] a practical knowledge of video production on its own will help demystify the world of television, necessarily promoting a more analytical, critical perspective. There is, however, little evidence to support such an assumption. On the contrary, we have found that students are apt to be seduced by the form, to try to imitate commercial television. (p. 115)

To distinguish between experiences that replicate the status quo in media industries and those that challenge it, Blanchard and Christ (1993) made a distinction between workshops (which replicate the management structure, forms, and content of current media) and laboratories (which challenge the status quo). They recommend that programs should be challenging the status quo. Media literacy efforts should encourage those students who want to become practitioners to make the industry news outlets better.

Scholars who study curriculum for media literacy across countries have noticed a wide variety of ways that media literacy has been incorporated into curricula (Brown, 1991, 1998; Kubey, 1997; Masterman, 1997). For example, Masterman (1997) finds four basic models in Europe: media studies as a specialist discipline in it own right; media education as a coherent element taught within an already established curriculum subject; media education across the curriculum; and aspects of media studies as a topic within an integrated (nonsubject-based) curriculum and generally taught by an interdisciplinary team. This form of media education is often found within primary school curricula. Hobbs (1998) says one of the big issues with media literacy is the debate about whether it should be taught as a "specialist subject" or integrated into existing courses so that it would permeate the entire curriculum. If it is a special subject, then it seems too isolated and reduced far below what its importance should be. Also, many school systems might not offer just another course, and those that offer it as an elective might not get many students to take it. On the other hand, if media literacy issues are to permeate all courses, the training problem is huge.

Once it is decided where media literacy should be situated in the curriculum, the components of the curriculum (see Brown, 1991, 1998; Hobbs, 1998) need to be determined. That is, what are the elements that are inherent in a successful media program? What are the guidelines for an effective media literacy program? This leads into questions of teaching and assessment.

D. Teaching Issues

Media literacy scholars have questioned the traditional role of the teacher in education (see Bazalgette, 1997; Brown, 1991, 1998; Buckingham, 1990; Kubey, 1998; Masterman, 1980, 1985, 1997; Sholle & Denski, 1994). There is a sense that the very act of studying media can help democratize the teacher-student relationship, because the act of critique is one of "reflection and dialogue" (Masterman, 1997, p. 44). There is even a sense that media literacy demands a different type of teaching that is democratic and non-hierarchical (Bazalgette, 1997; Masterman, 1980, 1985, 1997). Buckingham (1993b) challenges those who argue that teaching media literacy can be both proscriptive and nonhierarchical; trying to demystify students while using a nonhierarchical pedagogy, he says, "clearly places the teacher in a contra-dictory position—on the one hand, as the bearer of a 'truth' that is not avail-able to the students, yet on the other as an equal partner in dialogue" (p. 287). If the goal of media programs in higher education is to educate students to become reflective, self-directed communication citizens and, perhaps, practitioners, then the process of teaching can be seen as moving students from dependency to self-direction (Grow, 1990). Ultimately, espousing a New Professionalism for students that combines liberal arts and professional education means that, ultimately, media education needs to encourage student self-direction and "students' rights, obligations, and responsibility for their own education" (Blanchard & Christ, 1993, p. 134). By carefully looking at the teacher-student relationship, media literacy also suggests the need to investigate not only teaching styles but also student learning styles (Potter, 1993; Potter & Clark, 1991; Potter & Emanuel, 1990). Students have profoundly different motivations and agendas for their education. Unless we as educators recognize this and plan our teaching to meet these challenges, our efforts will fail to engage large segments of students, who will expect media education to be something radically different than we offer.

Active mediation in the schools has been shown to help children think more critically about television messages (Abelman & Courtright, 1983; Ball & Bogatz, 1970; Corder-Bolz, 1980; Desmond et al., 1985; Dorr, Graves, & Phelps, 1980; Hobbs & Frost, 1997; Matthews & Desmond, 1997; Rapaczynski, Singer, & Singer, 1982; Reiser, Tessmer, & Phelps, 1984; Roberts, Christenson, Gibson, Mooser, & Goldberg, 1980; Singer, Zuckerman, & Singer, 1980; Watkins, Calvert, Huston-Stein, & Wright, 1980). The key seems to be to keep children active by asking questions and challenging what is happening (Reiser et al., 1984). In fact, it appears that the questioning alone is more important than getting answers to those questions from an outside person (Reiser, Williamson, & Suzuki, 1988). Thus, the key is being an active viewer; once children are active, they become more skeptical, and accomplishing that alone is worthwhile. Also, once they begin asking questions, children become oriented toward constructing their own meaning.

Teachers of reading—traditional literacy—have been debating approaches to the teaching of reading for a long time. Of the two dominant approaches, one is skills-based reading instruction, and the other is text-based literary interpretation. Both teach students to find the meaning in the text. In one, the teacher's role is to impart information about the properties of the text, focusing attention on structure, language, and conventions. The instructional goal is comprehension, and readers demonstrate this by "their command of factual information in the text" (Vacca & Newton, 1995, p. 283). Comprehension of a literary text is called interpretation, explication, or exegesis; it is demonstrated by identifying the truth or deep meaning buried in the literary text. This latter approach, sometimes called the whole-language approach, is more dominant now. Under this approach, teachers believe that reading should be meaning based. Therefore, students should write daily in their journal, and they should do lots of silent and oral reading of literature. Students should not learn individual meanings, so they do not use flash cards, phonic drills, memorization, or a focus on the component tasks of reading (Ehri, 1995).

To put this debate in terms of the cognitive model of media literacy, the reading debate is whether to teach reading as a meaning-matching or meaning-construction task. Clearly, both are needed. At the beginning stages of reading, teachers need to treat this as a meaning-matching task in which students are taught to recognize symbols and match the denoted meaning to those symbols. That is foundational; unless students acquire these competencies, they will be unable to learn how to construct their own meaning. Both tasks are part of reading, and in a larger sense, both are required for processing information from any type of media message.

Whether reading is taught as a meaning-matching or a meaning-construction task, several teaching techniques have been found to work well. For example, Carver (1995) talks about the apprenticeship approach to reading, in which the teacher must be a master or expert of the relevant content. Apprenticeship also implies learning relationships for a significant period of time. Also, Holubec, Johnson, and Johnson (1995) talk about cooperative learning. They caution that it is not the same as group work. In group learning, students are still responsible only for themselves; in cooperative learning, members are responsible for each other's learning as well as their own, with high positive interdependence. In group learning, assignments are discussed with little commitment to each other's learning; in cooperative learning, members promote each other's success and support each other's efforts to learn. In group learning, teamwork skills are ignored as a leader is appointed; in cooperative learning, teamwork skills are emphasized, and leadership is shared. In group learning, individual accomplishments are rewarded; in cooperative learning, all members process the quality of the work, and continuous improvement is emphasized. Clearly, cooperative learning has more advantages. Teachers of media literacy would do well to be trained in techniques of cooperative learning.

E. Assessment Issues

In the United States, assessment of educational effectiveness is a large part of the accountability movement. Parents, legislative bodies, administrators, and accrediting associations all want evidence that educational resources are being spent wisely and that students are learning. K through 12 schools are under pressure to continually assess their effectiveness (Rosenbaum, 1994).

The troublesome question underlying all assessment is what is evidence of learning? This is especially a problem with media literacy where there is so much disagreement about the goals. In the United States, there is no national standard. Perhaps the closest to an attempt at a certified national standard has been articulated by the National Communication Association, which has taken a lead in communication and media assessment efforts. That group released 23 national standards with 2 applying to media literacy:

> Standard 22: The effective media participant can demonstrate the effects of the various types of electronic audio and visual media, including television, radio, the telephone, the Internet, computers, electronic conferencing, and film, on media consumers.

> Standard 23: The effective media participant can demonstrate the ability to identify and use skills necessary for competent participation in communication across various types of electronic audio and visual media.

Even if people could accept these standards as a goal, many decisions still need to be made. What should be assessed? Knowledge? Skills? Behaviors? Attitudes? Values? And what is the standard? Is a B average in all courses the mark of literacy, or are assumptions of literacy tested with assessment strategies (Christ, 1994, 1997; Christ, McCall, Rakow, & Blanchard, 1997).

Assessment schemes vary by curriculum. For example, one curriculum model is to integrate the teaching of media literacy fully across the entire curriculum. If this is done well, media literacy ends up being invisible. This invisibility may be a positive characteristic from a curriculum point of view, but this presents an impossible task from an assessment point of view.

Clearly, we are at the very beginning of the huge challenge posed by assessment. Before we can make any progress with the task of assessment, we first need to solve the problems of goals, standards, and curriculum design.

F. Critique of Curriculum Concerns and Recommendations

The problems over curriculum can be traced back to a lack of a useful definition of media literacy. To be useful, a media literacy definition must be clear and compelling. If it is clear, it can be understood by everyone. To be compelling it must provide strong reasons for the value of media literacy, so that people believe that it is not only worth the considerable costs but also— and more important—essential. This can be achieved if it is convincingly shown that media literacy is fundamental to all education, that is, that all information today comes to the student either directly or indirectly through some form of media and that the development of skills to process this information is generic to all educational endeavors.

A useful definition focuses attention on what needs to be achieved. Once people have a common goal, the challenge shifts to the less abstract tasks of implementation, that is, how to recruit and train teachers, how to develop materials, and how to structure courses and curriculum. With a clear and common goal, assessment is a more manageable challenge. This is the first step. Without a clear and compelling definition, the effort spent on all downstream educational tasks will have little lasting payoff.

Next, what is needed is a body of knowledge to guide the preparation of materials, courses, and ultimately the overarching curriculum. This body of knowledge needs to be affirmative. This means that there needs to be a designation of what works rather than criticism of negative practices. This knowledge needs to be tested through research rather than speculation. While speculation is good to direct research efforts, the tests are essential to develop confidence in certain knowledge principles that could guide pedagogy and do so in an efficient manner.

Some thought needs to be given to calibrating effort with payoff. That is, we need to start small with sound successes, then build on them to become more ambitious step by step until a full course is developed, then build toward a curriculum. We need to be realistic with our limited resources and start with those things that have smaller costs in relation to their payoffs. For example, some scholars have argued that students need to learn production skills in order to be media literate. Of course, these skills would help, but the cost of teaching them is high, and the payoff is marginal. People can learn many more fundamental ideas about media literacy without having to take a production course. Also, compared to production skills, many other skills are more central to media literacy and more transferable to other courses and to life itself.

In essence, I support the bottom-up approach that we currently have. We must be realistic about how the educational institution in this country is structured. It relies on a bottom-up approach, and it is most successful when it operates this way rather than responding to procrustean mandates coming down from bureaucrats who are removed from the local culture. However, to make more progress, we also need to be more systematic in sharing information so that the wheel does not have to be reinvented in hundreds of scattered classrooms. We need to find good examples of media literacy programs that work, that is, where teachers and students are committed to a common goal in which learning creates energy. For example, Bernhardt and Antonacci (1995) write about thinking environments. People should find places where there is successful learning and approach them much like an anthropologist would. Look at the social interactions as an ethnographer does. Study the physical world and its artifacts. When we find these media-literacy thinking environments, we can share the success stories, and that would seem to have the best chance of stimulating others to want to do the same.

III. Summary

The topic of helping others become more media literate is a large one, with writings scattered across many fields of scholarship (such as media studies, education, psychology, sociology, and English, to name a few) as well as the popular press and practitioners' materials such as Web sites, memos, state directives, and so on. Therefore, this chapter could not present a definitive treatment. Instead, this chapter addressed the more modest task of sketching out the parameters of thinking on this topic.

The chapter first dealt with the research and thinking about interpersonal techniques; then, it examined the more macro issue of providing help through the institution of education. It was argued that the thinking in these areas is strong on breadth and creativity. What is missing is a unified perspective that can guide research, thinking, and practices. Such a perspective can guide researchers to the most pressing questions, channel that research into programs that efficiently use resources to increase knowledge about what works, and make the task of synthesizing findings much more meaningful. Also, such a perspective can help parents understand the tasks they face when trying to help their children maximize the benefits from media exposures while avoiding potential negative effects. Such a perspective can help in curriculum design, teacher training, and learning assessment.

My thesis in this book has been that we need a cognitive theory of media literacy to help us understand more about media literacy. In this chapter, the thesis takes the more specific form that such a theory can help guide the design of practices used by individuals and institutions. To make progress, especially with few resources, we need to be clearer about what the advantages of media literacy are, as well as the related costs. Also, we need a better sense of what kinds of mediations work and why. Finally, we need a good sense of the value of all this if we are to be successful in institutionalizing media literacy into public education.

Appendix A
Definitions of Literacy

This appendix displays a range of definitions of media literacy put forth by a variety of scholars. It is organized into two sections: Definitions focusing primarily on skills and definitions focusing primarily on knowledge. Within each of these two sections, the definitions are presented chronologically from earliest to most recent.

Definitions Focusing Primarily on Skills

☐ Sholle and Denski (1995) emphasize three skills: (a) re-reading the media, (b) affective reflexivity, and (c) rewriting and the vital strategy of authorship.

☐ Hobbs (1996) lists analysis, reasoning, communication, and self-expression skills.

☐ Hobbs (1997b) says the component skills are access, analyze, evaluate, and communicate.

☐ Desmond (1997b) says people need to be critical consumers of entertainment and advertising fare, and they need to have insight and information from which they can watch.

☐ The National Leadership Conference on Media Literacy says, "A media literate person . . . can decode, evaluate, analyze, and produce both print and electronic media" (in Aufderheide, 1997, p. 79).

☐ Messaris (1998) argues that "a central component of media literacy should be an understanding of the representational conventions through which the users of media create and share meanings," especially visual representations (p. 70).

☐ Brown (1998) says that traditionally media literacy "has involved the ability to analyze and appreciate respected works of literature, and by extension, to communicate effectively by writing well. In the past half-century it has come to include the ability to analyze competently and to utilize skillfully print journalism, cinematic productions, radio and television programming, and even computer-mediated information and exchange (including real-time interactive exploration through the global internet)" (p. 44).

☐ Hobbs (1998a) says media literacy is "the process of critically analyzing and learning to create one's own messages in print, audio, video, and multimedia" (p. 16).

☐ Silverblatt, Ferry, and Finan (1999) say there are five types of analysis to media literacy: ideological analysis, autobiographical analysis, nonverbal communication analysis, mythic analysis, and analysis of production techniques.

☐ Rafferty (1999) says people need to be critical consumers of ideas and information. This involves interpreting media messages (creating personal meaning from codes and conventions) as well as thinking critically about them.

☐ Adams & Hamm (2000a) define it as "composing, comprehending, analyzing, and appreciating the multiple print and nonprint symbol systems" (p. 4).

Definitions Focusing Primarily on Knowledge

☐ Pattison (1982) argued that people need to have knowledge about the questions posed by language, regardless of the medium that transmits that language.

☐ Silverblatt (1995) said there are four keys that people need to interpret media messages. These are the understanding of the process, context, structure, and production values.

☐ A national leadership conference on media came up with a list of five ideas its members could agree were parts of media literacy. These are: (a) media messages are constructed; (b) media messages are produced within economic, social, political, historical, and aesthetic contexts; (c) the interpretation meaning-making processes involved in message reception consist of an interaction between the reader, the text, and the culture; (d) media have unique languages, characteristics that typify various forms, genres, and symbol systems of communication; and (e) media representations play a role in people's understanding of social reality (Aufderheide, 1993).

☐ Hobbs (1997a) says that media literacy is based on the following "key analytic concepts": all messages are constructions; messages are representations of social reality; individuals negotiate meaning by interacting with messages; messages have economic, political, social and aesthetic purposes; each form of communication has unique characteristics.

☐ Masterman (1997) analyzed the media literacy movement in Europe between 1970 and 1990 and says there are eight component ideas:

1. The central and unifying concept of media education is that of representation. This means that the media do not reflect reality but represent it.

2. A central purpose of the media education is to "denaturalize" the media. This means creating an understanding that the media messages are constructions and do not occur naturally.

3. "Media education is primarily investigative. It does not seek to impose specific cultural values. It aims to increase students' understanding of how the media represent reality. Its objective is to produce well-informed citizens who can make their own judgements on the basis of the available evidence. In so far as media education deals with value judgements, it does so in the ways which encourage students to explore the range of value judgements made about a given media text and to examine the sources of such judgements (including their own) and their effects. It does not seek to impose ideas on what constitutes 'good' or 'bad' television, newspapers, or films" (p. 41).

4. Media education is organized around key concepts, which are analytical tools rather than an alternative content. They do not seek to replace "bad" content with "better" content.

5. Media education is a lifelong process.

6. Media education aims to foster not simply critical understanding but critical autonomy.

7. The effectiveness of media education may be evaluated by two principal criteria (a) the ability of students to apply what they know (their critical ideas and principles) to new situations, and (b) the amount of commitment, interest, and motivation displayed by students.

8. Media education is topical and opportunistic. It seeks to illuminate the life situations for the learners by harnessing the interest and enthusiasm generated by the media's coverage of topical events.

Definitions Combining Skills and Knowledge

Bazalgette (1997) said that media literate people need knowledge about "a range of critical theories from sociology, or cultural studies, or art history," knowledge "of certain key texts (usually films)," knowledge "of the industrial and economic structures of media industries," and "a general awareness of the economic and ideological functions of media texts" (pp. 73-74).

☐ Messaris (1998) says "Media literacy can be defined as knowledge about how the mass media function in society. . . . Ideally, this knowledge should encompass all aspects of the workings of the media: their economic foundations, organizational structures, psychological effects, social consequences, and, above all, their 'language,' that is the representational conventions and rhetorical strategies of ads, TV programs, movies, and other forms of mass media content" (p. 70).

☐ Meyrowitz (1998) says there is a range of knowledge people should possess, because there are multiple literacies. He says a media literate person needs an understanding of media content (understanding of the conduits that hold and send messages), of media grammar (understanding of the language or aesthetics of each medium), and of the medium (understanding of the type of setting or environment).

☐ Zettl (1998) argued that a definition for media literacy should be built on an understanding of what he called "contextual media aesthetics. He says "we need to know how the basic aesthetic building blocks are used to create and shape our cognitive and affective mental maps" (p. 81).

Appendix B
Purpose of Media Literacy

This appendix displays a range of visions for the purpose or role of media literacy. It is organized into three sections: Improvement role, teaching role, and activism role.

Improvement Role

☐ Anderson (1983), in a review of television literacy projects up until the early 1980s, listed 11 objectives that he found to be prevalent in those projects. All of these were focused on improving the individual in some way.

☐ Masterman (1985) believes the goal of media education is to help people understand how the media distort aspects of reality as they manufacture their messages and how symbol systems mediate our knowledge of the world.

☐ Buckingham (1993a) points out that television has been regarded, especially in America, as having powerful negative influence on children, such as being addictive, harming mental health and personal relationships, and causing social unrest and disintegration. The purpose of literacy is to blunt the negative effects of television.

☐ Everette Dennis (1993), who is the executive director of the Freedom Forum Media Studies Center at Columbia University in New York, refers to media illiteracy as "potentially as damaging and poisonous to the human spirit as contaminated water and food is to our physical well-being" (p. 4). The metaphor of pollution is an apt one. The media industries provide us with many products that we desire—products that are good for us—but these same media industries are also producing harmful by-products and dumping them into our culture. If we are not literate, we don't know the difference and we consume the bad with the good.

☐ Hobbs (1996) says that "the goal of media literacy is to promote autonomy" (p. iii).

☐ The National Leadership Conference on Media Literacy says, "The fundamental objective of media literacy is critical autonomy in relationship to all media . . . including informed citizenship, aesthetic appreciation and expression, social advocacy, self-esteem, and consumer competence" (Aufderheide, 1997, p. 79–80).

☐ Lewis and Jhally (1998) say "the goal of media literacy is to help people become sophisticated citizens rather than sophisticated consumers" (p. 109).

☐ Brown (1998) says "the purpose of media literacy is to help recipients of mass communication become active, free participants in the process rather than static, passive, and subservient to the images and values communicated in a one-way flow from media sources" (p. 47).

Teaching Role

☐ Buckingham (1993b points out that the pedagogical role of television literacy has been for educators to defend those who are believed to be less capable of defending themselves from negative effects. Furthermore, he challenges those who argue that teaching media literacy can be both proscriptive and nonhierarchical when he writes that the aim to "demystify" students while using a nonhierarchical pedagogy "clearly places the teacher in a contradictory position—on the one hand, as the bearer of a 'truth' that is not available to the students, yet on the other as an equal partner in dialogue" (p. 287).

☐ The National Communication Association (formerly the Speech Communication Association, 1996), which has taken a lead in communication and media assessment efforts, released 22 national standards, with 2 applying to media literacy:

Standard 22: The effective media participant can demonstrate the effects of the various types of electronic audio and visual media, including television, radio, the telephone, the Internet, computers, electronic conferencing, and film, on media consumers.

Standard 23: The effective media participant can demonstrate the ability to identify and use skills necessary for competent participation in communication across various types of electronic audio and visual media.

□ Aufderheide (1997, p. 80) believes that media educators hold the following ideas in common: Media are constructed, and construct reality; media have commercial implications; media have ideological and political implications; form and content are related in each medium, each of which has a unique aesthetic, codes, and conventions; receivers negotiate meaning in media.

□ The Council of Europe Resolution on Education in Media and New Technologies says, "Pupils should be given an understanding of the structures, mechanisms, and messages of the mass media. In particular, pupils should develop the independent capacity to apply critical judgement to media content. One means to this end, and an objective in its own right, should be to encourage creative expression [of] the pupils' own media messages, so that they are equipped to take advantage of opportunities for the expression on particular interests in the context of participation at local level" (Masterman, 1997, p. 15).

□ Masterman (1997) argues that there is a sense that the very act of studying media can help democratize the teacher-student relationship because the act of critique is one of "reflection and dialogue" (p. 44). There is even a sense that media literacy demands a different type of teaching that is democratic and nonhierarchical (Bazalgette, 1997; Masterman, 1980, 1985, 1997).

□ The Council of Europe Resolution on Education in Media and New Technologies, which was adopted by European Ministers of Education, says, "Education in the new technologies and the media should play an empowering and liberating role, helping to prepare pupils for democratic citizenship and political awareness" (Masterman, 1997, p. 15).

□ Some believe that the purpose of media literacy education is the same as the purpose of education in general, that is, to educate people to be aware of their place in the world as well as to become empowered citizens and consumers (Blanchard & Christ, 1993; McLaren, Hammer, Sholle, & Reilly, 1995; Sholle & Denski, 1994).

Activism Role

Anderson (1983) uses the term *impact mediation,* meaning stimulated by social issues that are influenced by the media, for example, violence, materialism, nutrition, body image, distortion in news reporting, and stereotyping by race, class, gender, and sexual orientation.

☐ Lewis and Jhally (1998) contend that media literacy should go beyond textual analysis into ideological/political economy issues. They challenge the way much of media literacy is taught today.

☐ In Great Britain, academics and practitioners were able to agree that media education should foster "collaboration with professional people and agencies in both fields" (Commission 1, 1992, pp. 222-223).

References

Abelman, R. (1999). Preaching to the choir: Profiling TV advisory ratings users. *Journal of Broadcasting & Electronic Media, 43,* 529–550.

Abelman, R. (2000). Profiling parents who do and don't use the TV advisory ratings. In B. S. Greenberg, L. Rampoldi-Hnilo, & D. Mastro (Eds.), *The alphabet soup of television program ratings.* Cresskill, NJ: Hampton Press.

Abelman, R., & Courtright, J. (1983). Television literacy: Amplifying the cognitive level effects of television's prosocial fare through curriculum intervention. *Journal of Research and Development in Education, 17,* 46–57.

Adams, W. C. (1978). Local public affairs content of TV news. *Journalism Quarterly, 55,* 690–695.

Adams, D. M., & Hamm, M. E. (1989). *Media and literacy: Learning in an electronic age: Issues, ideas, and teaching strategies.* Springfield, IL: Charles C Thomas.

Adams, D., & Hamm, M. (2001). *Literacy in a multimedia age.* Norwood, MA: Christopher-Gordon.

Alvarado, M., & Boyd-Barrett, O. (Eds.). (1992). *Media education: An Introduction.* London: British Film Institute.

Alvermann, D. E., Moon, J. S., & Hagood, M. C. (1999). *Popular culture in the classroom: Teaching and researching critical media literacy.* Newark, DE: International Reading Association.

Anderson, C. A. (1997). Effects of violent movies and trait hostility on hostile feelings and aggressive thoughts. *Aggressive Behavior, 23,* 161–178.

Anderson, J. A. (1981). Receivership skills: An educational response. In M. Ploghoft & J. A. Anderson (Eds.), *Education for the television age.* Springfield, IL: Charles C Thomas.

Anderson, J. A. (1983). Television literacy and the critical viewer. In J. Bryant & D. R. Anderson (Eds.), *Children's understanding of television: Research on attention and comprehension* (pp. 297–327). New York: Academic Press.

Anderson, D. R., & Lorch, E. P. (1983). Looking at television action or reaction? In J. Bryant & D. Zillmann (Eds.), *Children's understanding of television: Research on attention and comprehension* (pp. 1–33). New York: Academic Press.

Anderson, D. R., Lorch, E. P., Field, D. E., Collins, P. A., & Nathan, J. G. (1986). Television viewing at home: Age trends in visual attention and time with TV. *Child Development, 57,* 1024–1033.

Atkin, C. K. (1985). Informational utility and selective exposure to entertainment media. In D. Zillmann & J. Bryant (Eds.), *Selective exposure to communication* (pp. 63–91). Hillsdale, NJ: Lawrence Erlbaum.

Aufderheide, P. (Ed.). (1993). *Media literacy: A report of the National Leadership Conference on Media Literacy.* Aspen, CO: Aspen Institute.

Aufderheide, P. (1997). Media literacy: From a report of the National Leadership Conference on Media Literacy. In R. Kubey (Ed.), *Media literacy in the information age: Current perspectives, information, and behavior* (Vol. 6, pp. 79–86). New Brunswick, NJ: Transaction.

Austin, E. W. (1993a). Exploring the effects of active parental mediation of television content. *Journal of Broadcasting & Electronic Media, 37,* 147–158.

Austin, E. W. (1993b). The importance of perspective in parent-child interpretations of family communication patterns. *Journalism Quarterly, 70,* 558–568.

Austin, E. W., Bolls, P., Fujioka, Y., & Engelbertson, J. (1999). How and why parents take on the tube. *Journal of Broadcasting & Electronic Media, 43,* 175–192.

Austin, E. W., Knaus, C., & Meneguelli, A. (1998). Who talks how to their kids about TV: A clarification of demographic correlates of parental mediation patterns. *Communication Research Reports, 14,* 418–430.

Austin, E. W., & Meili, H. K. (1995). Effects of interpretations of television alcohol portrayals on children's alcohol beliefs. *Journal of Broadcasting & Electronic Media, 39,* 417–435.

Austin, E. W., & Pinkleton, B. E. (1997, May). *Parental mediation as information source use: Political socialization effects.* Paper presented at the annual conference of the International Communication Association, Montreal, Quebec, Canada.

Austin, E. W., & Pinkleton, B. E. (2001). The role of parental mediation in the political socialization process. *Journal of Broadcasting & Electronic Media, 45,* 221–240.

Aversa, J. (1999, May 5). Government employees get no respect on TV. *Tallahassee Democrat,* p. 3A.

Baesler, E. J., & Burgoon, J. K. (1994). The temporal effects of story and statistical evidence on belief change. *Communication Research, 21,* 582–602.

Bagdikian, B. (1992). *The media monopoly* (4th ed.). Boston: Beacon.

Ball S. J., & Bogatz, G. A. (1970). *The first year of Sesame Street: An evaluation.* Princeton, NJ: Educational Testing Center.

Bandura, A. (1986). *Social foundations of thought and action: A social cognitive theory.* Englewood Cliffs, NJ: Prentice Hall.

Bandura, A. (1994). Social cognitive theory of mass communication. In J. Bryant & D. Zillmann (Eds.), *Media effects* (pp. 61–90). Hillsdale, NJ: Lawrence Erlbaum.

Barsalou, L. W. (1988). The content and organization of autobiographical memories. In U. Neisser & E. Winograd (Eds.), *Remembering reconsidered: Ecological and traditional approaches to the study of memory* (pp. 193–243). Cambridge, UK: Cambridge University Press.

Barsalou, L. W. (1992). *Cognitive psychology: An overview for cognitive scientists.* Hillsdale, NJ: Lawrence Erlbaum.

Bartlett. F. C. (1932). *Remembering: A study in experimental and social psychology.* Cambridge, UK: Cambridge University Press.

Barton, D., & Hamilton, M. (1998). *Local literacies: Reading and writing in one community.* London: Routledge.

Bash, A. (1997, June 10). Most parents don't use ratings to guide viewing. *USA Today,* p. 3D.

Bazalgette, C. (1989). *Primary media education: A curriculum statement.* London: BFI.

Bazalgette, C. (1997). An agenda for the second phase of media literacy development. In R. Kubey (Ed.), *Media literacy in the information age: Current perspectives, information, and behavior* (Vol. 6, pp. 69–78). New Brunswick, NJ: Transaction.

Bennett, W. L., & Lawrence, R. G. (1995). News icons and the mainstreaming of social change. *Journal of Communication, 45*(3), 20–39.

Berger, C. R. (2000). Quantitative depictions of threatening phenomena in news reports: The scary world of frequency data. *Human Communication Research, 26*(1), 27–52.

Berger, P. L., & Luckmann, T. (1966). *The social construction of reality.* Garden City, NY: Doubleday.

Berlyne, D. E. (1960). Conflict, arousal, and curiosity. New York: McGraw-Hill.

Bernhardt, R., & Antonacci, P. (1995). In search of thinking environments. In C. N. Hedley, P. Antonacci, & M. Rabinowitz (Eds.), *Thinking and literacy: The mind at work* (pp. 241–255). Hillsdale, NJ: Lawrence Erlbaum.

Bianculli, D. (1992). *Teleliteracy: Taking television seriously.* New York: Continuum.

Bickham, D. S., Wright, J. C., & Huston, A. C. (2001). Attention, comprehension, and the educational influences of television. In D. G. Singer & J. L. Singer (Eds.), *Handbook of children and the media* (pp. 101–119). Thousand Oaks, CA: Sage.

Biocca, F. (1991). Some limitations of earlier "symbolic" approaches to political communication. In F. Biocca (Ed.), *Television and political advertising: Vol. 2. Signs, codes, and images* (pp. 11–25). Hillsdale, NJ: Lawrence Erlbaum.

Blanchard, R. O., & Christ, W. G. (1993). *Media education and the liberal arts: A blueprint for the new professionalism.* Hillsdale, NJ: Lawrence Erlbaum.

Bleske, G. L. (1995, August). *Schematic frames and reader learning: The effect of headlines.* Paper presented at the annual meeting of the Association for Education in Journalism and Mass Communication, Washington, DC.

Broadbent, D. E. (1958). *Perception and communication.* London: Pergamon.

Broadbent, D. E. (1984). The Maltese cross: A new simplistic model for memory. *Behavioral and Brain Sciences, 7,* 55–94.

Brosius, H.-B., & Bathelt, A. (1994). The utility of exemplars in persuasive communications. *Communication Research, 21,* 48–78.

Brown, J. A. (1991). *Television "critical viewing skills" education: Major media literacy projects in the United States and selected countries.* Hillsdale, NJ: Lawrence Erlbaum.

Brown, J. A. (1998). Media literacy perspectives. *Journal of Communication, 48*(1), 44–57.

Brown, J. A. (2001). Media literacy and critical television viewing in education. In D. G. Singer & J. L. Singer (Eds.) *Handbook of children and the media* (pp. 681–697). Thousand Oaks, CA: Sage.

Brown, J. D., Childers, K. W., Bauman, K. E., & Koch, G. G. (1990). The influence of new media and family structure on young adolescents' television and radio use. *Communication Research, 17,* 65–82.

Bruner, J. S., Goodnow, J., & Austin, G. A. (1956). *A study of thinking.* New York: John Wiley.

Buckingham, D. (Ed.). (1990). *Watching media learning, making sense of media education.* Basingstoke, UK: Falmer.

Buckingham, D. (1993a). *Changing literacies: Media education and modern culture.* London: Tufnell Press.

Buckingham, D. (1993b). *Children talking television: The making of television literacy.* Washington, DC: Falmer.

Buckingham, D. (1998a). Media education in the UK: Moving beyond protectionism. *Journal of Communication, 48*(1), 33–43.

Buckingham, D. (Ed.). (1998b). *Teaching popular culture: Beyond radical pedagogy.* London: University College London Press.

Buckingham, D., & Sefton-Green, J. (1997). Multimedia education: Media literacy in the age of digital culture. In R. Kubey (Ed.), *Media literacy in the information age* (pp. 285–305), New Brunswick, NJ: Transaction.

Bucy, E. P., & Newhagen, J. E. (1999). The emotional appropriateness heuristic: Processing televised presidential reactions to the news. *Journal of Communication, 49*(4), 59–79.

Bushman, B. J., & Huesmann, L. R. (2001). Effects of television violence on aggression. In D. G. Singer & J. L. Singer (Eds.), *Handbook of children and the media* (pp. 223–254). Thousand Oaks, CA: Sage.

Bybee, C., Robinson, D., & Turow, J. (1982). Determinants of parental guidance of children's television viewing for a special subgroup: Mass media scholars. *Journal of Broadcasting, 26,* 697–710.

Cantor, J. (2001). The media and children's fears, anxieties, and perceptions of danger. In D. G. Singer & J. L. Singer (Eds.), *Handbook of children and the media* (pp. 207–221). Thousand Oaks, CA: Sage.

Cantor, N., & Mischel, W. (1977). Traits as prototypes: Effects on recognition memory. *Journal of Personality and Social Psychology, 35,* 38–48.

Cantor, N., & Mischel, W. (1979). Prototypes in person perception. In L. Berkowitz (Ed.), *Advances in experimental social psychology* (Vol. 12, pp. 3–52). New York: Academic Press.

Cantor, J., & Wilson, B. J. (1984). Modifying fear responses to mass media in preschool and elementary school children. *Journal of Broadcasting, 28,* 431–443.

Carlson, C. I. (1990). Assessing the family context. In C. R. Reynolds & R. W. Kamphaus (Eds.), *Handbook of psychological and education al assessment of children: Personality, behavior, and context* (pp. 546–575). New York: Guilford.

Carver, S. M. (1995). Cognitive apprenticeships: Putting theory into practice on a large scale. In C. N. Hedley, P. Antonacci, & M. Rabinowitz (Eds.), *Thinking and literacy: The mind at work* (pp. 203–228). Hillsdale, NJ: Lawrence Erlbaum.

Caughey, J. L. (1986). Social relations with media figures. In G. Gumpert & R. Cathcart (Eds.), *Inter/Media* (pp. 219–252). New York: Oxford University Press.

Chaffee, S. H., & McLeod, J. M. (1972). Adolescent television use in the family context. In G. A. Comstock & E. A. Rubinstein (Eds.), *Television and social behavior: Vol 3. Television and adolescent aggressiveness* (pp. 149–172). Washington, DC: Government Printing Office.

Chaffee, S. H., McLeod, J. M., & Atkin, C. K. (1971). Parental influences on adolescent media use. *American Behavioral Scientist, 14,* 323–340.

Chomsky, N. (1972). *Language and mind* (2nd ed.). New York: Harcourt Brace Jovanovich.

Christ, W. G. (Ed.). (1994). *Assessing communication education: A handbook for media, speech, and theatre educators.* Hillsdale, NJ: Lawrence Erlbaum.

Christ, W. G. (Ed.). (1997). *Media education assessment handbook.* Mahwah, NJ: Lawrence Erlbaum.

Christ, W. G. (1998). Multimedia: Replacing the broadcast curriculum. *Feedback, 39*(1), 1–6.

Christ, W. G., & Hynes, T. (1997). Missions and purposes of journalism and mass communication education. *Journalism and Mass Communication Educator, 52*(2), 73–100.

Christ, W. G., McCall, J., Rakow, L., & Blanchard, R. O. (1997). Assessing media education in an integrated communications program. In W. G. Christ (Ed.), *Media education assessment handbook* (pp. 23–56). Mahwah, NJ: Lawrence Erlbaum.

Christ, W. G., & Potter, W. J. (1998). Media literacy, media education, and the academy. *Journal of Communication, 48*(1), 5–15.

Clark, H. H., & Marshall, C. R. (1981). Definite reference and mutual knowledge. In A. K. Joshi, B. Webber, & I. Sag (Eds.), *Elements of discourse understanding* (pp. 10–63). Cambridge, UK: Cambridge University Press.

Collins, A. M., & Quillian, M. R. (1969). Retrieval time from semantic memory. *Journal of Verbal Learning and Verbal Behavior, 8,* 240–247.

Commission 1 (reported by M. Huguier). (1992). Involving the media in media education. In C. Bazalgette, E. Bevort, & J. Savino (Eds.), *New directions in media education worldwide* (pp. 220–223). London: British Film Institute.

Comstock, G. A. (1980). *Television in America.* Beverly Hills, CA: Sage.

Comstock, G. (1989). *The evolution of American television.* Newbury Park, CA: Sage.

Comstock, G. A., Chaffee, S., Katzman, N., McCombs, M., & Roberts, D. (1978). *Television and human behavior.* New York: Columbia University Press.

Comstock G., & Scharrer, E. (2001). The use of television and other film-related media. In D. G. Singer & J. L. Singer (Eds.), *Handbook of children and the media* (pp. 47–72). Thousand Oaks, CA: Sage.

Considine, D. M. (1997). Media literacy: A compelling component of school reform and restructuring. In R. Kubey (Ed.), *Media literacy in the information age* (pp. 243–262). New Brunswick, NJ: Transaction.

Conway, M. A. (1996). Autobiographical knowledge and autobiographical memories. In D. C. Rubin (Ed.), *Remembering our past: Studies in autobiographical memory* (pp. 67–93). Cambridge, UK: Cambridge University Press.

Corder-Bolz, C. R. (1980). Mediation: The role of significant others. *Journal of Communication, 30*(3), 106–118.

Cotton, J. L. (1985). Cognitive dissonance in selective exposure. In D. Zillmann & J. Bryant (Eds.), *Selective exposure to communication* (pp. 11–33). Hillsdale, NJ: Lawrence Erlbaum.

Cowan, N. (1995). *Attention and memory: An integrated framework.* New York: Oxford University Press.

Crigler, A. N., Just, M., & Neuman, W. R. (1994). Interpreting visual audio messages in television news. *Journal of Communication, 44*(4), 132–149.

Cutting, J. E. (1991). Why our stimuli look as they do. In G. R. Lockhead & J. R. Pomerantz (Eds.), *The perception of structure* (pp. 141–152), Washington, DC: American Psychological Association.

D'Alessio, D., & Allen, M. (2000). Media bias in presidential elections: A meta-analysis. *Journal of Communication, 50*(4), 133–156.

Davies, M. M. (1997). Making media literate: Educating future media workers at the undergraduate level. In R. Kubey (Ed.), *Media literacy in the information age* (pp. 263–284). New Brunswick, NJ: Transaction.

DeGaetano, G., & Bander, K. (1996). *Screen smarts: A family guide to media literacy.* Boston: Houghton Mifflin.

Dennis, E. E. (1993, April 15). *Fighting media illiteracy: What every American needs to know and why.* Presented as the Roy W. Howard Lecture in Journalism and Mass Communication. Number 4, Indiana University, School of Journalism.

Desmond, R. (1997a). Media literacy in the home: Acquisition versus deficit models. In R. Kubey (Ed.), *Media literacy in the information age* (pp. 323–343). New Brunswick, NJ: Transaction.

Desmond, R. (1997b). TV viewing, reading, and media literacy. In J. Flood, S. B. Heath, & D. Lapp (Eds.), *Handbook of research on teaching literacy through the communicative and visual arts* (pp. 23–30). New York: Macmillan.

Desmond, R. J., Singer, J. L., Singer, D. G., Calam, R., & Colimore, K. (1985). Family mediation patterns and television viewing: Young children's use and grasp of the medium. *Human Communication Research, 11*, 461–480.

Detenber, B. H., Simons, R. F., & Bennett, G. G., Jr. (1998). Roll 'em!: The effects of picture motion on emotional responses. *Journal of Broadcasting & Electronic Media, 42*, 113–127.

Deutsch, J. A., & Deutsch, D. (1963). Attention: Some theoretical considerations. *Psychological Review, 70*, 80–90.

Devine, P. G. (1989). Stereotypes and prejudice: Their automatic and controlled components. *Journal of Personality and Social Psychology, 56*, 5–18.

Dorr, A., Graves, S. B., & Phelps, E. (1980). Television literacy for young children. *Journal of Communication, 30*(3), 71–83.

Dorr, A., Kovaric, P., & Doubleday, C. (1989). Parent-child co-viewing of television. *Journal of Broadcasting & Electronic Media, 33*, 35–51.

Douglas, D., & Olsen, B. M. (1996). Subversion of the American family? An examination of children and parents in television families. *Communication Research, 23*, 73–99.

Ehri, L. C. (1995). Teachers need to know how word reading processes develop to teach reading effectively to beginners. In C. N. Hedley, P. Antonacci, & M. Rabinowitz (Eds.), *Thinking and literacy: The mind at work* (pp. 167–188). Hillsdale, NJ: Lawrence Erlbaum.

Entman, R. M. (1993). Framing: Towards clarification of a fractured paradigm. *Journal of Communication, 43*(4), 51–58.

Eveland, W. O., & McLeod, D. M. (1999). The effect of social desirability on perceived media impact: Implications for third-person perceptions. *International Journal of Public Opinion Research, 11*, 315–333.

Fischhoff, B. (1982). For those condemned to study the past: Heuristics and biases in hindsight. In D. Kahneman, P. Slovic, & A. Tversky (Eds.), *Judgment under uncertainty: Heuristics and biases* (pp. 335–351). Cambridge, UK: Cambridge University Press.

Fischhoff, B. (1988). Judgment and decision making. In R. J. Sternberg, & E. E. Smith (Eds.), *The psychology of human thought* (pp. 153–187). New York: Cambridge University Press.

Fiske, S. T., & Taylor, S. E. (1991). *Social cognition* (2nd ed.). New York: McGraw-Hill.

Foehr, U. G., Rideout, V., & Miller, C. (2000). Parents and the TV ratings system: A national study. In B. S. Greenberg, L. Rampoldi-Hnilo, & D. Mastro (Eds.), *The alphabet soup of television program ratings.* Cresskill, NJ: Hampton Press.

Fowler, R. (1991). *Language in the news: Discourse and ideology in the press.* London: Routledge.

Freire, P. (1985). *The politics of education: Culture, power, and liberation.* South Hadley, MA: Bergin & Garvey.

Gaertner, S. L., & McLaughlin, J. P. (1983). Racial stereotypes: Associations and ascriptions of positive and negative characteristics. *Social Psychology Quarterly, 46*, 23–40.

Gamson, W. A. (1992). *Talking politics*. Cambridge, UK: Cambridge University Press.

Gantz, W. (1981). An exploration of viewing motives and behaviors associated with television sports. *Journal of Broadcasting, 25*, 263–275.

Gardiner, W. L. (1997). Can computers turn teaching inside-out, transform education, and redefine literacy? In R. Kubey (Ed.), *Media literacy in the information age* (pp. 359–376). New Brunswick, NJ: Transaction.

Gardner, R. W. (1968). *Personality development at preadolescence*. Seattle: University of Washington Press.

Geer, J. G., & Kahn, K. F. (1993). Grabbing attention: An experimental investigation of headlines during campaigns. *Political Communication, 10*(2), 175–191.

Gerbner, G., Gross, L., Signorielli, N., & Morgan, M. (1980). Aging with television: Images on television drama and conceptions of social reality. *Journal of Communication, 30*(1), 37–47.

Gerbner, G., Gross, L., Signorielli, N., Morgan, M., & Jackson-Beeck, M. (1979). The demonstration of power: Violence profile No. 10. *Journal of Communication, 29*(3), 177–196.

Gibson, R., & Zillmann, D. (1994). Exaggerated versus representative exemplification in news reports, *Communication Research, 21*, 603–624.

Goleman, D. (1995). *Emotional intelligence*. New York: Bantam Books.

Goodwin, A., & Whannel, G. (Eds.). (1990). *Understanding television*. New York: Routledge.

Gordon, D. R. (1971). *The new literacy*. Toronto: University of Toronto Press.

Graber, D. (1988). *Processing the news: How people tame the information tide* (2nd ed.). New York: Longman.

Graber, D. A. (1990). Seeing is remembering: How visuals contribute to learning from television news. *Journal of Communication 40*(3), 134–155.

Graesser, A. C., Millis, K. K., & Long, D. L. (1986). The construction of knowledge-based inferences during story comprehension. In N. E. Sharkey (Ed.), *Advances in cognitive science* (Vol. 1, pp. 125-157). New York: John Wiley.

Greenberg, B. S., Edison, N., Korzenny, F., Fernandez-Collado, C., & Atkin, C. K. (1980). Antisocial and prosocial behaviors on television. In B. S. Greenberg (Ed.), *Life on television: Content analysis of U.S. TV drama* (pp. 99–128). Norwood, NJ: Ablex.

Greenberg, B. S., Ericson, P. M., & Vlahos, M. (1972). Children's television behaviors as perceived by mother and child. In E. A. Rubinstein, G. A. Comstock, & J. P. Murray (Eds.), *Television and social behavior: Television in day-to-day life: Patterns of use* (Vol. 4, pp. 395–409). Washington, DC: Government Printing Office.

Greenberg, B. S., & Rampoldi-Hnilo, L. (2001). Children and parent responses to the age-based and content-based television ratings. In D. G. Singer & J. L. Singer (Eds.), *Handbook of children and the media* (pp. 621–634). Thousand Oaks, CA: Sage.

Greenberg, B. S., Rampoldi-Hnilo, L., & Hofschire, L. (2000). Young people's responses to the age-based ratings. In B. S. Greenberg, L. Rampoldi-Hnilo, & D. Mastro (Eds.), *The alphabet soup of television program ratings.* Cresskill, NJ: Hampton Press.

Grodin, D., & Lindlof, T. R. (Eds.). (1996). *Constructing the self in a mediated world.* Thousand Oaks, CA: Sage.

Grow, G. (1990, August). *Enhancing self-direction in journalism education.* Paper presented at the Association for Education in Journalism and Mass Communication convention, Minneapolis, MN.

Grusec, J. E. (1973). Effects of co-observer evaluations on imitation: A developmental study. *Developmental Psychology, 8,* 141.

Gunther, A. C., & Chia, S. C.-Y. (2001). Predicting pluralistic ignorance: The hostile media perception and its consequences. *Journalism & Mass Communication Quarterly, 78,* 688–701.

Gunther, A. C., & Christen, C. T. (1999). Effects of news slant and base rate information on perceived public opinion. *Journalism & Mass Communication Quarterly, 76,* 277–292.

Hammond, K. R. (1996). *Human judgment and social policy: Irreducible uncertainty, inevitable error, unavoidable justice.* New York: Oxford University Press.

Hampton, J. A. (1982). A demonstration of intransitivity in natural concepts. *Cognition, 12,* 151–164.

Hansen, C. H., & Hansen, R. D. (1988). How rock music videos can change what is seen when boy meets girl: Priming stereotypic appraisal of social interaction. *Sex Roles, 19,* 287–316.

Hart, A. (1997). Textual pleasures and moral dilemmas: Teaching media literacy in England. In R. Kubey (Ed.), *Media literacy in the information age* (pp. 199–211). New Brunswick, NJ: Transaction.

Hartman, T. (1999, March 22). Movie characters aren't reaping what they sow. *Tallahassee Democrat,* p. A1.

Hawkins, R. P., Pingree, S., Bruce, L., & Tapper, J. (1997). Strategy and style in attention to television. *Journal of Broadcasting & Electronic Media, 41,* 245–264.

Hawkins, R. P., Yong-Ho, K., & Pingree, S. (1991). The ups and downs of attention to television. *Communication Research, 18*(1), 53–76.

Harwood, J. (1997). Viewing age: Lifespan identity and television viewing choices. *Journal of Broadcasting & Electronic Media, 41,* 203–213.

Heeter, C., & Greenberg, B. (1985). Cable program choice. In D. Zillmann & J. Bryant (Eds.), *Selective exposure to communication* (pp. 203–224). Hillsdale, NJ: Lawrence Erlbaum.

Herr, P. M. (1986). Consequences of priming: Judgment and behavior. *Journal of Personality and Social Psychology, 51,* 1106–1115.

Hicks, D. J. (1968). Effects of co-observer's sanctions and adult presence on imitative aggression. *Child Development, 39,* 303–309.

Hilton, M. (1996). *Potent fictions: Children's literacy and the challenge of popular culture*. New York: Routledge.

Himmelweit, H., Oppenheim, A., & Vince, P. (1958). *Television and the child*. London: Oxford University Press.

Hobbs, R. (1997a). Expanding the concept of literacy. In R. Kubey (Ed.), *Media literacy in the information age* (pp. 163–183), New Brunswick, NJ: Transaction.

Hobbs, R. (1997b). Literacy for the information age. In J. Flood, S. B. Heath, & Lapp, D. (Eds.), *Handbook of research on teaching literacy through the communicative and visual arts* (pp. 7–14). New York: Macmillan.

Hobbs, R. (1998). The seven great debates in the media literacy movement. *Journal of Communication, 48*(1), 16–32.

Hobbs, R. & Frost, R. (1997, May). *The impact of media literacy education on adolescents's media analysis and news comprehension skills*. Paper presented at the annual conference of the International Communication Association, Montreal, Quebec, Canada.

Hoffner, C. (1997). Children's emotional reactions to a scary film: The role of prior outcome information and coping style. *Human Communication Research, 23*, 323–341.

Hoffner, C., & Cantor, J. (1991). Perceiving and responding to mass media characters. In J. Bryant & D. Zillmann (Eds.), *Responding to the screen* (pp. 63–101). Hillsdale, NJ: Lawrence Erlbaum.

Hogan, M. J. (2001). Parents and other adults: Models and monitors of healthy media habits. In D. G. Singer & J. L. Singer (Eds.), *Handbook of children and the media* (pp. 663–680). Thousand Oaks, CA: Sage.

Hollenbeck, A., & Slaby, R. (1979). Infant visual and vocal responses to television. *Child Development, 50*, 41–45.

Holubec, E. J., Johnson, D. W., & Johnson, R. T. (1995). Cooperative learning in reading and language arts. In C. N. Hedley, P. Antonacci, & M. Rabinowitz (Eds.), *Thinking and literacy: The mind at work* (pp. 229–240). Hillsdale, NJ: Lawrence Erlbaum.

Holz, J. (1998). *Measuring the child audience: Issues and implications for educational programming* (Survey No. 3). Philadelphia: University of Pennsylvania, Annenberg Public Policy Center.

Houk, A., & Bogart, C. (1974). *Media literacy: Thinking about*. Pflaum/ Standard.

Huston, A. C., & Wright, J. C. (1983). Children's processing of television: The informative functions of formal features. In J. Bryant & D. R. Anderson (Eds.), *Children's understanding of television: Research on attention and comprehension* (pp. 37–68). New York: Academic Press.

Huston, A. C., & Wright, J. C. (1989). The forms of television and the child viewer. In G. Comstock (Ed.), *Public communication and behavior* (Vol. 2, pp. 103–158). San Diego, CA: Academic Press.

Iyenger, S. (1991). *Is anyone responsible? How television frames political issues*. Chicago: University of Chicago Press.

Iyenger, S., Peters, M. D., & Kinder, D. R. (1982). Experimental demonstrations of the "not-so-minimal" consequences of television news programs. *American Political Science Review, 76,* 848–858.

Jensen, C. (1997). *20 years of censored news.* New York: Seven Stories Press.

Johnson, J. T., & Taylor, S. E. (1981). The effect of metaphor on political attitudes. *Basic and Applied Social Psychology, 2*(4), 305–316.

Johnson, L. L. (2001). *Media, education, and change.* New York: Peter Lang.

Jordan, A. B. (2001). Public policy and private practice: Government regulations and parental control of children's television use in the home. In D. G. Singer & J. L. Singer (Eds.), *Handbook of children and the media* (pp. 651–662). Thousand Oaks, CA: Sage.

Josephson, W. L. (1987), Television violence and children's aggression: Testing the priming, social script, and disinhibition predictions. *Journal of Experimental Psychology: Learning, Memory, and Cognition, 26,* 441–455.

Kagan, J., Rosman, D., Day, D., Albert, J., & Phillips, W. (1964). Information processing in the child: Significance of analytic and reflective attitudes. *Psychological Monographs, 78,* 1.

Kahneman, D., & Tversky, A. (1973). On the psychology of prediction. *Psychological Review, 80,* 237–251.

Kaiser Family Foundation. (1998, May). *Parents, children, and the television ratings system: Two Kaiser Family Foundation surveys.* Menlo Park, CA: Author.

Kaiser Family Foundation. (1999). *Parents and the V-chip.* Menlo Park, CA: Author.

Kawamoto, K. (2003). *Media and society in the digital age.* Boston: Allyn & Bacon.

Kellner, D. (1995). Preface. In P. McLaren, R. Hammer, D. Sholle, & S. S. Reilly (Eds.), *Rethinking media literacy: A critical pedagogy of representation* (pp. xiii–xvii). New York: Peter Lang.

Kelly, M. R. (1983). *A parents' guide to television: Making the most of it.* New York: John Wiley.

King, P. M. (1986). Formal reasoning in adults: A review and critique. In R. A. Mines & K. S. Kitchenor (Eds.), *Adult cognitive development: Methods and models* (pp. 1–21). New York: Praeger.

Kolodner, J. L. (1984). *Retrieval and organizational strategies in conceptual memory.* Hillsdale, NJ: Lawrence Erlbaum.

Koziol, R. (1989, August). *English language arts teachers' views on mass media consumption education in Maryland high schools.* Paper presented at the annual conference of the Association of Education in Journalism and Mass Communication, Washington, DC.

Krcmar, M. (1996). Family communication patterns, discourse behavior, and children's television viewing. *Human Communication Research, 23,* 251–257.

Krcmar, M. (1998). The contribution of family communication patterns to children's interpretations of television violence. *Journal of Broadcasting & Electronic Media, 42,* 250–264.

Krcmar, M., & Cantor, J. (1996, May). *Discussing violent television: Parents, children, and TV viewing choices.* Paper presented at the annual conference of the International Communication Association, Montreal, Canada.

Kress, G. (1992). Media literacy as cultural technology in the age of transcultural media. In C. Bazalgette, E. Bevort, & J. Savino (Eds.), *New directions: Media education worldwide* (pp. 190–202). London: British Film Institute.

Krosnick J. A., & Kinder, D. R. (1990). Altering the foundations of support for the president through priming. *American Political Science Review, 84,* 497–512.

Kubey, R. (1997). A rationale for media education. In R. Kubey (Ed.), *Media literacy in the information age* (pp. 15–68). New Brunswick, NJ: Transaction.

Kubey, R. (1998). Obstacles to the development of media education in the United States. *Journal of Communication, 48*(1), 58–69.

Kuhlthau, C. C. (1997). Literacy in the information age school: Skills for lifelong learning. In R. Kubey (Ed.), *Media literacy in the information age* (pp. 441–448). New Brunswick, NJ: Transaction.

Kulleseid, E. R., & Strickland, D. S. (1989). *Literature, literacy, and learning.* Chicago: American Library Association.

Kunkel, D. (2001). Children and television advertising. In D. G. Singer & J. L. Singer (Eds.), *Handbook of children and the media* (pp. 375–393). Thousand Oaks, CA: Sage.

Kunkel, D., Cope, K. M., Fainola, W. J. M., Biely, E., Rollin, E., & Donnerstein, E. (1999). *Sex on TV: Content and context.* Menlo Park, CA: Kaiser Family Foundation.

Kunkel, D., Farinola, W. J. M., Farrar, K., Donnerstein, E., Bielby, E., & Swarun, L. (2002). Deciphering the V-chip: An examination of the television industry's program rating judgments. *Journal of Communication 52*(1), 112–138.

Kunkel, D., & Gantz, W. (1992). Children's television advertising in the multi-channel environment. *Journal of Communication, 42*(3), 134–152.

Lang, A. (2000). The limited capacity model of mediated message processing. *Journal of Communication, 50*(1), 46–70.

Lang, A., Bolls, P., Potter, R. F., & Kawahara, K. (1999). The effects of production pacing and arousing content on the information processing of television messages. *Journal of Broadcasting & Electronic Media, 43,* 451–475.

Lang, A., Potter, R. F., & Bolls, P. D. (1999). Something for nothing: Is visual encoding automatic? *Media Psychology, 1,* 145–163.

Lang, A., Zhou, S., Schwartz, N., Bolls, P. D., & Potter, R. F. (2000). The effects of edits on arousal, attention, and memory for television messages: When an edit is an edit can an edit be too much? *Journal of Broadcasting & Electronic Media, 44,* 94–109.

Large, P. (1984). *The micro revolution revisited.* Totowa, NJ: Rowman & Allanheld.

Lau, R. R. (1986). Political schemata, candidate evaluations, and voting behavior. In R. R. Lau & D. O. Sears (Eds.), *Political cognition* (pp. 95–126). Hillsdale, NJ: Lawrence Erlbaum.

Lawrence, F., & Wozniak, P. (1989). Children's television viewing with family members. *Psychological Reports, 65*(2), 395–400.

Lewis, J., & Jhally, S. (1998). The struggle over media literacy. *Journal of Communication, 48*(1), 109–120.

Liebert, R. M., & Schwartzberg, N. S. (1977). Effects of mass media. *Annual Review of Psychology, 28*, 141–173.

Limburg, V. E. (1994). Internships, exit interviews, and advisory boards. In W. G. Christ (Ed.), *Assessing communication education: A handbook for media, speech, and theatre educators* (pp. 181–200). Hillsdale, NJ: Lawrence Erlbaum.

Lin, C., & Atkin, D. (1989). Parental mediation and rulemaking for adolescent use of television and VCRs. *Journal of Broadcasting & Electronic Media, 33*, 53–67.

Lippmann, W. (1922). *Public opinion.* New York: Macmillan.

Lometti, G., Reeves, B., & Bybee, C. (1977). Investigating assumptions of uses and gratifications research. *Communication Research, 4*, 321–338.

Lorch, E. P., Anderson, D. R., & Levin, S. R. (1979). The relationship of visual attention to children's comprehension of television. *Child Development, 50*, 722–727.

Luke, C. (1998). Pedagogy and authority: Lessons from feminist and cultural studies, postmodernism and feminist pedagogy. In D. Buckingham (Ed.), *Teaching popular culture: Beyond radical pedagogy* (pp. 18–41). London: University College London Press.

Lyle, J., & Hoffman, H. (1972). Children's use of television and other media. In E. A. Rubinstein, G. A. Comstock, & J. P. Murray (Eds.), *Television and social behavior: Vol 4. Television in day-to-day life: Patterns of use.* Washington, DC: Government Printing Office.

Lyman, P., & Varian, H. R. (2001, November 6). *How much information, 2000.* Retrieved from http://www.sims.berkeley.edu/how-much-info.

Mackey, M. (2002). *Literacies across media: Playing the text.* London: Routledge.

Maddison, J. (1971). *Radio and television in literacy: A survey of the use of the broadcasting media in combating illiteracy among adults.* Paris: UNESCO.

Malamuth, N. M., & Impett, E. A. (2001). Research on sex in the media: What do we know about effects on children and adolescents? In D. G. Singer & J. L. Singer (Eds.), *Handbook of children and the media* (pp. 269–287). Thousand Oaks, CA: Sage.

Manley-Casimir, M. E., & Luke, C. (Eds.). (1987). *Children and television: A challenge for education.* New York: Praeger.

Mares, M.-L., & Woodward, E. H. (2001). Prosocial effects on children's social interactions. In D. G. Singer & J. L. Singer (Eds.), *Handbook of children and the media* (pp. 183–205). Thousand Oaks, CA: Sage.

Marton, K., & Stephens, L. F. (2001). The *New York Times'* conformity to AAPOR standards of disclosure for the reporting of public opinion polls. *Journalism & Mass Communication Quarterly, 78*, 484–502.

Masterman, L. (1980). *Teaching about television.* London: Macmillan.

Masterman, L. (1985). *Teaching the media.* London: Comedia.

Masterman, L. (1997). A rationale for media education. In R. Kubey (Ed.), *Media literacy in the information age: Current perspectives, information, and behavior* (Vol. 6, pp. 15–68). New Brunswick, NJ: Transaction.

Masterman, L. (1998). Foreword: The media education revolution. In A. Hart (Ed.), *Teaching the media: International perspectives* (pp. vii–xi). Mahwah, NJ: Lawrence Erlbaum.

Mathews, J. (1992, April 13). To yank or not to yank? *Newsweek,* p. 59.

Matthews, D., & Desmond, R. (1997, May). *"To get you to buy:" Effects of a parent workshop on young children's understanding of television advertising.* Paper presented at the annual conference of the International Communication Association, Montreal, Quebec, Canada.

McArthur, L. Z., & Post, D. L. (1977). Figural emphasis and person perception. *Journal of Experimental Social Psychology, 13,* 520–535.

McDonald, D. G. (1986). Generational aspects of television coviewing. *Journal of Broadcasting & Electronic Media, 30,* 75–85.

McDonald, D. G., & Kim, H. (2001). When I die, I feel small: Electronic game characters and the social self. *Journal of Broadcasting & Electronic Media, 45,* 241–258.

McLaren, P., Hammer, R., Sholle, D., & Reilly, S. (Eds.). (1995). *Rethinking media literacy: A critical pedagogy of representation.* New York: Peter Lang.

McLeod, J. M., Fitzpatrick, M. A., Glynn, C. J., & Fallis, S. F. (1982). Television and social relations: Family influences and consequences for interpersonal behavior. In D. Pearl, L. Bouthilet, & J. Lazar (Eds.), *Television and behavior: Ten years of scientific progress and implications for the eighties: Vol. II. Technical reviews* (pp. 272–286). Rockville, MD: U.S. Department of Health and Human Services.

McQueen, A. (1999, November 19). Future voters come up short on knowledge of civics. *Tallahassee Democrat,* p. B1.

Meltzoff, A. N. (1988). Imitation of televised models by infants. *Child Development, 59,* 1221–1229.

Messaris, P. (1994). *Visual "literacy": Image, mind, and reality.* Boulder, CO: Westview.

Messaris, P. (1998). Visual aspects of media literacy. *Journal of Communication, 48*(1), 70–80.

Messaris, P., & Kerr, D. (1984). TV-related mother-child interaction and children's perceptions of TV characters. *Journalism Quarterly, 61,* 662–666.

Metallinos, N. (1999). The transformation of biological precepts into mental concept in recognizing visual images. *Journal of Broadcasting & Electronic Media, 43,* 432–442.

Metsger, B. (1996). *Winds of change.* Virginia: The Freedom Forum.

Meyrowitz, J. (1985). *No sense of place: The impact of electronic media on social behavior.* New York: Oxford University Press.

Meyrowitz, J. (1998). Multiple media literacies. *Journal of Communication, 48*(1), 96–108.

Mifflin, L. (1997, February 22). Parents give TV ratings mised reviews. *New York Times,* p. A6.

Minsky, M. A. (1975). Framework for representing knowledge. In P. H. Winston (Ed.), *The psychology of computer vision.* New York: McGraw-Hill.

Miron, D., Bryant, J., & Zillmann, D. (2001). Creating vigilance for better learning from television. In D. G. Singer & J. L. Singer (Eds.), *Handbook of children and the media* (pp. 153–181). Thousand Oaks, CA: Sage.

Murray, J. P. (1980). *Television and youth: 25 years of research and controversy.* Boys Town, NE: The Boys Town Center for the Study of Youth Development.

Naisbitt, J. (1984). *Megatrends: Ten new directions transforming our lives.* New York: Warner Books.

Nathanson, A. I. (1999). Identifying and explaining the relationship between parental mediation and children's aggression. *Communication Research, 26,* 124–143.

Nathanson, A. I. (2001a). Mediation of children's television viewing: Working toward conceptual clarity and common understanding. In W. B. Gudykunst (Ed.), *Communication yearbook* (Vol. 25, pp. 115–151). Mahwah, NJ: Lawrence Erlbaum.

Nathanson, A. I. (2001b). Parent and child perspectives on the presence and meaning of parental television mediation. *Journal of Broadcasting & Electronic Media, 45,* 201–220.

Nathanson, A. I. (2001c). Parents versus peers: Exploring the significance of peer mediation of antisocial television. *Communication Research, 28,* 251–274.

Nathanson, A. I. (2002). The unintended effects of parental mediation of television on adolescents. *Media Psychology, 4,* 207–230.

Nathanson, A. I., & Botta R. A. (2003). Shaping the effects of television on adolescents' body image disturbance: The role of parental mediation. *Communication Research, 30,* 304–331.

Nathanson, A. I., & Cantor, J. (2000). Reducing the aggression-promoting effect of violent cartoons by increasing children's fictional involvement with the victim: A study of active mediation. *Journal of Broadcasting & Electronic Media, 44,* 94–109.

Nathanson, A. I., Eveland, W. P., Park, H.-S., & Paul, B. (2002). Perceived media influence and efficacy as predictors of caregivers' protective behaviors. *Journal of Broadcasting & Electronic Media, 46,* 385–410.

Nathanson, A. I., & Yang, M.-S. (2003). The effects of mediation content and form on children's responses to violent television. *Human Communication Research, 29*(1), 111–134.

Neisser, U. (1976). *Cognition and reality: Principles and implications of cognitive psychology.* San Francisco, CA: W. H. Freeman.

Neuman, S. B. (1991). *Literacy in the television age: The myth of the TV effect.* Norwood, NJ: Ablex.

O'Gorman, H. J. (1986). The discovery of pluralistic ignorance: An ironic lesson. *Journal of the History of the Behavioral Sciences, 22,* 333–347.

Paivio, A. (1986). *Mental representations: A dual-coding approach.* New York: Oxford University Press.

Palmgreen, P., & Rayburn, J. (1982). Gratifications sought and media exposure: An expectancy value model. *Communication Research, 9,* 561–580.

Pan, Z., & Kosicki, G. (1993). Framing analysis: An approach to news discourse. *Political Communication, 10,* 55–76.

Parenti, M. (1986). *Inventing reality: The politics of the mass media.* New York: St. Martin's Press.

Pashler, H. (1998). *The psychology of attention.* Cambridge: MIT Press.

Pattison, R. (1982). *On literacy: The politics of the word from Homer to the age of rock.* Oxford, UK: Oxford University Press.

Payne, D. G., Klin, C. M., Lampinen, J. M., Neuschatz, J. S., & Lindsay, D. S. (1999). Memory applied. In F. T. Durso, R. S. Nickerson, R. W. Schvaneveldt, S. T. Dumais, D. S. Lindsay, & M T. H. Chi (Eds.), *Handbook of applied cognition* (pp. 83–113). New York: John Wiley.

Peiser, W., & Peter, J. (2000). Third-person perception of television-viewing behavior. *Journal of Communication, 50*(1), 25–45.

Perloff, R. M. (1999). The third-person effect: A critical review and synthesis. *Media Psychology, 1,* 353–378.

Perry, S. D., & Gonzenbach, W. J. (1997). Effects of news exemplification extended: Considerations of controversiality and perceived future opinion. *Journal of Broadcasting & Electronic Media, 41,* 229–244.

Piaget, J., & Inhelder, B. (1969). *The psychology of the child.* New York: Basic Books.

Piette, J., & Giroux, L. (1997). The theoretical foundations of media education programs. In R. Kubey (Ed.), *Media literacy in the information age: Current perspectives, information and behavior* (Vol. 6, pp. 89–134). New Brunswick, NJ: Transaction.

Pinker, S. (1997). *How the mind works.* New York: W. W. Norton.

Ploghoft, M. E., & Anderson, J. A. (Eds.). (1981). *Education for the television age.* Springfield, IL: Charles C Thomas.

Pomerantz, J. R., & Lockhead, G. R. (1991). Perception of structure: An overview. In G. R. Lockhead & J. R. Pomerantz (Eds.), *The perception of structure* (pp. 1–20), Washington, DC: American Psychological Association.

Posner, M. I., & Peterson, P. T. (1990). The attention system of the human brain. *Annual Review of Neuroscience, 13,* 25–42.

Posner, M. L., & Snyder, C. R. R. (1975). Attention and cognitive control. In R. L. Solso (Ed.), *Information processing and cognition: The Loyola Symposium* (pp. 55–85). Hillsdale, NJ: Lawrence Erlbaum.

Potter, W. J. (1987). Does television viewing hinder academic achievement among adolescents? *Human Communication Research, 14*(1), 27–46.

Potter W. J. (1990). Adolescents' perceptions of the primary values of television programming. *Journalism Quarterly, 67,* 843–851.

Potter, W. J. (1991). Examining cultivation from a psychological perspective: Component subprocesses, *Communication Research, 18,* 77–102.

Potter, W. J. (1993, April). *Instructional styles and student learning styles.* Paper presented at the annual meeting of the Broadcast Education Association, Las Vegas, NV.

Potter, W. J. (1997). The problem of indexing risk of viewing television aggression. *Critical Studies in Mass Communication, 14,* 228–248.

Potter, W. J. (1999). *On media violence.* Thousand Oaks, CA: Sage.

Potter, W. J. (2001). *Media literacy* (2nd ed.). Thousand Oaks, CA: Sage.

Potter, W. J. (2003). *The 11 myths of media violence.* Thousand Oaks, CA: Sage.

Potter, W. J. (2004). *Becoming a strategic thinker: Developing skills for success.* Upper Saddle River, NJ: Prentice Hall.

Potter, W. J., & Clark, G. (1991). Styles in mass media classrooms. *Feedback, 32*(1), 8–11, 24.

Potter, W. J., & Emanuel, R. (1990). Students' preferences for communication styles and their relationship to achievement. *Communication Education, 39,* 234–249.

Potter, W. J., Eyal, K., Fandrich, R., Mahood, C., McIlrath, M., & Riddle, K. (2003). *Judging the degree of violence in media portrayals.* Working paper, University of California at Santa Barbara.

Potter, W. J., & Smith, S. (1999). Consistency of contextual cues about violence across narrative levels. *Journal of Communication, 49*(4), 121–133.

Potter, W. J., & Vaughan, M. (1997). Aggression in television entertainment: Profiles and trends. *Communication Research Reports, 14,* 116–124.

Power, J. G., Murphy, S. T., & Coover, G. (1996). Priming prejudice: How stereotypes and counter-stereotypes influence attribution of responsibility and credibility among ingroups and outgroups. *Human Communication Research, 23,* 36–58.

Price, V., Tewksbury, D., & Powers, E. (1996, May). *Switching trains of thought: The impact of news frames on reader's cognitive responses.* Paper presented at the annual meeting of the International Communication Association Conference, Chicago.

Pritchard, D. A. (1975). Leveling-sharpening revised. *Perceptual and Motor Skills, 40,* 111–117.

Pritchard, D., & Hughes, K. D. (1997). Patterns of deviance in crime news. *Journal of Communication, 47*(3), 49–67.

Quin, R., & McMahon, B. (1997). Living with the tiger: Media curriculum issues for the future. In R. Kubey (Ed.), *Media literacy in the information age* (pp. 307–321), New Brunswick, NJ: Transaction.

Rafferty, C. S., (1999). Literacy in the information age. *Education Leadership, 57*(2), 22–26.

Rampoldi-Hnilo, L. & Greenberg, B. S. (2000). A poll of Latina and Caucasian mothers with 6 - 10 year old children. In B. S. Greenberg, L. Rampoldi-Hnilo, & D. Mastro (Eds.), *The alphabet soup of television program ratings.* Cresskill, NJ: Hampton Press.

Rapaczynski, W., Singer, D. G., & Singer, J. L. (1982).Teaching television: A curriculum for young children. *Journal of Communication, 32*(2), 46–54.

Reid, L. N. (1979). Viewing rules as mediating factors of children's responses to commercials. *Journal of Broadcasting, 23,* 15–26.

Reid L. N., & Frazer, C. F. (1980). Children's use of television commercials to initiate social interaction in family viewing situations. *Journal of Broadcasting, 24,* 149–158.

Reiser, R. A., Tessmer, M. A., & Phelps, P. C. (1984). Adult-child interaction in children's learning from Sesame Street. *Educational Communication and Technology Journal, 32,* 217–223.

Reiser, R. A., Williamson, N., & Suzuki, K. (1988). Using Sesame Street to facilitate children's recognition of letters and numbers. *Educational Communication and Technology Journal, 36,* 15–21.

Rhee, J. W. (1997). Strategy and issue frames in election campaign coverage: A social cognitive account of framing effects. *Journal of Communication, 47*(3), 26–48.

Rice, M., & Wartella, E. (1981). Television as a medium of communication: Implications for how to regard the child viewer. *Journal of Broadcasting, 25,* 365–372.

Rips, L. J., Shoben, E. J., & Smith, E. E. (1973). Semantic distance and the verification of semantic relations. *Journal of Verbal Learning and Verbal Behavior, 12,* 1–20.

Roberts, D. R. (1973). Communication and children: A developmental approach. In I. DeS. Pool, W. Schramm, F. W. Frey, N. Maccoby, & E. B. Parker (Eds.), *The process and effects of mass communication* (rev. ed., pp. 596–611). Urbana: University of Illinois Press.

Roberts, D. F., & Christenson, P. G. (2001). Popular music in childhood and adolescence. In D. G. Singer & J. L. Singer (Eds.), *Handbook of children and the media* (pp. 395–413). Thousand Oaks, CA: Sage.

Roberts, D. F., Christenson, P., Gibson, W. A., Mooser, L., & Goldberg, M. E. (1980). Developing discriminating consumers. *Journal of Communication, 30*(3), 94–105.

Roberts, D., Foehr, U., Rideout, V., & Brodie, M. (1999). *Kids and media @ the new millennium: A comprehensive national analysis of children's media use.* Menlo Park, CA: Kaiser Family Foundation.

Rogers, W. A., Rousseau, G. K., & Fisk, A. D. (1999). Applications of attention research. In F. T. Durso, R. S., Nickerson, R. W. Schvaneveldt, S. T. Dumais, D. S. Lindsay, & M. T. H. Chi (Eds.), *Handbook of applied cognition* (pp. 33–55). New York: John Wiley.

Rosch, E. (1978). Principles of categorization, In E. Rosch & B. B. Lloyd (Eds.), *Cognition and categorization.* Hillsdale, NJ: Lawrence Erlbaum.

Rosenbaum, J. (1994). Assessment: An overview. In W. G. Christ (Ed.), *Assessing communication education: A handbook for media, speech, and theatre educators* (pp. 3–29). Hillsdale, NJ: Lawrence Erlbaum.

Roskos-Ewoldsen, D. R., Roskos-Ewoldsen, B., & Carpenter, F. R. D. (2002). Media priming: A synthesis. In D. Zillmann & J. Bryant (Eds.), *Media effects: Advances in theory and research* (pp. 97–120). Hillsdale, NJ: Lawrence Erlbaum.

Ross, M., & Sicoly, F. (1979). Egocentric biases in availability and attribution. *Journal of Personality and Social Psychology, 37*, 322–336.

Rothschild, N., & Morgan, M. (1987). Cohesion and control: Adolescents' relationships with parents as mediators of television. *Journal of Early Adolescence, 7*, 299–314.

Rowland, W. D., Jr. (1999). Media education. In W. G. Christ (Ed.), *Leadership in times of change: A handbook for communication and media administrators* (pp. 41–59). Mahwah, NJ: Lawrence Erlbaum.

Rubin, A. M. (1977). Television use by children and adolescents. *Human Communication Research, 5*, 109–120.

Rubin, A. M. (1981) An examination of television viewing motivations. *Communication Research, 8*, 141–165.

Rubin, A. M. (1983) Television uses and gratifications: The interactions of viewing patterns and motivations. *Journal of Broadcasting, 27*, 37–51.

Rumelhart, D. E., & Norman, D. A. (1988). Representation in memory. In R. C. Atkinson (Ed.), *Stevens' handbook of experimental psychology: Vol 2. Learning and cognition* (2nd ed., pp. 511–587). New York: John Wiley.

Salomon, G. (1977). Effects of encouraging Israeli mothers to co-observe Sesame Street with their five-year-olds. *Child Development, 48*, 1146–1151.

Salwen, M. B., & Dupagne, M. (2001). Third-person perception of television violence: The role of self-perceived knowledge. *Media Psychology, 3*, 211–236.

Sang, F., Schmitz, B., & Tasche, K. (1992). Individuation and television coviewing in the family: Development trends in the viewing behavior of adolescents. *Journal of Broadcasting & Electronic Media, 36*, 427–441.

Sapolsky, B. S., & Tabarlet, J. (1990). *Sex in prime time television: 1979 vs. 1989.* Unpublished manuscript, Department of Communication, Florida State University, Tallahassee.

Schacter, D. L. (1987). Implicit memory: History and current status. *Journal of Experimental Psychology: Learning, Memory and Cognition, 13*, 501–518.

Schank, R. C. (1982). Depths of knowledge. In B. de Gelder (Ed.), *Knowledge and representation* (pp. 170–216). London: Routledge & Kegan Paul.

Schank, R. C., & Abelson, R. P. (1977). *Scripts, plans, goals, and understanding: An inquiry into human knowledge structures.* Hillsdale, NJ: Lawrence Erlbaum.

Schenck-Hamlin, W. J., Procter, D. E., & Rumsey, D. J. (2000). The influence of negative advertising frames on political cynicism and politician accountability. *Human Communication Research, 26*, 53–74.

Scheunemann, D. (Ed.). (1996). *Orality, literacy, and modern media.* Columbia, SC: Camden House.

Schmitt, K. (2000). *Public policy, family rules, and children's media use in the home.* Washington, DC: University of Pennsylvania, Annenberg Public Policy Center.

Schramm, W., Lyle, J., & Parker, E. B. (1961). *Television in the lives of our children.* Palo Alto, CA: Stanford University Press.

Scribner, S., & Cole, M. (1981). *The psychology of literacy.* Cambridge, MA: Harvard University Press.

Shamir, J., & Shamir, M. (1997). Pluralistic ignorance across issues and over time. *Public Opinion Quarterly, 61,* 227–260.

Shiffrin, R. M. (1988). Attention. In R. A. Atkinson, R. J. Herrnstein, G. Lindzey, & R. D. Luce (Eds.), *Stevens' handbook of experimental psychology: Vol. 2. Learning and cognition* (pp. 739–811). New York: John Wiley.

Sholle, D., & Denski, S. (1994). *Media education and the (re)production of culture.* Westport, CT: Bergin & Garvey.

Sholle, D., & Denski, S. (1995). Critical media literacy: Reading, remapping, rewriting. In P. McLaren, R. Hammer, D. Sholle, & S. S. Reilly (Eds.) *Rethinking media literacy: A critical pedagogy of representation* (pp. 7–31). New York: Peter Lang.

Shum, M. S., & Rips, L. J. (1999). The respondent's confession: Autobiographical memory in the context of surveys. In M. G. Sirken, D. J. Herrmann, S. Schechter, N. Schwarz, J. M. Tanur, & R. Rourangeau (Eds.), *Cognition and survey research* (pp. 95–109). New York: John Wiley.

Silverblatt, A. (1995). *Media literacy: Keys to interpreting media messages.* Westport, CT: Praeger.

Silverblatt, A., & Eliceiri, E. M. E. (1997). *Dictionary of media literacy.* Westport, CT: Greenwood Press.

Silverblatt, A., Ferry, J., & Finan, B. (1999). *Approaches to media literacy: A handbook.* Armonk, NY: M. E. Sharpe.

Simon, H. A. (1957). *Administrative behavior* (2nd ed.) Totowa, NJ: Littlefield, Adams.

Sinatra, R. (1986). *Visual literacy connections to thinking, reading and writing.* Springfield, IL: Charles C Thomas.

Singer, J. L., Singer, D. G., & Rapaczynski, W. S. (1984). Family patterns and television viewing as predictors of children's beliefs and aggression. *Journal of Communication, 34*(2), 73–89.

Singer, D. G., Zuckerman, D. M., & Singer, J. L. (1980). Helping elementary school children learn about TV. *Journal of Communication, 30*(3), 84–93.

Sizer, T. R. (1995). Silences. *Daedelus, 124*(4), 77–83.

Slater, M. D., & Rouner, D. (2002). Entertainment-education and elaboration likelihood: Understanding the processing of narrative persuasion. *Communication Theory, 12,* 173–191.

Slattery, K., Doremus, M., & Marcus, L. (2001). Shifts in public affairs reporting on the network evening news: A move toward the sensational. *Journal of Broadcasting & Electronic Media, 45,* 290–02.

Slattery, K. L., & Hakanen, E. A. (1994). Sensationalism versus public affairs content of local TV news: Pennsylvania revisited. *Journal of Broadcasting & Electronic Media, 38,* 205–214.

Smith, E. E., Shoben, E. J., & Rips, L. J. (1974). Structure and process in semantic memory: A featural model for semantic decisions. *Psychological Review, 81,* 214–241.

Smith, E. R. (1999). New connectionist models of mental representation: Implications for survey research. In M. G. Sirken, D. J. Herrmann, S. Schechter, N. Schwarz, J. M. Tanur, & R. Rourangeau (Eds.), *Cognition and survey research* (pp. 251–264). New York: John Wiley.

Speech Communication Association. (1996). *Speaking, listening, and media literacy standards for K through 12 education.* Annandale, VA: National Communication Association.

Spelke, E. Hirst, W., & Neisser, U. (1976). Skills of divided attention. *Cognition, 4,* 215–230.

Stanger, J. (1997). *Television in the home: The second annual survey of parents and children in the home* (Survey Series No. 2). Philadelphia: University of Pennsylvania, Annenberg Public Policy Center.

Statistical Abstract of the United States (2002). N. 1135: *Households with computers and internet access by selected characteristic: 2001.* Retrieved January 9, 2004 from http://www.census.gov/prod/2003pubs/02statab/infocom.pdf

Sternberg, R. J., & Berg, C. A. (1987). What are theories of adult intellectual development theories of? In C. Schooler & K. W. Schaie (Eds.), *Cognitive functioning and social structure over the life course* (pp. 3–23). Norwood, NJ: Ablex.

Stoneman, Z., & Brody, G. H. (1982). An in-home investigation of maternal teaching strategies during Sesame Street and a popular situation comedy. *Journal of Applied Developmental Psychology, 3,* 275–284.

Taylor, S. E. (1981). The interface of cognitive and social psychology. In H. Harvey (Ed.), *Cognition, social behavior, and the environment* (pp. 189–211), Hillsdale, NJ: Lawrence Erlbaum.

Thaler, R. H. (1980). Toward a positive theory of consumer choice. *Journal of Economic Behavior and Organization, 1,* 39–60.

Tolan, P. H., Gorman-Smith, D., Huesmann, L. R., & Zelli, A. (1997). Assessment of family relationship characteristics: A measure to explain risk for antisocial behavior and depression among urban youth. *Psychological Assessment, 9,* 212–223.

Treisman, A. M., & Geffen, G. (1967). Selective attention: Perception of response? *Quarterly Journal of Experimental Psychology, 19,* 1–17.

Tulving, E. (1983). *Elements of episodic memory.* Oxford, UK: Oxford University Press.

Tversky, A. (1972). Elimination by aspects: A theory of choice. *Psychological Review, 79,* 281–299.

Tversky, A., & Kahneman, D. (1983). Extensional versus intuitive reasoning: The conjunction fallacy in probability judgment. *Psychological Review, 90,* 293–315.

Tyner, K. (1998). *Literacy in a digital world: Teaching and learning in the age of information.* Mahwah, NJ: Lawrence Erlbaum.

U.S. Department of Justice, Federal Bureau of Investigation. (1999, October 17). *Crime in the United States 1998: Uniform crime statistics.* Washington, DC: Author.

Vacca, R. T., & Newton, E. V. (1995). Responding to literary texts. In C. N. Hedley, P. Antonacci, & M. Rabinowitz (Eds.), *Thinking and literacy: The mind at work* (pp. 283–302). Hillsdale, NJ: Lawrence Erlbaum.

Valkenburg, P. M., Krcmar, M., & de Roos, S. (1998). The impact of a cultural children's program and adult mediation on children's knowledge of an attitudes toward opera. *Journal of Broadcasting & Electronic Media, 42*, 315–326.

Valkenburg, P. M., Krcmar, M. Peeters, A. L., & Marseille, N. M. (1999). Instructive mediation, restrictive mediation, and social coviewing. *Journal of Broadcasting & Electronic Media, 43*, 52–66.

Valkenburg, P. M., & Van der Voort, T. H. A. (1995). The influence of television on children's daydreaming styles: A 1-year panel study. *Communication Research, 22*, 267–287.

Van der Voort, T. H. A. (1986). *Television violence: A child's-eye view.* Amsterdam: North-Holland.

van der Voort, T. H. A., Nikken, P., & van Lil, J. E. (1992). Determinants of parental guidance of children's television viewing: A Dutch replication study. *Journal of Broadcasting & Electronic Media, 36*, 61–74.

Walker, J., & Ferguson, D. (1998). *The broadcast television industry.* Needham Heights, MA: Allyn & Bacon.

Watkins, B., Calvert, S., Huston-Stein, A., & Wright, J. C. (1980). Children's recall of television material: Effects of presentation mode and adult labeling. *Developmental Psychology, 16*, 672–674.

Weaver, B., & Barbour, N. (1992). Mediation of children's televiewing. *Families in Society: The Journal of Contemporary Human Services, 73*, 236–242.

Whitman, D. (1996, December 16). I'm OK, you're not. *U.S. News & World Report,* pp. 24–30.

Wildavsky, B. (1999, October 11). Kids don't have the write stuff. *U.S. News & World Report,* p. 28.

Wilson, B. J., Smith, S. L., Potter, W. J., Kunkel, D., Linz, D., Colvin, C. M., & Donnerstein, E. (2002). Violence in children's television programming: Assessing the risks. *Journal of Communication, 52*(1), 5–35.

Witkin, H. A., & Goodenough, D. R. (1977). Field dependence and interpersonal behavior. *Psychological Bulletin, 84*, 661–689.

Woods, D. D., & Cook, R. I. (1999). Perspectives on human error: Hindsight biases and local rationality. In F. T. Durso, R. S., Nickerson, R. W. Schvaneveldt, S. T. Dumais, D. S. Lindsay, & M. T. H. Chi (Eds.), *Handbook of applied cognition* (pp. 141-171). *Chichester*, UK: Wiley.

Wulff, S. (1997). Media literacy. In W. G. Christ (Ed.), *Media education assessment handbook* (pp. 123–142). Mahwah, NJ: Lawrence Erlbaum and Speech Communication Association.

Wyer, R. S., Jr., & Gruenfeld, D. H. (1995). Information processing in social contexts: Implications for social memory and judgment. *Advances in Experimental Social Psychology, 27*, 49–91.

Zettl, H. (1998). Contextual media aesthetics as the basis for media literacy. *Journal of Communication, 48*(1), 81–95.

Zillmann, D. (1982). Television viewing and arousal. In D. Pearl, L. Bouthilet, & J. Lazar (Eds.), *Television and behavior: Ten years of scientific progress and implications for the eighties: Vol. 2. Technical reviews* (pp. 53-67). Washington, DC: Government Printing Office.

Zillmann, D. (1991) Television viewing and physiological arousal. In J. Bryant & D. Zillmann (Eds.), *Responding to the screen: Reception and reaction processes* (pp. 103–133). Hillsdale, NJ: Lawrence Erlbaum.

Zillmann, D., & Bryant, J. (1985). Affect, mood, and emotion as determinants of selective exposure. In D. Zillmann & J. Bryant (Eds.), *Selective exposure to communication* (pp. 157–190). Hillsdale, NJ: Lawrence Erlbaum.

Zillmann, D., Taylor, K., & Lewis, K. (1998). News as nonfiction theater: How dispositions toward the public cast of characters affect reactions. *Journal of Broadcasting & Electronic Media, 42*, 153–169.

Index

Abelson, P. R., 52, 53
Abilities, 89-90
Abstraction, 134-135
Academic achievement, 16-17, 87
Access to information, 3-4
    avoidance and, 5, 9
    coupling knowledge
        structures and, 198
    currency, maintenance of,
        5-7, 6 (table)
    inert knowledge and, 198
    information production and, 5
    inside sources, 194-198
    outside sources, 193-194
    vehicles of, 4-5, 159-160
    See also Automatic processing;
        Information
Accuracy of information, 62, 193
Action Coalition for Media Education, 24
Active mediation, 234-235, 238-239, 250
Active searching, 50, 142-144
Adams, D. M., 27, 29, 30, 31, 33, 258
Adams, W. C., 150
Advertising, 5-6, 6 (table)
    audience attention to, 45, 111
    content formula in, 76, 77
    framing process in, 211-212
    info-mercials, 8, 45
    subconscious patterning and,
        10, 12, 14
    values messages within, 77
Aesthetic information, 60

Albert, J., 107
Allen, M., 211
Alliance for a Media Literate America, 24
Alvarado, M., 32
Alvermann, D. E., 30
Ambiguity, 106
American Association for
    Public Opinion Research, 203
American Psychiatric Association, 24
Analysis, 125
    component analysis, 125-126
    critical analysis, 14
    focal plane analysis, 125
    framing process, 210-213
    knowledge structures and, 126
    message elements and, 126
    outline analysis, 126
    unit selection and, 213
    unit sizing and, 213-214
Analytical strength, 14, 106, 109
Anderson, C. A., 213
Anderson, D. R., 151, 174
Anderson, J. A., 27, 32, 261, 264
Anecdotal information, 19
Antonacci, P., 254
Arousal process, 90-91, 154
Associations:
    absorption process, 169-170
    choice in meanings and, 123
    coupling knowledge
        structures and, 198
    meaning construction and, 121

About the Author

W. James Potter is currently a professor in the Department of Communication at the University of California at Santa Barbara. He holds a Ph.D. in Communication Theory and another Ph.D. in Instructional Systems Technology. He has taught a wide variety of students at Florida State University, UCLA, Indiana University, Stanford University, and Western Michigan University. He has served as editor of the *Journal of Broadcasting and Electronic Media* and is the author of many journal articles and books, including the following SAGE titles: *Media Literacy 2/e, On Media Violence,* and *How to Publish Your Communication Research* (with Alison Alexander), and most recently *The 11 Myths of Media Violence.*